Rebecca Smith is a non-fiction author and journalist from Cumbria. She worked for BBC Radio for over a decade, producing a variety of programmes including news and features, and has written for *The New York Times*, the *Guardian* and the *Sunday Times*. She has a Masters in Creative Writing at Glasgow University and now lives in central Scotland with her children and partner. This is her f

A BBC RADIO 4 *FRONT ROW* B(

T0337250

Praise for *Rural*

'[T]his intensely personal investigation of rural people's working lives … is both eye-opening and persuasive … effective and affecting. Smith is trying to understand what it means to work on the land but not own it … This is not just a polemical book. It is more generous and ambitious. "It feels we are only at the beginning of understanding how our country was really built," Smith writes. And books like this, which look at history from new vantage points, and with fresh eyes, are part of that new beginning'   ***SUNDAY TIMES***

'Its most memorable passages resound with all the get-off-our-land fury of a gamekeeper's shotgun … How we manage people's competing claims to ownership of places is one of the great questions for the world in the twenty-first century. As *Rural* shows, the British country-side is a good example of how not to do it'   ***OBSERVER***

'[An] intelligent, multifaceted exploration of working-class life in the British countryside … it is to Smith's huge credit that she achieves her aim with the book, of revealing parts of society that are too often simply forgotten'   ***INDEPENDENT***

'A brilliant book about another side of working-class life, not a tower block in sight. Clever and honest, tackling slavery, loss and aspiration with humour and candour. I loved it'

KIT DE WAAL, author of *My Name is Leon*

'*Rural* is a book about the vast social changes that are often difficult to spot from the outside, and the villages where an appearance of timeless serenity is maintained by heritage paints and second-homers'

TIMES LITERARY SUPPLEMENT

'Part memoir and part historical document, what emerges is a love letter to life in the countryside and a distinctive rural working-class identity. As Smith and countless others attest, rural life may be challenging, but it's a lifestyle worth defending' **DAZED**

'[A] considered and considerate book ... her analysis is acute and dislodging and revelatory. It is also very self-aware, in a good way, the author constantly cross-examining herself on the ambiguities and paradoxes of what the rural life really means ... Smith has written something which does not reduce the world to easy answers but revels in its difficulty' **THE SCOTSMAN**

'The author's understanding of the land, innate curiosity of people that live off it, and emotional connection to it makes her book an educational and moving read that I believe no matter where you fit in society, you can enjoy ... But most importantly, her work is a voice for working class people in rural communities from the past to the present day whose voices have so often been overlooked ... Smith beautifully stitches together the beauty, tragedy and comedy that underpins rural communities today, making her book a fascinating history lesson' **SCOTSMAN MAGAZINE**

'Smith is alert to the fact that when we aestheticise the countryside we mistake natural beauty for something that has been largely shaped by human labour, and, because we define that beauty as belonging to nature, we fail to value the labour and the lives of working people who live on the land today ... unsentimental, clear-sighted accounts of the realities of rural life' **LITERARY REVIEW**

'A thoughtful, moving, honest book that questions what it means to belong to a place when it can never belong to you: a timely and illuminating exploration of the lives of the countryside working class. *Rural* reminds us that human stories lie at the heart of the land ownership debate – and that a feeling for place traverses the class divide' **CAL FLYN**, author of *Islands of Abandonment*

'A shrewd, inquisitive and enlightening guide to a vitally important aspect of the nation … While *Rural* has an undertone of melancholy with centuries-old social injustice burning through every chapter, Smith's writing is good enough and the personal anecdotes uplifting enough to keep the book a lively rather than depressing read. It feels like the introduction of an important new voice to landscape writing in post-Brexit Britain and, importantly, one speaking from a perspective too long underrepresented' ***NEW EUROPEAN***

'Smith explores these issues without turning the book into a polemic, leaving room for nuance and difficult questions … *Rural* explores the diverse lives and industries entangled in the natural landscape and how they've changed. It's a personal and insightful read for anyone who wants to get under the skin of Britain's green and pleasant land'
GEOGRAPHICAL MAGAZINE

'*Rural* sets out to identify some of the huge and near-invisible changes to rural life that have occurred in recent decades … should be considered by anyone with an interest in the future of the British countryside'
COUNTRY LIFE MAGAZINE

'[Smith's] perspective is nuanced, coming to positions through discovery and weighing all views rather than lecturing the reader. That makes her critiques all the more powerful: she persuasively shows how Britain has treated its rural working classes – past and present – with contempt, harshness and insecurity. With rural workers too often absent from conversations on British industrial history, books like Smith's are a welcome corrective' ***NEW HUMANIST***

'*Rural* tenderly reveals the precarious lives that underpin the beauty and the wealth of our countryside. Essential reading for lovers of the land and its people'   **KATHERINE MAY**, author of *Wintering*

'*Rural* is a refreshing and necessary reminder that … we should all aspire to be generous caretakers of rural environments and properly appreciate the skills, resilience and perspectives of the working people that sustain them'   *QUIETUS*

'A corrective to a one-sided story of ownership and control … restores the drowned voices of those who weren't heard in their own lifetimes. Her style gives the lie to the lingua franca of scholarly pursuit – at once entertaining and conversational, the reader is surprised by Smith's depth of investigative acuity … [Smith] has an extraordinary feeling for the past and its underpinning of the present'
      YORKSHIRE TIMES

'Brilliant … deeply thought out … packed with affecting scenes'
      CUMBRIA LIFE MAGAZINE, Book of the Month

'It is a wonderful book, beautifully conceived in its movement between different dimensions of a rural working life, Smith's and her family's and all the others, both past and present. So immediate and clearly seen, so gracefully and gently written'
      ADAM NICOLSON, author of *Life Between the Tides*

'*Rural* ascends to beauty because it manages something more than simple reportage. Smith is of the land; rural life is her blood and her history. She narrates the pregnancy that bloomed during her research, the writing poignantly undershot with a sense of belonging she worries her children won't have'
      KIRSTIN INNES, *THE PRESS AND JOURNAL*

Rural

The Lives of the
Working Class Countryside

REBECCA SMITH

WILLIAM
COLLINS

William Collins
An imprint of HarperCollins*Publishers*
1 London Bridge Street
London SE1 9GF

WilliamCollinsBooks.com

HarperCollins*Publishers*
Macken House, 39/40 Mayor Street Upper,
Dublin 1, D01 C9W8, Ireland

First published in Great Britain in 2023 by William Collins
This William Collins paperback edition published in 2024

2

Typeset in Adobe Garamond Pro by
Palimpsest Book Production Ltd, Falkirk, Stirlingshire

Printed and bound in the UK [using 100% renewable electricity
at CPI Group (UK) Ltd]

This book contains FSC™ certified paper and other controlled sources
to ensure responsible forest management.

For more information visit: www.harpercollins.co.uk/green

To Mum and Dad.
Without whom none of this would be possible.

Contents

Prologue

Often, I think, people assume I am something I am not. My childhood was spent making dens within rhododendron bushes in the hidden corners of landscaped gardens and wandering the woods full of baby pheasants being fattened up for the shoot. I had lake shores to paddle in and a dinghy that we bumped down the field to the private beach.

My dad was the forester on a small country estate. 'It's the middle of nowhere,' people said when they visited. If it was 'nowhere', then there was a lot of it. And it was all mine. I roamed the hills listening to my Walkman – a modern Brontë sister – while my brother skinned rabbits on the wall as tourists slowly drove past. Written down, it sounds slightly ridiculous. Well, that's what it was like. And, of course, it wasn't all mine. None of it was.

I didn't realise that only the very wealthy, or sometimes lucky, had this kind of life. I was stepping in the footsteps of the upper classes, with access to the kinds of views that nature writers and landscape painters have been describing for hundreds of years. I had unlimited access *inside* the walls of a managed, affluent landscape, which, now, people pay a fortune to holiday in, let alone live in. But stepping in the footsteps of the upper classes did not mean I wore their shoes. Our lives ran parallel, but our worlds were very different. My brother and I played Kick the Can and rode our bikes too fast over the speed bumps, racing with the plumber's kids, the farmer's kids and the electrician's kids, but I can count on one hand the number of times I saw the children from the Big House. They spent most of their time away at boarding school. As I grew into adulthood, I worked as soon as I could, and at 13 I started saving up. For what, I didn't know yet. But I knew our family didn't have property, savings or a business to fall back on.

And yet, this upbringing seemed to come with a class ambiguity that I still can't put my finger on. When I talked about the lake, the garden and the treehouse my dad built, people assumed we had money. We did not. When I talk about the estate, people assume I had a connection with the landowners. There was one, to some extent, once. For a time, they threw parties for the estate residents and their families, but the gap grew large enough for the eldest son of the estate not to recognise me when I served him in the local pub. Did other communities in rural areas feel the same? Did growing up with access to so much nature change the way I looked at the world? Or did it change the way the world looked at me?

When my dad became the estate forester, we were given a house. A lodge house, no less. Almost as grand as the manor house, with bay windows and a round, castle-like turret. But, of course, it was much, much smaller than the Big House. It was a 'tied cottage', which meant we didn't pay rent and my dad's wages reflected that. For seven years, my brother and I played in the gardens, made rhododendron perfume to sell to the visitors and swung on an old tractor tyre underneath a beech tree. But things were changing. When I was 16, the estate decided not to employ a forester anymore; Dad became self-employed, and we started paying rent.

Looking back, it was a time of transformation. There were blurred lines between the old sepia lifestyle and the new digital era, in more ways than one. I had no idea that the way a rural community was held together was changing. Big landowners were modifying how they made money. They no longer needed a workforce in the same way. It was possible to make more money letting property to families like mine than providing households with jobs. Or better still, letting the houses out to tourists, for which you could earn the same in a week as you would have otherwise in a month. For better or worse, communities that had grown up for generations providing for one family, one name or one business, dispersed.

Tied cottages are mainly a thing of Britain's past. They were abundant for hundreds of years, springing up to facilitate a whole range of rural industries. Coal companies built rows of damp miners' cottages by their pits, and textile manufacturers designed mill towns by waterfalls. The Forestry Commission built settlements so remote it took foresters' wives all day (often hitching lifts in the timber lorries) just to get out to do the shopping. At the peak of the Industrial Revolution, temporary wooden huts appeared so hundreds of men could build reservoirs that took years to complete. And private landowners, big estate owners – the original landlords, if you like – built houses for their own private world. A country estate could have homes for the blacksmith, the butler, the gamekeeper, the housekeeper, the gardener, the plumber, the joiner. A world inside a world. Microcosms of society. A whole raft of tenants and their families lumped together to manage the estate.

Today, the coal mines are gone. Forestry has adapted to using machines, which makes the job much quicker, cheaper and safer. We don't need to create communities to build huge engineering projects like dams and reservoirs. Machines can shift far more soil than a gang of hardy men can. It is often tourism that now employs the bigger slice of the pie in rural areas, and it is here you will find staff housing. Well, you would. If there were any houses left in rural areas. I used to think tied housing was a bad thing – the Scottish expression 'on a shoogly peg' always sprang to mind. Yes, the miners, the mill workers, the foresters' wives were all living on a shoogly peg, precariously, tied by circumstance. There was always the fear you could be kicked out of your home if you lost your job. But now we are faced with almost the opposite problem. A lack of homes in rural areas means the actual jobs in those areas are redundant. And it's killing the countryside. There are already a limited number of houses in areas renowned for their natural beauty and, of those houses, a huge percentage don't belong to people who actually live there – in some areas, 80 per cent of villages are now second homes. It's not rocket science. If there is nowhere to live, there is nowhere to work. Or go to school. Or to shop. If there isn't a house for the teacher, the doctor, the farmer, the shopkeeper, we lose those assets.

This book is about land, housing and rural industry. But it's also about family and community. I was pregnant when I wrote the bulk of it, plagued with awful morning sickness for months. I dragged my kids, partner and my poor parents halfway around the country for research trips. We travelled to mill towns, reservoirs high up in valleys and slate islands. After I had the baby, I did more research. The three-month-old and I found ourselves stuck on the Isle of Arran in a January storm. Being pregnant or with young children in these environments shed a new light onto the lives of generations past, and for families now living in rural areas.

This is in no way a full account of all the rural industries that had houses come with the jobs. There are so many more sorts of mining I don't even touch on: salt mining, tin mining, lead mining. Then there is iron ore, shale and the mills that smelted the lead or iron. Railway building and canal building all provided temporary housing. Lockkeepers, lighthouse keepers, vicars, doctors and nurses, policemen. This is not a full account of land use or housing issues either. That would be impossible, and there are other books out there that attempt to explain these issues much better than I ever could anyway.

What I hope the book does is reveal a part of society that has been largely forgotten. I am tired of reading stories about landowners, lairds, the Big House and rich people who always seem to get their own way. I am tired of reading a tourist's view of the countryside. Yes, the mountains are spectacular and mushrooms are pretty, but tourists quite often forget that this beautiful place is a working environment. People actually live here. I hope this book tells the stories of the families who are making a living within this natural world and have done so for generations. I hope it tells the stories of tenants whose lives went unrecorded. When reading about forestry villages, I recognised the stories about the foresters who would walk 15 miles to 'go to the pub'. Our nearest pub was only three miles away in a small settlement by the lake, so it wasn't such a trek for Dad to walk there and back in all kinds of weather. I recognised the stories of the dreaded food shop. Mum went to town once every two weeks to do the 'big shop'. This *did* feel like a trek, even with a car. She filled the boot with bags and bags of food, bringing a freezer box so the frozen food wouldn't melt on the journey home. I recognised the stories of spending a few days in autumn felling a tree and then chopping endless logs to fill up the shed, ready for the winter ahead. I recognised the stories of kids sledging down hills and nearly crashing into sheep. I recognised the stories of adders in the kitchen and mistaking a severed deer leg for a log for the fire. I recognised the stories of saving up and going away to work, then realising you belong in the hills, after all. I recognised the stories of moving away and bringing up

your children elsewhere as you can't afford to live in the place you know is home.

These are not your usual working-class stories; they are the stories of the rural working-class.

1

Land

The tyres rattle over the cattlegrid as the stable block appears on our left. We park behind the building, in the shadow of the beech trees that have grown further across the sky than I ever remember them being.

'You didn't tell us it was like this,' my son Ellis says.

I falter. I thought I did.

'It didn't look like this when I lived here. It's much fancier now.'

I see Phil, my partner, smile, possibly at the word 'fancier', possibly at Ellis's remark.

The stable block was once, as the name suggests, the home for the horses of the estate and the people who looked after them. Three blocks of two-storey buildings form the three sides of a square. The fourth edge was enclosed by a low wall that we used to sit and climb on as kids, with the gateway in the centre of it. There was a clock tower at the back of the square, which had never seemed to tick, even when I lived here. All the buildings are now freshly painted, the white render of the top storey shines bright and the grey mock-Tudor panels are rich against it. It looks very smart. There is a line of expensive cars in the car park alongside us.

I point up to the back of the building. There is a small window that looks onto the car-park area, almost the same height as the biggest beech branches.

'There used to be an old woman who lived there. She used to

look out of the window. She was terrifying.' Ellis, who is ten, and Jess, only three, look up. The window looks dark, the space around it crowded with the branches of the trees. It still looks spooky now. I have no idea who the woman was, or what she did on the estate. Maybe we made her up.

I had always known the stable block as homes, rather than where horses were kept. The housekeeper and her husband lived in one of the end houses. When you walked into their small living room that smoky, dry heat of the open fire hit you. The plumber and his kids lived in the house opposite. They had bats in their loft, which sometimes ended up in their bathroom. I remember the shock of seeing the dark mass of the bat in the corner of the room and the plumber's wife screaming when it started flapping about upstairs.

Today, the stable block has a shiny new sheen about it. The flats have been converted to a higher standard. Some are let out long term, some as holiday flats. I can see why it might look different from what I had told Ellis.

It is difficult to work out the exact number of estates there are left in Britain today. Some of them, like Chatsworth and Blenheim, are still huge landowners with hundreds of thousands of acres. They are also big local employers. Chatsworth, for example, employs more than 800 people. There are lots of smaller estates that continue to maintain the house and the grounds, employing a core member of staff for the kind of business they run now – often holiday homes.

Some estates were sold to the National Trust, unable to stay in the family due to death duties, or because the upkeep of the old, elaborate house was simply too expensive. The National Trust now looks after 300 historic houses in England alone.

Some have been bought by local councils. Where there were once designed gardens, there are now play parks. Some of these grand homes have been so neglected that the only evidence that there was once a privately owned estate there are the remnants of walls and burnt-out buildings. It is said that nearly 2,000 stately homes have been demolished or ruined in England alone over the last 200 years.

These changes have been under way for decades now. Whereas, once, income used to come from rent from tenants, and the pursuits of farming, forestry or mining on the land, now it comes from tourism, weddings, safari parks and hotels. The practice of shooting deer and grouse is still lucrative (in Scotland there are around 340 sporting estates in the Highlands and Islands covering around 5.2 million acres of land), but some landowners are moving towards rewilding and ecotourism.

Whatever state these estates are in, one thing is certain: they cover a huge amount of the UK's rural landmass and are a whole industry in themselves.

Until the age of 18, I lived on three private country estates. First in Yorkshire, then Bedford, then, lastly, Graythwaite Estate in Cumbria. I was four when my dad was given the job of head forester of this small estate, overseeing 500 acres of woodland. My parents drove up from Bedford and went for the interview, with Tom and me in tow. They gave us KitKats to keep us quiet in the reception area. When they saw where we would be living, they knew this was the place for us.

The job came with a house. It was a three-bedroom lodge house, a bungalow, with an open fire, a huge walk-in pantry and a bay window to watch the south gates from. Legend says the house once had an upstairs, but the landowner didn't like the way the top floor ruined his view. He literally sliced it in half, taking the top off like a Victoria sponge cake. I'm not sure how likely this is.

For us, and many like us, it was simply impossible to buy a house on a regular rural wage. On Graythwaite, a house came with the job of the plumber, the housekeeper, the electrician, the farmer, the estate manager. Our homes were old, damp and cold, and we were four miles from any kind of shop.

But it was idyllic. We were surrounded by gardens and woodland, and Windermere lake was only a mile away down a private path.

In the summer, I would climb out of my bedroom window when I should have been asleep and ride my bike up and down the estate road. I just wanted to be outside. And in the autumn, I lay in bed listening to stags rutting, the roar of them, both unnerving and exciting. It *was* idyllic, and none of us paid rent.

I lead Phil and the kids along the road that led to our old lodge house. Naturally, it looks smaller now. Even the trees look smaller, the rockery less steep and the hill down past the wall more like a slope. The wall that ran around the house and the estates garden, however, looks bigger than ever. I point out the places where we made dens, where the farmer's daughter and I used to hold discos in the rhododendron bushes, decorating the branches with my mum's silvery thread from the sewing box. The coal bunker has gone, the shed is new, but the steps to the front door are exactly as I remember them. There are no cars by the house so I assume no one is in. It doesn't even look like anyone lives there but I can't bring myself to get too close and look in the windows to check. Phil takes a picture of me and the kids outside the bay windows, but I am keen to leave. It feels odd being here.

The huge beech tree that our tyre swing had hung from is still standing in what we called the back garden, but obviously the playhouse Dad built has gone. I tell them that, one day, Tom and his best mate, Adam, the plumber's son, borrowed some white paint and covered the playhouse in it. They tried to hide their paint-stained denim jackets under the boards of the playhouse but we could see their white glossy footprints all the way back up the steps.

We carry on around the paths. It's summer, so people are allowed to walk around the gardens, but there is no one else around. We can hear an engine – a ride-on lawnmower going up and down the field above the river. I don't want to be seen or to explain what we are doing here, so I hurry everyone along, past the beck and back to the stable block. Ellis asks about the people in the Big House. Who they were, what they are doing now. I only know what Mum told me: that the children of the estate – there were five of them; I was the same age as the second eldest – are all grown up. At least one of them has married another landowner and has not only children of her own, but her own land too. The eldest son now runs this place, I tell him. I wonder what Ellis thinks of this, but we have reached the car and we are all hungry. We change our plan of having a picnic by the lake and eat our sandwiches as we drive under the trees to the village.

My dad had a new knee a few weeks ago. He is still stuck at home, bored, resting, exercising it, so I call and ask him how we ended up there in Cumbria, living on an estate, in the playground of the upper classes.

'It was all I knew. My dad worked for estates, so I did too.'

My paternal grandfather was the head forester for the Osberton estate in Nottingham. Dad and his siblings also lived in a lodge house, very like the one we grew up in at Graythwaite. Dad would help Grandad in the woods, learning to love it as much as we would one day too. Their landowner was horse mad and set up the now-famous horse trials at Osberton, where Princess Anne competed in 1973, my dad having made all the jumps for the horses.

At 18, Dad applied for a forestry degree at university, but he didn't get the grades. Instead, he was offered a place studying geology at Leicester University. It might not have been his first choice, but it's easy to see why understanding the history of the land, learning why rocks are formed and why, ultimately, the landscape looks and behaves the way it does made for a good start to a life working outside. Needless to say, this was back in the time when university was free to attend and wouldn't otherwise have been an option.

When he graduated he started looking for jobs. He had met my mum when he was 18 and she 16, in the back of a Mini on the way to a Pink Floyd concert. They were married just a few years later and were hoping to start a family.

'The first place I worked wasn't keen on giving your mum and me a house, as they thought I wouldn't stick it, being a graduate. They gave us one in the end. Reluctantly.' The house was small and cold, but it was their first home together. They had geese and ducks and met friends in the pub nearby. My mum missed her mother terribly and her parents paid for a phone line to be installed so they could keep in touch.

For the estates Dad worked for, a degree meant nothing. Especially as it wasn't in the industry he wanted to work in – forestry. 'I was

at the bottom of the ladder again. I needed to learn from scratch.'
He did, taking a step up at each estate we moved to until, when I
was four and Tom was two, he got the job in Cumbria.

'We knew we were very lucky there,' he says. An image of South
Lodge and the path to the lake forms in my mind. As a parent
now, the lack of something solid to call our own would make me
nervous.

'Did you ever worry about not owning the house?' I ask.

'It clicked for me about the time you kids were teenagers. I
thought, "What are we going to do now?" But I was fortunate
enough to have married your mum. She's brighter than me.'

He's right. Without her, I'm not sure where we would have ended
up. She's always been the savvier one, more forward thinking. Dad's
head never really left the woods, whereas Mum managed the house
with us two kids on a low wage in an isolated place.

'Your mum worked hard to keep us afloat. Remember that guest
house next to the school? She used to clean there, then work in the
kitchen at lunchtime.'

I was a nervous kid at primary school, so having Mum in the
kitchen as a dinner lady settled something in me for a while.

'We were lucky too, as the estate started giving me commission
on timber.'

To encourage Dad to think more commercially, the estate gave
him a 2-per-cent commission on timber sales. After a particularly
good sale of wood, they received a small lump sum. They saved and
added more to this and then used it to buy a house in Worksop,
Nottingham, the town where Mum grew up. They rented it to
Mum's sister, who had recently been divorced. Her rent paid their
mortgage.

'It was the best we could do at the time. We knew we could
never buy in the Lakes.'

I imagine if our old lodge house ever came on the open market, it
would go for a lot of money. But it never will. Lodge houses are

part of the country estate as much as the Big House is. They are the first thing visitors see. They act like sentries, statements of intent that open out onto the road to the main house like a scene from a film.

Who can forget how Elizabeth Bennet changed her view of Mr Darcy when the road opened up to a view of his house behind the lake? Or the way the new Mrs de Winter described the drive that 'twisted and turned as a serpent' and then Manderley house, 'lovelier than I had ever dreamed'.

Personally, the Big House never interested me. In fact, it was always a place I avoided at all costs. It represented a space that was not for me. When I was young, I didn't like how I couldn't see into their windows (there were so many of them), but I knew that, if anyone was in there, they could see me. The Victorian Gothic style of the house of Graythwaite seemed to have a life all of its own. Without being told why, all the kids kept well away from it, as though it had some kind of repelling forcefield around it. We played our games firmly away from its gaze.

It was the wider estate gardens that were our territory. Or it felt like it. There were towering larch trees and dinky slate bridges over rivers. A stone staircase led to a pet graveyard with all the beloved dogs belonging to the estate family over hundreds of years. Socks, Indy, Lady. (There was one cat.) These gardens, designed well over

Land

a hundred years before, were not as well kept as they would have been in their heyday, but they were still lovely to be in, especially when the rhododendrons started to bloom. As they were open to the public every spring and summer, my brother and I would stand at the side of the path in shorts and mucky knees and sell mashed-up flowers in jam jars to the people who came to see the gardens, calling it perfume. Mum said we had to stop doing this. We couldn't really ask people to give us money on someone else's land without permission, no matter how small the profit was.

The estate had an incredible wall, as all private country estates do. The wall ran around the parklands and gardens from lodge house to lodge house, a stone ribbon pulling in the most managed, designed areas owned by the family. It was 10 feet high and built with huge chunks of red and cream sandstone with lime mortar between the gaps. There was no way you could climb it.

The south gates that stood in front of our house were mighty wrought-iron things that were always chained shut. I assume they used to open when horses and carriages travelled from the main road into the heart of the estate, but now they were padlocked tight. There were two side gates for people entering on foot. The whole thing was intricately designed with spikes and twisted iron spirals, beautiful and formidable. The family's crest was etched on shields melded onto the gates and there was a bell lodged into one of the stones. I can't remember if this worked, or even how it would work. It was ridiculously grand. I look for photos as, again back at home, I am a little worried I have exaggerated the memories of the gate and the sheer size of the wall. I have not. I find a picture of Tom and I waiting by the side gates for the school taxi, our lodge house in the background. We are standing in the turning space for carriages, my school bag in my hand, my brother with his head in a book. I am about nine, wearing black patent shoes and white socks up to the knees, and Sally, our collie dog, stands beside us with the same white furred socks.

Sometimes, a minibus picked us up for school, sometimes just a car; it changed every year, depending on how many children had to be collected this far out. Here, on the threshold of the gated estate, my mum sometimes had to pick me up and physically put me – crying my eyes out – on the school minibus. I had a stage – and most kids go through it; I know my own did – when I did not want to leave the safe, walled environment with my mum and go to school. I liked it there.

Sometimes I take Jessie to the old estate of Muiravonside in Central Scotland before we pick up Ellis from school. It is a woody, peaceful place now, owned by the local council. The foundations of the old house stand in the clearing just up the banking from the River Avon. When the weather is warm, we paddle in the water or go and see the animals at the farm park, where the farm steading was originally.

Jessie likes to walk on the foundations of the old house as the wall is low, just reaching below my knees, but the width of it is sturdy, measuring over 2 feet. She carefully steps on the stone, following the skeleton of the property as an architect would draw a plan. I'm always amazed an entire house was placed on these walls, but I suppose the act of walking on it can diminish it somehow. I have no doubt that if the house at Muiravonside was left standing, I would have avoided it much like I did Graythwaite Hall as a child. The fact that we can walk on the foundations of the Big House appeals very much to me now.

Muiravonside House was once a grand place, originally built in the sixteenth century, and the surrounding estate is rich in history. It seems it ticks every box in the life cycle of a country estate with links to the slave trade, illegitimate children, family disputes, soldiers and battles, and a hand in all the typical rural industries.

In the mid-eighteenth century, the man who owned Muiravonside, Alexander McLeod, was at the centre of the Jacobite rebellion. Geoff Bailey, a local historian, has researched Muiravonside's history. He writes that Alexander MacLeod was:

a major messenger between the Scottish Jacobites and Prince Charles Edward Stuart in the spring of 1745. He fought in all the actions of the '45 Campaign and stood beside the Prince at the Battle of Culloden Moor. He was one of the few who accompanied the Prince from the field. His servant, Ned Burke, helped guide Prince Charles to safety.

Not only did Alexander, the laird of Muiravonside, follow Bonnie Prince Charlie in the battlefield, but his servant had to as well.

Before Alexander died – as an old man, surprisingly, and not on the battlefield – it was understood that he had two illegitimate sons with a servant called Louisa Mowat. Here follows an almost soap-opera chapter of Muiravonside life. A story circulated that the cook had poisoned Alexander, persuaded to do so by either the local school master, who loved the servant Louisa himself, or possibly by Alexander's niece, Elizabeth, who wanted to prevent him from marrying Louisa and legitimising their sons' claim on the estate.

Whether this was true or not, Elizabeth, his niece, did indeed inherit Muiravonside.

Illegitimate children were not uncommon on estates like this. Quite often the gentleman of the house took a fancy to a servant. One account by Margaret Powell, who worked as a kitchen maid on an English estate in 1910, explains how her friend, the under-parlourmaid, was dismissed when they found out she was pregnant. She lists the ways she tried to remedy her situation, including hot mustard baths and Beechams pills, and 'when it was her day off she used to go in the park, climb on the park benches and then keep jumping off. It sounds amusing but it was a terrible thing for her.' They dismissed the under-parlourmaid with a month's worth of wages, which made them suspect the father was the nephew of the house.

It makes you wonder how many people are actually lost descendants from a Big House somewhere in the country.

Unfortunately for the niece who inherited Muiravonside, she and her husband went on to find themselves 'financially embarrassed' and declared bankruptcy some years later. Muiravonside was sold again. Another Alexander MacLeod purchased it. He had been an attorney in Spanish Town, Jamaica, and was responsible for managing plantations there that used slave labour. He is named as a 'slave-factor' (or manager) for at least four voyages to Jamacia.

In the last few years the National Trust has been researching the stately homes they own and their links to slavery. They've produced a report naming 93 properties so far, but this number is expected to be much higher. We are only just beginning to understand how the grandest of buildings, the artwork, the silver and the ornate furniture inside them derive from the profits of the slave trade. It irrevocably changes the way we see some of the places the public seem to love best.

Alexander MacLeod was no exception here. He expanded the house and its grounds with the profits he made abroad. An unusual summerhouse was built in a precarious position in the side of a gorge. It is still there today, although there is nothing summery about it. It is sunken into the embankment, the roaring weir of the River Avon below, its sandstone walls and vaulted roof now covered in plants and earth. Once it would have had views across the valley, but the trees have grown too high for this. The summerhouse feels more like a witch's cottage now.

Over the centuries, Muiravonside also made money through forestry; they built a sawmill, they mined coal, and limekilns were also constructed in the nineteenth century. Lime, used by farmers on the local clay soil to improve crop productivity, was also sent along the canal, which runs through the estate, for the construction of the New Town in Edinburgh. The history of Muiravonside shows how even a small estate had connection not only to the local area, but to the wider world.

In the late nineteenth century, the owner, Charles Stirling of Drumpellier, thought that connection to the local area was important for everyone. His grandson wrote about Charles:

My grandfather, a man of strong convictions, had believed that everyone should be mutually helpful; that his tenants troubles were his own; that employment should be found on the estate for all his men's children, and that everything in use on the estate should be produced, if possible, by the estate itself. Consequently his suits were made of cloth woven from the wool of his own sheep and his boots were made by a local shoemaker. His money, little of which was spent outside, was in constant circulation among his tenants.

The post of coachman seemed to be hereditary. James, the holder of the title when I was a boy, was a giant of a man, with red hair and a flaming spade-shaped beard which reached right down to the third button of his livery. That great growth on the box seat was considered out of place by the more fashionable members of the family, but James resolutely declined to shave it off. Eventually it was decided that the only possible solution was to have chestnut horses harnessed to the coach to match the colour of James's beard.

The recollection of changing the horses to match the coachman, rather than the other way around, lends a sweet insight into how the estate was run at this point. It was around then that Charles started a tradition of inviting the children from the local school to the Big House where they were given Christmas treats. It was a Christmas party on our estate that I remember as the only time I was in the Big House. It felt like everyone was there: the housekeeper, the gamekeeper, the plumber, Mum and Dad – all in their best clothes, in a room with a huge fireplace laden with garlands of holly and ivy. People looked different – smarter and taller; the women in high heels and with tiny glasses of sherry in their hands. My brother and I found the other estate kids and slipped off, leaving the adults to their mince pies. We were terrified to go too far, so a bunch of us lingered on a staircase, which climbed up in a square. We sat on the red carpet and frightened each other with stories of the portraits' moving eyes.

Muiravonside House continued to be owned by the Stirling

family, whether through direct descendants of children or sometimes cousins. But often, the house was not lived in and was rented out.

In 1925, it was advertised for rent in the *Scotsman* newspaper and boasted four public rooms, six bedrooms, two dressing rooms and the luxury of 'electric light'. The entrance hall is noted to have 'a tiled hearth, a Persian copper kettle, four oak hall chairs and an antique mahogany drawing table'.

During the Second World War, it was used by the army. The 1st Light Anti-Aircraft Regiment of the Polish Forces stayed at Muiravonside House, and huts were built near the house for accommodation. Incredibly, in 2003, a digger accidentally uncovered a box-load of grenades, which had been deliberately hidden in the ground just to the north of the house.

The Polish soldiers became a regular sight in the area, and one newspaper article describes how the members of a Polish unit held a party at Muiravonside House.

The dining hall, where tea was served, was tastefully decorated for the occasion with flags, flowers and evergreens. After tea, the floor was cleared and the company, which numbered 80 couples, spent the rest of the evening in dancing to music provided by the Polish Lala Band.

In 1978, Falkirk Planning Department purchased the estate of Muiravonside to use as a country park. They bought the 170 acres for £70,000. After years of neglect and vandalism, the house was deemed too far gone to restore. It was demolished in 1979. People have barbecues and parties here now on the old walls of the Big House. We held Ellis's fifth birthday party here. It was a *Star Wars*-themed party and Dad came out from underneath the sweet chestnut trees dressed as Darth Vader.

Remnants of estates like Muiravonside sit underneath our parks, our roads, our schools and our hospitals. There are usually clues left behind. The Big Houses may have gone but the huge walls that surrounded the gardens are often still intact. Sometimes, only sections of them run alongside a road or are integrated within a more modern wall. We are so used to seeing them we forget that they marked boundaries between landowners. These walls were built to prove a point, to make a statement. They are the barricades to keep the unwanted masses out.

It is very difficult to find any facts or statistics about how many people lived and worked for places like this. The bigger estates might have kept records of people who worked for them, but, short of contacting every estate in the UK and compiling a list, any number would only ever be a rough estimate. It almost feels like a hidden sector. Although occasionally staff could stay on for generations, like James, the red-haired coachman at Muiravonside, it was also the case that estates changed hands regularly due to bankruptcy. If the estate had no money, staff inevitably would have been let go.

One former gamekeeper in Scotland said, 'Everyone's thinking, you've got a house there that you live in, but I had nothing, because if that guy doesn't like me and makes me homeless, where am I going to stay? You're thinking it's great, but I had a pittance of a wage.'

The Hopetoun estate is only a 20-minute drive from where we live. It's a particularly grand estate that spans over 6,500 acres in West Lothian, and we often visit for events or to walk in the grounds. Some way through the Covid pandemic, when community events were mostly still cancelled, Hopetoun put on a dazzling light show in its woodland. After dusk had fallen, we were shepherded around the grounds, the trees backlit to create fairy-tale-like scenes. Jessie loved the magic of it. I had also been in the Big House before – a Christmas fair a few years before. The front façade of the house is never-ending, with rows of windows climbing four floors high, numerous chimneys pitched into the sky and a stone staircase up to the front doors, which would make a mother with a buggy cry.

Of course, it is beautiful inside, with those staircases, the fireplaces and the library especially. But the same feelings always creep up on me: this place isn't for you. Of course it isn't; I know it isn't. The idea of eating in such a huge dining room is unnerving and unappealing. Even the rooms with the fireplaces to read and relax in look cavernous and unwelcoming. When visiting houses like this, I move from room to room quickly and breathe a little more easily when I'm in the grounds outside rather than in the long corridors inside. I find myself wondering what it would be like to live on an estate like this again, as an adult.

Phil and I were cycling part of the coastal path between Kincardine Bridge and Edinburgh, which runs through the Hopetoun estate, Jessie bouncing away in the cycle seat behind her dad, when we bumped into a mutual friend. It was November, so the fields around the house were wet and muddy; a herd of deer were far away in the top field. In spring there are lambs, in summer the sound of grasshoppers and in autumn, pheasants dashing from one copse of trees to the next. We stopped at a kissing gate as the woman and her husband were closing it.

'Oh, hello,' I said, recognising her, and then tactlessly, 'You live *here*?!' I sounded shocked but it really masked a sudden flash of jealousy.

'Just at the end of this road.' She pointed the way we had cycled.

I looked back and saw the lodge house next to the cattlegrid. I had often looked through the window as we'd walked past and seen cookbooks on the deep windowsill and Blu-Tacked pictures on the fridge in the background.

'I grew up in a house like that!' In a rush, I told her about my estate and how this – I gestured around at the fields, the cattlegrids, the deer – was what my childhood looked like.

'It's like time travelling,' I said.

'We love it here. The kids do too.'

For the rest of the bike ride, I was quiet. At home, I looked up the estate online to see if there was any property to rent. There was one place available, a big, stone-built house just outside the walls, the rent costing almost double our mortgage.

When I was eleven, we moved into our second home on our estate. I had just started secondary school and the travel catchment changed, so, instead of paying for the taxi to school, we asked the estate to move us a mile closer to the village so the school would still provide transport. But other things were changing too. A few years after we moved, the estate decided they didn't want to employ a forester anymore. Big landowners were beginning to modify the way they made money. Dad was made redundant, along with the plumber and the electrician. The other families moved into the village or further away into the towns, but we stayed put. Dad became self-employed and we started paying rent. All of a sudden, the pressure was on to make it work. Dad started looking for clients and as Mum was good with numbers, she found work doing the books for a couple of the pubs in the village.

Our new house was previously the estate's social club. It had none of the grandeur of the lodge house and was more utilitarian, a classic house a kid would draw with three windows in the front, a chimney and a pitched slate roof. The only door in was at the side of the house. When it was the estate's social club, people used to come to play cards there and sit in front of the open fire, catching up, gossiping. Now we sat in front of the fire, watching cartoons after school, as it was the warmest place in the house.

The area around the house had a more industrial feel as it was alongside the estate woodsheds and the sawmill. We were well and truly outside the managed walls and the designed gardens now, and our garden was not a garden at all. It was a jungle of rhododendrons and fir trees. We spent years cutting it back, burning it up and making space for plants to grow. We had so many bonfires. We revealed the beck, whose water course ran right under the house and seeded a small patch of grass next to a section of it. This was our only bit of lawn. Years later, in the summer, on my split shifts in the pub, I lay on the grass in the sun, careful not to sit too close to the adders that would swim in the water nearby. Once, we found an adder in the kitchen. We had seen the snake, its diamond markings wrapped around its body, snug alongside the base of the washing machine. It had found its way in between the water pipes. After one failed attempt at catching it, Tom stood by the kitchen table for hours, his air rifle pointed at the base of the kitchen cupboards, ready to 'get it'. Mum, never one to miss a conical moment, took a photo of him doing this. She finally caught the snake in the biscuit tin and released it near the beck at the top of the garden.

The adders lived in the warm piles of wood shavings from the sawmill just behind our house. I avoided this area, not only for fear of standing on a nest of snakes, but because this was where the sheds for hanging the venison were. Hanging deer improved the texture and flavour, apparently, but all I remember is the stench of dead flesh. No matter how sealed the building was meant to be, the smell still somehow seeped out of the shed. It made my stomach turn.

Every winter, the estate threw big hunting parties. Men came from all over the world to shoot there, mainly pheasant but with a few deer hunts too. The gamekeeper bred pheasants in the woods near our house and in winter they were released in designated areas. Range Rovers started appearing, parked in rows at the side of the woods, and shots would echo off the fells behind our house on cold mornings. It is estimated that 35 million pheasants are released every year for shooting. Many of those shot now end up on the dining plates of restaurants around the country.

I once joined the shoot as a beater. I tagged along with a few other estate kids and the dogs to 'flush out' the birds from the copse of trees or bushes. I hated it. I don't think it was the actual shooting of the pheasants I didn't like. I had grown up alongside the idea of this, although, thinking about it now, I'm much more uncomfortable about the practice of shooting for sport. What felt so unsettling was the clear divide between the two parties. I was tramping through the cold, wet grass for the benefit of someone else's so-called fun. As a child, it felt troubling on many levels, which I just couldn't pick apart yet. I knew I didn't want to do it twice, and my parents never suggested it again.

Years later, as an adult, I was invited on another pheasant shoot by an old boss in Scotland. I went, intrigued (and admittedly thrilled) to be part of the other side of the party. I sat in the Range Rover, high up on the heated seats, and reeled as we drove from site to site. I watched the beaters and their dogs go ahead and scare the pheasants into the sky. I felt like I had put on the wrong shoes. I didn't really understand why I had been invited. I was nothing like anyone else on the shoot; I didn't own a business or a property empire or have a rich family like the rest of them. I don't drink sherry.

I *think* I was invited because, somehow, growing up the way I did has given me a kind of class ambiguity. Or maybe an absence of class. I'm not sure exactly. But Dad always said, when working for estates and landowners you have to have a foot in both fields. To fit in with the workers, but also the owners.

Maybe I inherited this classlessness. Maybe my old boss saw that. As a teenager I answered the phone in our hallway and if it was someone for Dad, one of his landowners, I learned to change my accent. It came naturally, almost an imitation of the person on the phone. Keeping this up for a whole day, however, is near impossible.

Nature writer Nicola Chester lived on the Highclere estate (where *Downton Abbey* is set) and recognises this. She tells me she also changed her voice when speaking to the farrier, or the master or the farmer. Her book, *On Gallows Down*, draws out this magical but sometimes unsettling lifestyle.

She writes, 'The past was tangible. We felt, sometimes resentfully, part of the ghost of an old order of things. It was there when a low feudal mist cut us off from the outside world, when the Queen or wealthy Arabs visited, when we were allowed to collect firewood, cut ourselves a Christmas tree, or accept a brace of pheasants.'

We never had anyone as fancy as the Queen, but, yes, for all its advantages and disadvantages, this was it exactly. Every year we walked into the woods and chose our Christmas tree. Dad chopped it down and dragged it back. Not only were we neither comfortably one class nor the other, it also felt we were not quite living in the present either.

Andy Wightman, who worked as a stalker's ghillie in the 1980s, wrote, 'The work was straightforward but the cultural practices were out of the Edwardian period. The whole glen was infused with such malfunctioning social norms and the insidious power struggles between landowners, the tenants and the visiting public.'

I was oblivious to this as a child. But now, living on an estate seems almost an impossible lifestyle to me, both difficult to maintain with the power struggles between landowners and tenants, and difficult to believe with the somewhat antiquated existence.

*

A mutual friend grew up on a huge estate and for one of the first times in adulthood, I speak to someone who recognises my own experiences precisely. She says there was 'sledging in the farmer's field, lots of den building, treasure hunts, tree climbing. We had a playing field with a massive log we used to play on. We made our own rope swings.' I want to tell her about our rope swings, our dens. The tractor-tyre swing that filled with rainwater, which would swish out as we swung on it.

'It was great fun living on the estate as a child and I now look back and realise how lucky we really were. My two children are now in the same situation, and I keep telling them how lucky they are also. It is like one large family.'

This is where our experiences diverge. Whereas she moved back onto the estate with her children, I have moved away from that life. I am, once again, struck by jealousy.

Her father, who started as a gardener and became the chauffeur was given a house to retire in, but, she says, the estate stopped doing this some years ago. As most estates have. Her husband currently works as a landscape manager, and they live in the house that comes with that job.

'I hope we can stay in our house; we love the setting and the way of life.'

I ask whether she ever feels she needs to own a property. 'I always feel we should buy a house and rent it out in case anything happened to my husband's job, but I would hope that if this happened, we would get the opportunity to rent our current property.'

I find out later that Dad applied for a job on that estate when Tom and I were kids. 'I didn't even get an interview,' he laughs. Maybe I could have been part of that community. I could have grown up alongside her. Maybe I would have returned, like she did, given half the chance.

2

Wood

It is autumn and we are scattered about the wood my brother lives in. We do not know it yet, but this will be the last time in months we are all together. The next time we meet, the pandemic will have eased for the second time, I will be a few months pregnant, in the throes of morning sickness, and Lesley, my brother's girlfriend, will once again be having regular chemotherapy. But today, it is perfect. The air is cool and fresh, and we are helping Tom clear a beech tree he has felled. It lies across a small spring, covering it entirely with a mass of branches, and we are tasked with dragging the branches up and away, to clear the beck. He has been digging out the normally boggy area, encouraging the spring to run clearly and using the clay for plastering the walls inside his cabin. There are now plants and herbs growing on the banking, and he is hoping for tadpoles in the future.

I often tell people my brother lives in the woods, but it always sounds a little odd, almost too fairy-tale-like. So much so that sometimes Mum holds back on telling people what he does, as they don't quite believe it. He spends most the year in a small patch of woodland in Cumbria near Bouth, in a similar way to how coppice workers and charcoal burners lived over a hundred years ago. Like them, Tom spends the warmer seasons within the trees, hoping to stretch it out as long as the weather will allow. He stays at Lesley's house across the country in Gateshead when he needs to. And sometimes, when he really needs to, he goes to Mum and Dad's house a few miles away for a bath. He makes a living from the forest around him, managing the woodland, encouraging diversity in the species. He is not what you would call a forester, an ecologist or an environmentalist but sits somewhere in between all these things. He understands how a forest works, so when he fells a tree, he ensures the cut will allow more sunlight onto the forest floor for plants to flourish. Then, he will use the chainsaw to carve the trunk of it into a hare, a horse or a bear. He sells these online and at country shows.

My son, Ellis, usually loves to help him mine the muddy clay but today he is chopping branches off the tree with an axe, watched closely by Tom. He is eleven and the idea of working with what can only be described as dangerous tools appeals to him. Mum, Jessie and I are dragging the branches, piling them up into a makeshift wall to provide habitat for beasties, as well as creating a natural screen to camouflage the area from any walkers that happen to pass. Not that many do. Tom's single-room wooden cabin sits behind the scenes like something Henry David Thoreau might write about. Inside, there is a small kitchen area and a wooden bed that my dad built for Tom when we were kids. When we are tired, Mum unpacks the cake and milk for coffee, and we sit by the fire in the clearing. Tom is having a go at making charcoal using an old oil drum. The vents at the base of the drum glow red hot. He wants the charcoal for forging, to get hot enough to hammer metal into shape, so it needs to be good quality and strong. For this, the draught of the fire is important – it needs to travel backwards. Tom fills the drum with logs and lights it from the top. The vents at the bottom suck the air out that way. Eight hours later, hopefully, the wood will have turned black, any moisture in it cooked out.

The scene from *Swallows and Amazons* pops into my head: when the children come across a group of charcoal burners, the men speak of the fire as if it's got a character all of its own.

Wood

'We want ours to burn good and slow. If he burns fast he leaves nowt but ash. The slower the fire the better the charcoal.'

These woods are no stranger to charcoal burning. For hundreds of years, groups of men set up camps in the forests around the UK to make charcoal for iron smelting, glass making and working precious metals. Tom's woods were used to supply the local gunpowder works a mile down the road. The fire would burn for six to eight days under a huge kiln the men built with earth.

Today, small sparks of the fire escape from the tiny air holes at the bottom of the drum. The smoke is grey – for really good charcoal, the smoke will turn blue. Sometimes we hear the sheep in the field at the edge of the wood. Sometimes we hear the low rumble of a passenger plane flying overhead. But mainly all we hear is birdsong and the crackle of the hidden fire. I heard a cuckoo for the first time in years there last spring. I sit on a log next to Lesley. She is over for a few days from Gateshead. Busy town, then busy woods, literally swapping high heels for wellies. They don't have a toilet here, running water or heating. She had cancer last year, which changed everything. She left her office job and has started spending more time here, taking up painting, creating artwork on the wooden boards Tom has lying around. She'll probably use the charcoal made today to draw with.

After a few hours of working, we have cleared a small area and can see the source of the beck. The water is still full of leaves, a patchwork of colours, a messed-up work by Andy Goldsworthy. There is a lot more to do but Tom is in no rush. As we collect our coats from the porch, something flutters past and lands on a post in one of the wood stores. It flashes bright at us, orange with black polka dots, and then is camouflaged against the wood.

'It's a comma butterfly,' Tom says – named for the tiny white mark on the underside of the wings shaped like a punctuation mark. We stand on tiptoes to get a better look and I lift Jessie up. We stare at the tatty edges of the butterfly's wings. It is one of the few species in the UK that is bucking the trend and increasing its population. It is looking for somewhere cosy and warm to settle down and hibernate until spring. Maybe, for the time being, it will make its home here in the woods like Tom and Lesley have done. It will find a tree trunk, a fallen branch or a log pile – Tom has plenty of them – and sleep, occasionally waking for the warmer winter days. Hidden within the warmth of the woods sounds like a good way to see through the winter months to me.

It feels inevitable that Tom ended up living in the woods, as forestry runs in the family. Grandad Morris was a forester, working in the Dukeries in Nottingham, part of what was once the vast Sherwood Forest, walking the same paths that Robin Hood supposedly did. Grandad Morris started working in forestry before machines and chainsaws were introduced. A day invariably started as early as possible, 6 a.m. in the summer – but in winter as soon as it was light – and finished either at 5 p.m. or when it was too dark to see. There were many roles within the job of a forester: planting, ditch digging, road building, felling, harvesting. Not only did you need the physical strength to use the saws, but you had to engineer how to get the timber out, understand how the tree would fall and manoeuvre a huge log without injury. They would have used a two-man cross-cut saw to fell a tree. Which then would have to be stripped of the branches and made 'clean' for the sawmill. The logs were then dragged off site by horses. Now huge machines do all these steps. It's easier on the back but doesn't make it any less dangerous.

After retiring, Grandad Morris lived within a small community not far from the ancient oak tree that legend says Robin Hood lived in. He spent his retirement years working away in his shed, leaving a trail of sawdust behind him.

My dad's generation of foresters has seen huge changes to the industry. Not only do they still do all the roles Grandad's did, they now have to understand the ecology of forestry. Personally, I think foresters have always understood the role of ecology. By the very nature of the job, you are working with ecosystems that support each other, and learning how landscapes and successful woodlands are created. There was a time when profit margins outweighed a responsibility to the wider environment – and bear in mind, foresters never gained from this; the landowners did, but foresters have always understood how interlinked the natural world is. How could you not when it takes your whole career, a whole lifetime, to see a forest grow, caring for it, spending time in it, watching the wildlife thrive beneath the branches?

I can understand why Tom has chosen this lifestyle. I can see the pull of the forest, or rather I *feel* it. It must do something to you, growing up in such close proximity to it. We watched saplings reach out of their tubes and rise big enough for birds to nest in. We looked for deer, searched for badgers, and Dad would point out the buzzards or kestrels circling above us as we ate our packed lunches on slabs of stone or wind-blown trees. We heard the trees creak as the winter storms picked off the weakest branches and foraged their timber for firewood. Forestry was never just planting and felling. There's a whole lifetime between that.

After the First World War, there was a chronic shortage of timber in the UK. Deforestation had been happening gradually since the Neolithic times when farmers started the process of clearing the land for grain and animals. When the *Domesday Book* was written, England's forests had already dwindled to cover only 15 per cent of England, cut down for materials or to give way to pasture. Most surviving woodlands were used for coppicing, which is the practice of cutting a tree down to its base to encourage regrowth. By repeatedly doing this, it creates a sustainable supply of thin timber strips, which are used for hurdles to make fencing, or for hedge laying or for building materials. Writer and academic Oliver Rackham wrote, 'The survival of almost any large tract of woodland suggests that there has been an industry to protect it against the claims of farmers.' Perhaps the industries of coppicing and charcoaling were the only thing that saved Tom's woods from becoming farmland, although I find it hard to imagine them as anything else.

Woodland cover dropped even further to just 10 per cent in the mid-twelfth century, but the Black Death in both the UK and across Europe halted any more decline. Huge areas of pastureland were abandoned as there was no one left to farm it. Cal Flyn writes, 'Between one fifth and a quarter of all settlements [in Europe] were abandoned. Harvests went unreaped, crops rotted in fields.' Many of the forests we see in Germany were the result of this period and much of the forest area across the UK stabilised. But even with this slowing of the ravishing of woodlands, 500 years later an agricultural survey in 1877 stated that forest cover in England was at 4 per cent.

By 1914 and the outbreak of the First World War, the UK was importing 90 per cent of its timber, much of it from Russia. This wasn't sustainable during a conflict that used naval blockades and the war effort demanded huge amounts of timber for the front line. Trenches needed pit props, planks, duckboards and posts for shelters, tunnels and fortifications. As the UK's supplies of timber declined ever faster, so did the forests in France, which were also exploited. Wood was essential and we were in danger of running out. Prime Minister David Lloyd George said that Britain had 'nearly lost the war for want of timber than of anything else'.

The First World War showed how vulnerable we were as a country without timber supplies, so, in 1919, the Forestry Commission was created. Its main aims were to restore the UK's woodlands and reduce the quantity of timber being imported. The third goal was to reduce the decline of the rural population across Britain – so many small communities had lost men in the war; rural villages must have looked and felt very different to the years previous.

The physical work of afforestation had the immediate advantage of bringing men and their families 'back to the land'. The Commission's intention was for millions of acres of forest to be replanted over the next 30 years, and the first Annual Report in 1921 showed they had already acquired over 100,000 acres throughout Britain and Ireland. The Acland Report, which ultimately formed the beginnings of the Forestry Commission, initially envisaged building smallholdings for families to live in. There were 624 holdings by 1924, which usually consisted of a cottage and a garden with 'enclosed agricultural or cultivable land to keep a couple of cows and to grow potatoes and other crops'.

These smallholdings, like Tom's, were only expected to be lived in for 150 days of the year, ideally when the weather was good in the spring and summer, but many people stayed year long, enjoying the lifestyle. It seemed it was a success.

By the late 1940s, swathes of forests were maturing across the country and a bigger workforce was needed to be close at hand for forest management and to be on the lookout for forest fires. But this was easier said than done. The third chair of the Forestry Commission, Sir John Stirling Maxwell, had noted that 'the planting of forest workers on the land is a more anxious and much more expensive business than the planting of trees'.

In light of this, the Commission started planning more than just the occasional smallholding, and instead drew up plans for whole communities of their workforce with village halls, schools and shops. It is reported that this new phase of social planning was the first one since the planned villages of the eighteenth and nineteenth centuries and could be considered a predecessor to the 'new' towns of the future.

The village of Ae, in Dumfriesshire in the south of Scotland, was the first Forestry Commission village to be designed in the UK. Eighty houses were planned in 1947, along with a school, playing fields and a pub. The Commission produced a guidebook to sell the benefits of Ae, in which it said, 'Those who live in the village will feel that they are not isolated; they will be members of an active community, and without the disadvantages of urban life.'

I wonder about this phrase, 'the disadvantages of urban life', and can only assume it means the areas in cities, such as in the Gorbals in Glasgow, where there was serious overcrowding. It seems families were shipped in from the 'slums' of cities to work for the Commission, and not all of them adapted to rural living as well as they hoped. In her book, *Voices of the Forest*, Mairi Stewart interviews previous residents. One said, 'People moved in and out a lot, came from the city. Some couldn't cope with no bus service, one shop and that sort of thing.' One man said he heard someone drove into the village, looked around and went straight back home again. George Ivison, a retired forester, reflected: 'You can't bring people from the middle of a city and dump them in the middle of nowhere.'

What better way to highlight the difference between 'city folk' and 'country folk' than putting them in each other's shoes? Or rather, what better way to look at the aspects of life we come to hold dearest, unable to live without. I have lived in cities and enjoyed parts of it – it was exciting to stumble home after the pub, to, on the spur of the moment, buy a coffee or visit an art gallery. But I never truly felt at home. I saw an old school friend at a country show a few years ago and I asked her where she was now living. 'Back at the farm,' she said. She and her husband had moved to a small town. I knew the one she mentioned – it had one main street, maybe four pubs and a few shops – but she shook her head: 'It wasn't for us. I can't imagine what it must be like in a city. Not for me, that's for sure.'

Until age 18 I grew up in these environments but never once felt isolated. We had the other children on the estate to play with;

our friends came from the village to ride their bikes up and down the estate roads, over the cattlegrids and speed bumps. In my teenage years, the huge advantage of living away from villages or towns were the parties. Isolation meant that no one was going to complain about how many teenagers were parked up outside the house. It didn't matter how loud the music was or where we wandered. We had parties in the bothy, an old stone building behind our house, which was Dad's office. The walls were covered in maps of woodlands, letters and postcards and the desk was a mass of papers in front of the huge grey bulk of the computer. We would drag the kitchen chairs up to the bothy and line the room with them and added camping chairs and invited as many friends as we could. We placed candles on every surface and stoked up the huge open fire to make it as hot as a sauna. We danced to Dad's tinny stereo and newly got-together couples wandered around the garden in the dark. Of course, there was always alcohol and quite often weed. But no one ever passed out or became paralytically drunk. I do remember one girl barging into the bathroom when Dad was brushing his teeth to empty her stomach in the toilet. It was probably the fresh air of the woods. I think the alcohol affects you more when the night air feels so alive. Or at least that was my excuse.

Even as older teenagers, my friends seemed to 'play' when they came to our house. I have photos of them putting on my dad's flat cap and chopping logs. My brother had an air rifle and they liked to play with that in the back garden, sometimes sitting on the swing with the air rifle in their arms.

Even though I never felt isolated, it was a different matter for Mum. Shopping was a huge issue. Our nearest Co-op was four miles away; the nearest big supermarket 20 miles away. Not so bad with a car but impossible with public transport, which was non-existent. Our car was our saviour. The wives in the forestry settlements in the 1950s often had no transport. If the shop was 20 miles away, you were lucky if there was a nearby bus. Hitching lifts in timber wagons was more likely. One woman said, 'I would cycle two miles, then take the train to Ballachulish, the ferry across, then the bus on the other side to Fort William, then I had two hours for shopping.' She could only buy what she could carry on her bike on the way back, though. Many villages were blessed with all sorts of weekly vans, such as the butcher's van, the fish van, the fruit-and-veg van. These were, and still are, a lifeline in isolated communities.

Rural industries, certainly rural communities, can be forgiven for thinking they were forgotten about by the central political forces that had a say in rural life. Before the NHS, 'friendly societies' were set up to help workers if they found themselves in debt due to illness, death or old age. Many forestry and estate workers joined these, paying a regular contribution that guaranteed help when they needed it most. Just before 1900 there were as many as 27,000 such societies in the UK.

In some areas, the Forestry Commission was seen as a good place to work, with decent wages and suitable housing. They helped new communities by providing logs for people, and 'supporting children's parties', which could have been anything from putting on galas to hosting Christmas events for them. In Falstone in Northumberland, the Commission provided a private healthcare system for 'a few coppers per week' to workers and their families. It didn't cover operations, but it included doctors' visits and prescriptions.

However, this wasn't always the case. In 1960, Sir Rupert Speir, MP for Hexham, set out in the House of Commons the issues his constituents had in the Forestry Commission village of Kielder in Northumberland.

They are provided with pretty well no amenities. They are charged the full economic rent for their houses, although they are tied houses. They are snowed up in winter, and for a large part of the summer they are consumed by midges from the forests and the trees.

Ah, yes, the seasons and therefore, always, the weather. Anyone who lives rurally, and especially those who work outside, keeps watch of the weather religiously. Each evening we used to watch the news at six o'clock, and during it my brother and I could mess about. But at 6.27 p.m., when the weather came on, we were dead quiet. The weather decides everything. What you do the next day. What you plan to do the next week. How you do the job. Where the job is. Whether or not you will even get *to* the job in hand. At the very start of the pandemic, I was struck how Covid-19 stopped cities as if the air had been taken out of them in the same way that big weather events can bring rural communities to their knees. Whereas offices, train stations and restaurants all ground to a halt, Dad and other rural businesses carried on. They had to. The farmers had to feed their cattle and see to the lambs, the foresters had to fell the trees and re-plant areas too. They were providing vital resources to the country. At home, we watched the weather, wary of storms that blew down trees and blocked roads. We watched the weather to be prepared for snow so deep the sheep were lost underneath it. We watched the weather and dreaded the floods that were so formidable that cattle were found 15 miles downstream. In those times, it became about surviving. Again.

Sir Rupert Speir then went on to note in his address to the House of Commons that in the village 'there are no trained nurses, the doctors are miles away over hilly roads, and the hospital is distant by 30 miles or more'. As a mother myself, this sends a shiver down my spine. Our nearest hospital was about an hour away. We didn't register with the doctor in the nearest village; we chose to register with one in a village on the way to the hospital. Mum figured if we were ill enough to see the doctor, we were likely to have to go all the way to the hospital anyway, so we may as well be halfway there. Looking back, I'm not so sure about her logic, but coming from a particularly clumsy household, I'm glad she made that decision. I've lost count the amount of times we ended up at the hospital. If my mum receives a phone call, even now, the first thing she establishes is that everyone is well.

Tom has broken a number of bones in his body: once playing football, once playing rugby (he collided with the post), and there was also an incident with a flying fox in our back garden. Dad had rigged up a wire that went from the tall larch tree to the rhododendron bushes on the other side of the garden. We called it the death slide. It snapped one day and Tom plunged into the beck. Mum, Dad and I were out at work, so he walked up to the nearest neighbour's house so they could phone the ambulance. His arm was broken and he had bloody gashes all over his face and chest. He must have looked like something from a horror movie, coming out of the bushes. We dismantled the death slide after that.

Forestry, however, is a whole other level of dangerous. Dad has dropped logs on his toes, broken various bones and cut his face too many times to recall. One worker joked that his 'native Indian name' would be 'man with a bleeding face'. He has driven himself to hospital with a broken foot. I think he even managed to drive over his own foot once – I'm not sure how. Chainsaws; huge, immovable trees; tractors; axes: it's a recipe for repeated hospital stays. The worst was when I was 13. The nurse phoned Mum at work and told her that, in fact, Dad had been lucky. He had fallen out of a tree and broken his back. I can almost feel the punch in the chest she would have experienced. The dread. He had been cutting some branches down that were hanging over phone wires. If the branches came down on the wire, the whole area would have no phone line, which happened quite regularly really. It was Dad, however, who came down. He slipped, lost his footing on the tree and fell 12 feet, landing on the tarmac road, but – and this was the lucky part – he managed to push the roaring chainsaw away from his body on the way down. He broke his bottom thoracic vertebra. He spent three months lying flat on his back, the doctors hoping it would heal without surgery. It did. He never 'nipped up' a tree without a harness again.

Thankfully, things are different now. We have GPS signals, 4G and helicopters. When foresters work at a site, an emergency procedure is always planned beforehand. Coordinates are arranged so they know the nearest spot for the rescue helicopter to land. So far, my brother has only been picked up by a helicopter once. Tom and the team were working alongside Coniston lake. Tom was chainsawing and, again, slipped. He sliced the inside of his calf, the saw brushing through the chainsaw trousers and into his muscle like it was silk. Chainsaw trousers are made of layers and layers of strong fibres that are meant to jam the chainsaw when it comes into contact with it. Tom's chainsaw trousers only had this super-strong fabric on the front of the leg, where most injuries occur. Somehow, he had managed to slash the fleshy bit on the back of his leg. It makes me shudder to think of the moments after it first happened – the shock, the mess. The men working with him clamped the wound as best they could and waited for the whirring sound of the rescue helicopter's arrival. They probably phoned Dad at that point, who then phoned Mum. Another dreaded phone call at work. The helicopter arrived within 20 minutes and landed in the arranged spot

— a nearby field. Tom was whisked away and sewn back up. He tells people his scar was from a shark attack.

In its heyday in the Fifties, the Forestry Commission owned thousands of properties. Dad was born in one in 1956. Before he was a forester, Grandad Morris was a farm labourer and then a gamekeeper. They moved to the Commission house in Walesby in Nottinghamshire in 1950, and Lin, Dad's older sister, remembers it well. She describes a small collection of semi-detached houses in a cul-de-sac, with the biggest house, where 'the boss' lived, at the top of the street. It certainly 'felt like a step up' from the previous house they had been in.

Our house was huge. It had three bedrooms with a kitchen-diner, and a wash house and a toilet just off the kitchen. The coal house and log house were attached to the kitchen so you didn't need to traipse out in the dark and get the coal. The hallway was so big your dad's pram could sit in it quite comfortably.

Although 'city folk' may not have always stayed for long in the more isolated forestry villages, often it was the mix of people in the villages that made them work so well. The village of Glenmore near Strathspey was built to help rejuvenate the forest that had both suffered a destructive fire in 1942 and been plundered for timber during the war. Rita Robertson was interviewed by Mairi Stewart for the book *Voices of the Forest*. Rita, who was just a teenager when she moved into Glenmore, echoed what Lin said about the house: 'We couldn't believe our luck. It was marvellous.' When Rita's father, Louie, returned from the war to work for the Forestry Commission, their newly built house had 'stairs, running water and a Rayburn cooker'. Although electricity was still a few years away, they had an indoor bathroom, which was a bonus.

The village had a mix of residents; one of Rita's neighbours, Edi, was Polish and had been forced into Hitler Youth at 17. It is said there might have been around 400,000 prisoners of war in the UK, mainly from Germany and Italy, by the end of the Second World War. They provided a much-needed workforce in rural areas that had lost so many of their men to the war. The POWs worked in farming and forestry, and, like many, Edi found he liked the lifestyle and the area, so stayed and married a local girl. Rita's father, who had also been a prisoner of war on the Continent, noted that the residents all got on well. Glenmore had been transformed into a small but bustling community.

Lin remembers that their life in Walesby did not revolve around Grandad's job as a forester: 'I remember he would wear certain clothes on certain days – huge toe-capped boots – but we didn't go out into the woods with him.' I find this funny as our childhood certainly did revolve around Dad's job. As young children, we played in the back of Dad's pick-up truck, trying on his chainsaw helmet. In the summer holidays, on hot days, we would follow the sound of chainsaws and deliver huge bottles of iced squash we had frozen in the freezer. I learned to drive in Dad's Land Rover in the tractor ruts of a Sitka spruce plantation. And in the back end of winter, I went planting with him as a teenager. As a self-employed forester by this point, he was managing a number of woodlands and estates. We set off before dawn, often picking up the other lads on the way, and went to some far-flung site to plant thousands of trees each season. It was always cold, always beautiful. I wasn't as strong as the others, so instead of making the hole for the tree or hammering

the stake in, my job was mainly planting the saplings and stamping them into the cold ground or tubing the trees. The thick, green tube acts as a mini greenhouse and also protects the trees from deer and rabbits. It was a cold, fiddly job, tying the tubes to the posts, and the only way to do it was gloveless. It took some time for my hands to warm up and on the way home, I would fight sleep in the Land Rover as the ancient heating system washed hot air over us.

There was always a mix of people working for Dad – local lads, friends of his, people who had just heard about this kind of work and wanted to give it a try. There was one guy who had spent his whole life in an office. He was so bored with it, he just upped and left. He told me this as we ate our packed lunch sitting on the stakes we were going to plant later that afternoon. He had no idea what he was going to do when the planting season was over, but he was so happy out in the cold planting trees with us. It didn't seem to matter.

The forest idyll didn't quite materialise in the way the Forestry Commission hoped – or rather, it wasn't set up to suit its workers indefinitely. As the 1960s arrived, more and more people began to question their future. One former deputy director-general of the Commission, George Ryle, noted in 1969 that, 'The main anxiety of several of the older folk was that nothing had been planned for accommodation of those who would soon be retiring.' This was true for foresters like Louie Robertson in Glenmore. After 46 years' service with the Commission, he retired and 'reluctantly' left his home for a one-bedroom house in nearby Aviemore. Having to leave not just your home, but also the area where you brought up your children, *and* to start paying rent, must have been an awful shock. Ryle was also keen to note that as houses could only be given to Commission workers, there was nothing for children to inherit.

By the 1980s, during the Thatcher era, privatisation enabled sitting tenants to buy their Commission home, but it was too late for most of the foresters who had already reached retirement age and had left their homes. At the same time there was a declining workforce as advances in technology meant mechanical equipment such as chainsaws were more widely available. The Commission stopped building new homes and the housing stock was gradually sold off.

As for Ae, the first Forestry Commission village, little there has changed. When the final house was completed in 1967, the total number of houses came to 54.

I drive to Ae one Sunday afternoon. I leave the children and Phil at home. I know they would like it down in the forest, but for some reason I want to go alone.

I follow the road along the River Ae, meeting a few cars who clearly know every bend and bump of the road, just as I did in the Lakes. The village appears on the hill and I pull over and look into the valley at the blocks of spruce trees growing, ready for harvest soon. It has a taste of Switzerland to it, all green and lush. I can hear the birds sounding from every direction, the distant sheep over the hills and much closer, the bees bustling around the clover in the grass.

Back in the car, I continue the half a mile to Ae where there is a small coffee shop on the edge of the forest. I sit outside and order tea and cake – I have to eat so often now, to stave off the pregnancy sickness. It is so bad some days, it almost floors me. The Forest of Ae is now a popular place to mountain-bike, so I watch the bikers vanishing beneath the branches of the plantation while I wait for the tea. I mention to the girl behind the counter that I am interested in the link to the Forestry Commission houses and Diane, who runs the café, comes to talk to me. She told me about her 'papa' who was a prisoner of war. Her gran, dad and auntie followed him over. Her dad, who was only fifteen, couldn't speak any English. They had rented a smallholding and later on her papa and her father both worked for the Commission. Back at home, I read that the reason they proposed building the village here in Ae was due to a local shortage in labour to look after the forest. An article from the time in the *Scottish Forestry Journal* states, 'At the present time some twenty men, together with fifty German prisoners of war (when available) are employed. This staff is in no way too large, and already there is danger of maintenance work getting into arrears.' I wonder if one of the 50 POWs might have been Diane's papa.

'I loved growing up here,' Diane says. 'Both in the village and going to see my papa in the woods at the smallholding. I remember throwing cowpats at my brother when we should have been clearing them.'

When the Forestry Commission sold off the land, Diane's family bought the house and her grandfather bought some land. Her children were brought up here just as she was. Her son now owns a house in the village too.

I say goodbye and head back into the heart of the village. The houses are much more substantial than the wooden huts the Commission originally built. They are made of brick with handsome pitched roofs. Mostly semi-detached, they are all painted with white rough cast and are well kept. I park next to the primary school to finish the hot tea and think about what Diane said about the school. When she was a kid here in the 1980s there were 70 children. By the early 2000s, only nine children went here. The current roll is 18. The school roll is a good way to judge the health of a community.

The Forest at Ae is now run by Forestry and Land Scotland and provides mountain-biking routes, walking trails and picnic areas as well as timber for the next generation. In 1999, the Forestry Commission started to divide responsibility for its forests between Wales, Scotland and England. At this point, it was the UK's biggest landowner, managing around 2.2 million acres (figures do vary and are hard to come by). In 2013, Natural Resources Wales took over the forests in Wales and in Scotland in 2019 Forestry and Land Scotland was created. Their website states: 'Many people think our work is timber production. That's true – but it's only part of the story. We also develop renewable energy schemes, create and maintain trails and visitor facilities and conserve habitats, wildlife and archaeological treasures.' Forestry is very much in the twenty-first century now.

Sitting next to the primary school in Ae, I look down at the houses with the hills of wooded trees behind them and watch two young girls of around eight years old kick a football around. Diane has given me an old booklet celebrating the 50-year anniversary of the village and I flick through, reading about its biggest moments: the galas, and the thrilling time a BBC radio programme came to broadcast from here in the Sixties. Then I see Diane's name beneath a black-and-white picture of a young girl who looks about seven years old, a crown of leaves and flowers in her hair. There are two young boys in kilts flanking her and an older girl behind her. In italic writing below the photo it says, *'Diane, Ae's Forest Queen, 1982.'* 'Forest Queen' makes me smile. It seems right that Diane, crowned queen of the woods decades ago, still lives here and, what's more, makes a living here, baking cakes on the edge of the forest.

3

Coal

Wherever I travel near home, the old chimney stack of what was once the biggest northern coal power station, Longannet, seeps into my view. If I am driving to take Ellis to his dad's, it follows me in the passenger window, a talisman flashing a warning to low aircraft. When I walk the local hills, it appears on the horizon, an oversized brick candlestick. I take Jessie to the foreshore to find shells and it stretches across the River Forth. I even see it out of Ellis's bedroom window as I close his curtains. It sits in the gap between the houses, like the last domino refusing to fall. To Jessie it is a magical fairy-tale place, the warning lights twinkling and flickering where its highest point reaches above the mist. It is Rapunzel's turret, sitting at odds with the natural landscape. She once asked if she could live there.

The chimney stack of Longannet is no longer producing smoke; the station closed down in 2016. But there is something about it that still feels very much alive, almost magnetic, as if the tower is the stationary spike of a mathematical compass, marking the very centre of things.

Longannet was once the largest coal-fired power station in Europe. It provided energy for a quarter of the homes in Scotland and hundreds of jobs for the people of Fife. It also consumed up to 4 million tonnes of coal per year, and in 2003 was named Scotland's biggest polluter at the time. It produced thousands of tonnes of ash a day, which was piped to nearby Preston Island in the Firth of Forth; in the same spot, centuries before, salt pans dotted the area. Like all behemoths of the fossil fuel industry, it consumed and spewed out, it provided and damaged. The coal came from local mines as well as mines further afield, in places such as Russia and Colombia, until 2002, when the conveyor belts in the heart of the plant stopped. Longannet was the last coal power station in Scotland, and it's strange to think of how recently – just 40 years ago – it was crucial for energy, jobs and the infrastructure of this community as it had been for centuries before.

We are walking along the River Forth, Jessie ahead of us on her bike, pedalling furiously and often veering off the path. Just along from the chimney stack of Longannet is the Royal Burgh of Culross. It is one of the best-preserved sixteenth-century industrial towns in Scotland, maybe in the whole of the UK. Lots of films and series have been filmed here, including *Outlander* and the 1971 version of *Kidnapped*. In the centre of the small town, the ground is cobbled, and the buildings are jammed together, like old friends swaying in a packed pub. Their old bricks and whitewashed walls seem to bulge with layers of history. Culross Palace, which is centred at the heart of the place, shines a bright mustard colour, limewashed with yellow ochre, which was a sure sign of ancient wealth. We like it here. There is a good-sized park for the kids, the path along the Forth is perfect for learning to ride a bike, and the pub serves good food and beer. Today, it is winter and I am keen for fresh air while the light is with us. We walk along the foreshore, beside an old railway line, which I guess used to take coal out towards Edinburgh. There is an information board and I read briefly how the first underwater pit was sunk here in 1575 by Sir George Bruce of Culross. He set up an Egyptian water wheel, pulled by three horses, where 36 buckets constantly brought the water up to keep the sea out of the pit. It is a scary thought. I look at where the pit would have been; the tide is coming in, and I think I wouldn't have liked to trust that method to keep the cold water of the Forth out of my boots.

The board also briefly explains serfdom, a truly horrific period in Scottish history when the coal miners and the salt miners in Scotland were essentially tied to their employers for life. In 1606, an act was passed, stopping anyone employing a collier or a salter unless he could produce a document releasing him from his previous master. This effectively meant that mine owners could keep their workers as long as they wanted.

Historian T. C. Smout notes, 'He became a piece of mining equipment that could be bought, sold and inherited by his master.'

The miners' children were even in on the bargain and were 'arled', meaning the mine owner gave a gift to the family in return for a promise that the child would be brought up a miner. Beggars and vagabonds were picked up off the street and sent to work in the mine. It wasn't until the Colliers and Salters Act of 1775 that the

laws on this improved. It made any new entrants to these jobs 'free labourers' but existing workers wouldn't enjoy the same freedom until 1779. I can't imagine there would be many of the original miners left 20 years later to benefit from the change of law. Many have compared the colliers and salters to slaves, and certainly the act that abolished their servitude describes it as a 'state of slavery and bondage', but it is interesting to read that Adam Smith said that, in fact, 'They had privileges which slaves have not. Their property after maintenance is their own, they cannot be sold but along with their work, they enjoy marriage and religion.' It's not something I would have liked my children 'arled' into, though. On the drive home, we pass Longannet and Jessie shouts in amazement, 'Ellis's tower! It's Ellis's tower.' She likes to watch the tip of it twinkle from Ellis's bedroom window. Mesmerising.

I have never been down a mine. Or in a power station. But somehow, coal feels intrinsically linked to my life. It keeps popping up, always at the edge of my view, like Longannet tower.

Most rural childhoods were arranged around the fire. I sat by ours watching TV, or to dry my hair. We toasted bread on it when the electricity went out. Boots, filled with newspaper were often stationed close by, steam rising off them. Sitting on the rug in front of the flames, I scraped letters and shapes with the poker in the coal dust on the back plate. I remember my mum carrying a brass bucket piled high; the coal fragments shone as the firelight hit it – black and silver glitter. Too much coal on the fire and you couldn't sit next to it. It became like a furnace, the huge black gems glowing with painful intensity. But a purely coal fire was rare. Given my dad's job, logs were always in reasonable supply. They spat and sparked at us as they burned, fast and hot; the rug was peppered with small burn holes.

Like all houses of this ilk, we had no central heating. The fire was the only way to heat the radiators and the water. In winter, when we went away for the weekend visiting family, my mum asked Mrs Dacre, the estate housekeeper who looked after the Big House, to light the fire before we were due home. Too long without one and the bones of the house got cold. It would take hours for warmth to creep back in. Every time we returned home, we opened the door, dragging our bags behind us, and the heat hit us. Mrs Dacre piled the coal up to create a searing temperature, a fire that could drive a steam engine. We couldn't go near it until it had died down, the house disconcertingly, brilliantly toasty. A purely coal fire was a Mrs Dacre fire.

I don't have a fire now. I live in a new house with central heating and no chimney. It's warm and cosy and reliable. I don't need to chop logs or get coal delivered. I don't move the pictures on the wall and see the true colour of the wallpaper, those patches untouched by soot.

Our new housing development was built just before Longannet closed its doors in 2016, but the shadow of coal still very much colours the area. Most of the old settlements in this central belt were once mining communities. If I take the old roads to Glasgow or Stirling, I drive through former mining village after mining village. Now they look quite different to what they would have done 150 years ago. The current houses, mainly council houses from the Fifties and Sixties, sit along the same lines as the old miners' cottages. The original homes weren't built to last. Sometimes there are traces of the timeworn buildings, but mostly the only thing left standing to commemorate the industry are the leftover bings, small or sometimes mighty hills of leftover material dug from the pit. Some villages have memorials for the men who died in the shockingly common pit disasters.

A short distance from where we live is the site of an old hamlet called Jawcraig, now a shooting centre. I like driving up this way. When Jessie refuses to sleep in the buggy, I sometimes take her out in the car (there is nothing worse than an overtired toddler). The road tends to be quiet around here and there is a desolate kind of beauty to the boggy moorland. A few farms are scattered about, with sheep grazing the muddy grass and the odd tree, bent slightly by the wind. But mainly, at first glance, there is not much here.

This was not the case in the 1850s when pits spread across Scotland's central belt like chicken pox.

In 1875, a *Herald* newspaper correspondent visited the mining communities in Scotland. His report notes that Jawcraig was the worst village for damp out of the whole country. He writes, 'The old woman who lives here told me that sometimes during the night, when the door is shut and a large fire burning, she sees steam rising from the floor.'

He visited another house in the row the day they were removing a large 'eight-day clock' (a clock that only needs to be wound once a week). He explains how the clock was six-foot tall, but the ceiling of the house was not quite as high as this, so the occupants had dug a hole in the floor to fit it in. As the clock was removed from the room, they realised the hole was full of water and the bottom of the clock fell out completely.

I drive near Jawcraig one day, waiting for Jessie to fall asleep, when I suddenly recognise this row of houses from the journalist's description. I pull in at the side of the road and look at Jessie in the back. Out for the count. The wind is squally and spitting rain, so I leave her sleeping while I walk across the road to see what is remaining of the miners' cottages. I stand on the banking and look down into them. The shapes of the houses are visible, but they are nothing more than sheep shelters now. One gable end is left standing, but the stones that made up the walls have collapsed both inside and out of the building. It's difficult to picture the huge clock in the reporter's description, the fireplace and the family that lived here. The wind rattles around the broken walls and I wrap my jacket closer to me. Even if it had four walls and a roof, it's hard to imagine being warm in this home.

A few miles away in the hamlet of Nappyfaulds, the journalist notes, 'During the night the people, while in bed, hear the miners blasting underneath.' That mine wound its way so directly below the miners' houses that some collapsed: a ripe metaphor for the impossible separation between work life and home. Mr Hay, the mine owner, offered the families accommodation elsewhere, but few took him up on it, and as the houses were robbed of their walls, Hay could no longer charge rent for them. 'They prefer to sit rent free in Nappyfaulds,' the report concludes. I guess the extra savings – money for food, or fuel, or life's necessities – were enough temptation to forego having four walls.

When I first moved to this area, I bought a house that was originally just two rooms. The walls were stone and almost 2-feet thick. We know it was built in the mid-1800s because when we refloored the loft (due to an ongoing issue where woodworm would drop from the ceiling onto the windowsills) we found layers of newspapers from 1864: an attempt at makeshift insulation. I read faded articles peppered with woodworm holes about how ribbons were back in fashion, until they crumbled in my hands.

The main room, then my living room, had the largest fireplace I had ever seen outside a stately home. It took up nearly half the wall (though it was a very small room) and some years ago, before I lived there, a real wood-burning stove had been installed. It warmed the room up so quickly I had to open the doors to the kitchen extension to cool it down. Yet, the whole house suffered from draughts under doors and through windows. The floorboards in the living room were placed on the bare ground – with just soil and stone underneath. There was no insulation beyond the newspaper stuffing. Nothing fitted properly, so the outside was let in all day and all night. This could have been remedied with a full overhaul: new floors, new windows, new walls. Or perhaps it should have been knocked down and started over. Of course, this required money – lots more than I had.

Living there meant waking up to the clues of a party of slugs, a glittery trail over the bean bag, the rug, the sofa. I took to placing a layer of salt around the edges of rooms like a witch. When I moved out, I bumped into my old neighbour who said the new homeowners had once caught 107 slugs in one night. I had never bothered to capture and count.

If this was what it was like in the twenty-first century with a working boiler, running water, leather sofas to sit on, carpets and electricity, what must it have been like when it was built? If I managed to stave away the damp with an Argos dehumidifier, what must it have been like with nothing but an open fire and a coal or wood store that you also had to keep dry? In my old cottage, at night especially, I found I could almost conjure up what it might have been like: life in a miner's house a hundred years ago. What I found impossible was imagining how it must have felt in those black pits of the earth underground.

If you look at a geological map of the United Kingdom, you can almost pinpoint at a glance where the coal-mining villages and towns are. They lie in neat seams across the natural coal fields, which proliferate in certain areas: the central belt of Scotland, South Yorkshire, South Wales, Northeast England.

Coal formed around 300 million years ago. During the Carboniferous Period, the atmosphere was warm and swampy; microorganisms hadn't quite worked out how to decompose plants yet, so when trees and vegetation died, they lay undisturbed. (Coal is much rarer after this period as the microorganisms figured out how to eat away at the dead trees.) Layer after layer of wood accumulated in the swamps, which created peat. And as more peat was buried, the high temperatures and pressure transformed it into coal.

The Carboniferous Period was also the time when the continents started to move around. Several continents crashed into each other, which gave England a huge shove, which, in turn, pushed up many small mountain ranges. Coal was preserved in the lower areas in between these.

When we realised how rich England, Scotland and Wales were in coal, and how useful coal was for the Industrial Revolution, no time was wasted in creating pits to dig it out. And in the late 1800s, we needed somewhere to house this growing workforce of coal miners, so isolated villages started popping up around mines. Denaby

Main in South Yorkshire was one such place. It grew from a small village surrounded by farmland to a huge community with around 2,500 employees at two collieries. It also housed workers from the nearby glassworks. Such was its growth that people visited it with interest and one reporter, writing for the *Christian Budget* in 1899, gave it the unfortunate accolade of being 'the worst village in England'.

> *If the dreams of some social reformers are true, Denaby Main ought to be a paradise. Every man there has ample work, wages are very high, and each family can have a house to itself for a very low rent. The eight hours day has been granted. The country around ranks amongst the most beautiful in England, undulating, well timbered, with bright streams running through it.*

The contrast of it being the 'worst village' in the 'most beautiful' countryside is striking. It *should* be a wonderful place to live, it *should* be a secure place to live, with a house for each family within the surrounds of nature. But it is not. Denaby Main had classic Industrial Revolution housing: poker-straight streets, with red-brick houses that ran parallel to each other. Two houses shared a backyard and a toilet. There were no trees or shrubs and even the pavements were red brick. It certainly doesn't sound like paradise.

The reporter describes how gambling had taken hold of the village, and to his abject horror, even the women partook. One woman said, 'If we don't do it, the men will. We might as well spend the money as anybody else.' The children were taught to swear and bet 'as soon as they could toddle', and the reporter concludes, 'It is safe to say that four out of five of them [the residents] enter the pawn-shop far more often than they go to church.'

Two weeks after the *Christian Budget* piece was published, someone signing themselves as J. F. wrote to the *Mexborough & Denaby Times* and took pains to defend the community of miners. He lists the successes of Denaby Main and the ways in which it was truly thriving, including the 'good and well-managed football club, which fought its way into the third round of the English cup ties' and the Denaby Main Orchestral Society, describing it as 'one of the best in the district'.

Despite admitting that the place had all the failings of a typical working-class community, he could see goodness in it.

[The writer] might have learnt that young men, residents in this dreadful place, who earn their bread in the mines, have won County Council scholarships, and actually qualified themselves for the important positions of Colliery managers and under managers.

These thriftless people have also a full 'Penny Bank' which has been in existence some years, and is well patronised. Again, the majority of the men are so thrifty, and have so much foresight as to be members of Friendly Societies. Very probably the writer would be surprised to meet the Denaby collier accompanied by wife and family at the seaside in summer, and actually residing there for a period. Men who can make such provision in friendly societies and for the annual summer outing cannot spend so much money in betting and beer.

Maybe J. F. lives in Denaby Main. Maybe he has seen the orchestra play in a nearby village. Maybe he grew up there himself. Whatever his connection to the town, I'm glad there was someone there to stick up for it.

Another characteristic of these mining communities was their resilience. Again, like in forestry, physical strength was needed to achieve the work; the men dug the coal out by hand in dark, cramped and dangerous conditions. But another kind of strength was necessary to survive: strength of mind. Catherine Bailey's book *Black Diamonds* explains how, 'In the absence of a benevolent coal owner, jeopardy and uncertainty were the keynotes of a collier's existence.' And no matter how benevolent the colliery owner was, no company paid compensation to a widow if her husband died underground from natural causes. This, Bailey explains, meant 'a dead man' would die twice.

'For the sake of the wives and children, the miners mutilated the bodies of the heart attack victims.' They dragged pit props on top of them, letting the muck from the pit cover them to make it look like an accident. The act of doing this, while seemingly barbaric, was really a kindness beyond what we, thankfully, can imagine now.

The proximity of death was common not just in the mines, but in the overcrowded cottages as well. Often corpses shared beds with other members of the family as there was simply nowhere else to put them. Bailey describes how one boy in a village not far from Denaby told his teacher he wasn't scared of sleeping next to his brother Ernest on the eve of his funeral. ''e carn't hurt ya, 'e's dead and wrapped in a sheet, so I sleep next 'im and our Alice next to me, an our Joe at t' bottom.' Poor lad.

The idea of a coal miner is, for many, also synonymous with strikes and disputes. For hundreds of years, miners have fought for better conditions and better pay. More often than not, they had to return to their job after some weeks, sometimes months, having lost the strike, the mine owners or, in more recent memory, the government winning the battle. In the cases where the miners' homes were owned by the colliery company, the striking miners knew they could be kicked out, no matter what the weather or their family situation. It must have taken a real belief in what they stood for to be faced with the loss of home *and* job.

In 1878, the *Evening Telegraph* in Scotland reported on the case in court of the eviction of 62 miners at Slamannan in Central Scotland. Strangely, the men were not arguing against their evictions (this was commonplace), but they were requesting more time to vacate their homes – two weeks as opposed to the usual four days. In some cases it was granted; for instance, when the miner's father was ill with 'chest disease', or another was 'confined to bed by rheumatic fever', which goes some way to illustrate the health of the residents in these situations. The rest weren't so lucky. The report concludes that 'in each warrant for ejectment, eight days were granted'. Sheriff Balfour said he had given the miners twice the number of days they were entitled to. 'They had got all they had asked, and therefore they had nothing to complain of.'

By our modern standards this is harsh beyond belief, but compared to some instances, this was a softer approach. Often the miners and their families were literally turfed out of their homes, their furniture thrown after them. Melvyn Jones, in his book *South Yorkshire Mining Villages*, describes a dispute in Denaby Main where 'large parts of the village had to be evacuated and the population dispersed to be temporarily housed in churches and chapels'. The infamous 'bag-muck strike' of 1902–3, when the colliery company refused to pay the miners for the removal of muck before even reaching the coal, lasted for weeks in the dead of winter. In January 1903, many families were evicted and had to sleep in tents with nothing more than sheets and blankets. Newspaper reports describe women and children huddled together at the side of the road, 'soaked to the skin' due to the icy rain. Their furniture, which had also been chucked out of their homes, ruined on the street in the cold winter weather. The miners lost the bag-muck strike and returned to the village, beaten once again.

Another dispute, in a place called Westwood Row, in the countryside between Barnsley and Sheffield, lasted 17 months. There is nothing left of the hundreds of houses built in Westwood Row, now a country park, but in 1870, it was the sight of 'one of the most determined contests between capital and labour which is to be found in the mining history of this or any other country' Jones writes. Westwood Row was built to house the 'blackleg miners' recruited by the mine owners when their own workers were striking. Some months before, the colliery reduced wages by 7.5 per cent and the workmen, understandably, refused to accept this. There were a number of pits in the area, and a number of settlements, and when the mine owners started evicting their own striking workers and placing their 'blacksheep' miners in them, the trouble started. Policemen were employed to 'protect the property and the men who had started work at the pits, against the men who are on strike'.

Months went by and, with no sign of a settlement from the colliery owner, crowds of up to 1,500 strikers took to Westwood Row, where the majority of the blackleg miners lived. 'Armed with pistols, some with bludgeons, the heads of which bristled with spikes, some with picks,' they set about destroying the houses. Doors and windows were smashed; furniture was wrecked and looted. About a hundred men were arrested and the strike continued for another seven months. But to no avail. The mine owners didn't budge; the wages stayed reduced by 7.5 per cent and former workers had to reapply for their jobs. Most, however, had been taken by the blackleg men, so employment was unlikely.

Not far away from Westwood Row, a little further south down the motorway, is the pit village of Cresswell near Worksop in Derbyshire, where in 1950, 80 miners died. For hundreds of years, pit disasters were commonplace; from 1873 to 1953, up to 85,000 men were killed. The worst pit disaster on record was Senghenydd in Glamorgan in 1913 where a gas explosion killed 439 men. Every single person in the community must have been affected. Fathers, sons, brothers – gone, in minutes, not unlike the fields in France during the First World War, which started only a year later. The Cresswell pit disaster was just another tragedy to add to the list. This, however, was the one that killed my gran's dad.

It was 26 September 1950 and the night shift was in full flow. Grandad Edward would have left his home just before 10 p.m., saying goodnight to his wife as she went to bed. He would have carried his sandwiches in a metal tin to protect them from the rats like all the other men. At the pit head, they all jammed themselves into the cage that took them down underground. Creswell was a relatively shallow mine at only 400 metres, so the journey was short. Some mines went as deep as 1,000 metres.

Coal

There were 1,144 men employed at Cresswell Colliery, and that night 232 of them were underground.

At 3.45 a.m. a fire started at a damaged conveyor belt. Grandad Edward worked as a 'ripper', which meant he dug the rock or coal out of the roof to gain height for the roadways. Toxic fumes from the fire spread along these roadways, travelling from one section to the other. Fifty-one miners who were working on the southwest part of the mine escaped quickly, but the rest were trapped. Over the next few hours, there was a breakdown in communications and any fire-fighting equipment they had failed to put the fire out. The trapped miners, all 80 of them, were overcome by carbon-monoxide poisoning. Grandad Edward nearly made it out; his was one of the first bodies to be dragged out on the morning of the accident, along with 46 others. His daughter, my Gran Nora, was just 15.

The fire, which was still roaring underground, had to be extinguished, so the tragic decision was made to seal up the mine to stop it. One miner reportedly worked on the seal knowing his father was still inside. No one in the community was unaffected by the disaster. One family lost three sons.

The photos of the wives and families waiting for news in the early hours of the morning are heart-breaking. But teenager Nora and her mother, Gran Lizzie, weren't part of the community. By a sad twist of fate, this was only Edward's second shift at the mine. He had been transferred from a nearby pit, so my gran and Gran Lizzie had stayed in the same house a few miles away. The news of the fire spread in the early morning, but Gran would not have known about it. She might have got up, made breakfast ready for Edward returning from his nightshift, then waited a while, the pot of tea getting colder. She did not know any of the other miners' wives who had lost their husbands, and they would not have thought to send a message to her. She could not share in the collective loss. When the compensation money finally came through, nearly six years later, Gran Lizzie bought a brand-new house in the nearby town of Worksop. She stayed there the rest of her life. She never remarried.

Some years before the Creswell pit disaster, Gran Nora's future husband, my Grandad Vic, also worked in the pits. In the area around Worksop, where almost all of my immediate family hail from, it's what you did. There wasn't much choice in career. And Grandad, much to his displeasure, was made a Bevin Boy during the Second World War. Named after Ernest Bevin, the wartime labour politician, the Bevin Boys numbered up to 48,000 and provided much-needed coal for the war effort, to keep people warm and to fuel industry and shipping.

But despite the importance of the job, it was a much-maligned role. Bevin Boys were picked out of a hat; every month, a ballot would take place in which two numbers were drawn out. The men whose National Service registration number ended with those numbers were sent to the mines. One in ten 18-year-olds were drafted into mines rather than the forces in this way. At 16, Grandad's numbers were picked, alongside his older brother James, who was 17.

There was sense among most Bevin Boys that they were missing out on their opportunity to fight abroad, and Grandad and his brother certainly felt this. As soon as James turned 18, he applied to the RAF as a pilot and was accepted. When Grandad turned 18, he applied for the Merchant Navy but was refused, the need for coal being so vitally important. He was stuck on the 'underground front' until the end of the war.

Not only did the young men feel they were missing out on the war, but they had to put up with a certain amount of resentment from the general public too. Local miners' families, whose own sons were fighting abroad, hated the 'outsiders' who had come to mine when their sons had been sent away essentially to be killed. People who saw the conscripted miners on the street also assumed they were cowards for not going to fight on the front line and were often stopped by the police as deserters.

Grandad's job in the mine was as an 'onsetter', which meant that he was at the bottom of the mine shaft and he exchanged full and empty corves, or buckets of coal. He was hit by a corve once and he spent several months recovering at a mineworkers' hospital. He told my Uncle Jim about working in the mine and said he saw many accidents, including some fatalities. 'One miner', Jim says, 'was crushed by a full corve and Grandad had to send his body up the shaft in several corves.' While at 17 Grandad was recovering a body in parts, at the same age, I was serving ice cream in a café in the Lakes. Worlds apart.

In 1945, when the war ended, Grandad knew he would do anything rather than go back in the pit. He studied in night school while working as a construction worker and, eventually, became an engineer. When Uncle Jim turned 11, he arranged for him to spend a shift with a miner friend, right at the coal face. He wanted to show him how bad it was, to encourage him to do well in his eleven-plus and stay away from the mines. Jim remembers the long journey down in the cage, the even further journey to the coal face and then the baths afterwards, when hundreds of men stripped off and washed a day's worth of coal dust off their skin. It worked. Uncle Jim passed his eleven-plus, went off to the local grammar school and found his way to university to study meteorology.

Back in Scotland, I visit my friend Fiona in the pretty mining village of Edgehead in East Lothian. A single street with cottages on both sides originally built to house the miners for the pit at the top of the road, which have aged better than the houses in Jawcraig and Nappyfaulds. There are established trees dotted up the street and the houses have the same thick walls, small windows and low roofs that my old cottage had. It seems these were built to last. The place is still very much a rural area with fields surrounding the village and homemade signs selling potatoes and eggs straight from the farm doorstep.

Fiona grew up in Edgehead and now lives in one of the new houses in a small development just at the top of the village. I have spent years visiting her in her parents' cosy cottage and now we drink mugs of tea in her own home – a large, modern, centrally heated house on old farmland. Her housing development of about 20 houses was built opposite the old mine, which is now a woodland where deer roam and the local kids build dens.

This mine was unusual as it also boasted a windmill to help bring the coal up.

We often walk past the converted windmill and look at it in envy – it is now a quirky, rather glamorous home, the kind you can imagine Kevin McCloud looking at admiringly. We plod around the woods with our children and talk, distracting the kids with sticks and feathers so we can try to catch up on life undisturbed.

I am around eight weeks pregnant and can't hide it from Fiona. I feel like I'm being poisoned. I have never enjoyed being pregnant, and the first five months are particularly tough. I feel sick every minute of the day, though it's a little better in the fresh air.

Fiona tells me how her street is named after a young girl who was a miner and I'm surprised. I remember learning about young boys going down the mine, but I had never heard much about female miners. But, I suppose, what difference does gender make? If your family was poor, you began labouring as soon as you could. If you lived in a cottage belonging to the mine owner, you had no choice but to send your children underground when they called for it. In fact, in a lot of cases, mining was a whole-family affair.

Women as well as children worked in British pits until 1842, when perhaps the predictable happened: scandal. It was so hot underground that men often worked without their shirts, sometimes naked, and as this occurred to the newspapers of the time, they began to print accounts and illustrations of women doing the same thing. Investigators actually only confirmed one pit where the women worked topless, but this was immaterial. The immorality shocked Victorian society so much that within three months the Mines and Collieries Act of 1842 was drawn up, banning boys under 10 from the pit and all women and girls. It was said that working in the mine 'made girls unsuitable for marriage and unfit to be mothers', so extinguishing a valuable source of income for families. Quickly, women started working above the mines, sorting the coal. These 'pit brow lassies' or 'tip girls' were paid half the amount of the men, though they reaped the benefits of working out in the fresh air, rather than in the hot and dangerous environment of the mills, which was another option for work. They wore trousers underneath their skirts, which again shocked and fascinated Victorian Britain. In a society where women's clothing meant skirts, cinched waists and frills, up sprung a decent trade in photographs and postcards, '*carte de visite*', of the pit lassies, posing in what seems to me now perfectly ordinary get-up.

Later, at home, I do some research into Elizabeth Dickson, the little girl whose name has been given to Fiona's street. She was interviewed along with many others as part of the Children's Commission, which went on to ban children under ten from the mines. Her words are ghostly when I read them

> *I draw with the ropes and chain and often fall and get crushed as the hurly comes down the brae; never off work long from the hurts. I am wrought with two brothers and two sisters below: we takes pieces of bread, and get nothing more till work is done: am never wrought less than 12 and 14 hours. I bend nearly double while at work, as all the roads are very low.*

It notes that Elizabeth 'reads very badly, and [is] much neglected'. She has not been at school for many years and, since her father was unable to work ('caught in the bad air'), the children have worked instead of him. There are many, many more accounts of girls and boys working long, dangerous, unhealthy hours in a mine from age seven and upwards. I lose a few hours reading the words recorded 150 years ago. Perversely, I cannot stop thinking of the mothers. How did Elizabeth's mother feel giving her and her siblings a single piece of bread each day as they left for a 14-hour shift in a pit?

Did her mother also work in the mine? Fiona and I, both with children around that age, talk briefly about the words of Elizabeth next time we are in the woods. But what else can we say but 'how terrible'? We watch our youngest kids burling on ahead and change the subject.

I like this idea of naming new streets for people who were walking the same paths years before. Elizabeth Dickson could never have imagined in her wildest dreams that the homes her name sits alongside are full of children who go to school and play with an endless supply of toys. She could not have imagined a life unconnected from coal. It is a contrast I find both unsettling, but also *just*, like we have finally gifted Elizabeth the lifestyle a 12-year-old girl deserves.

My own street is part of a large development of houses that tells the story of one of Scotland's biggest mining disasters. In my development there are 600 houses, built on old, pretty poor-quality farmland. The streets snake round in spirals, designed to create cul-de-sacs and safe areas for children to play. We are circled here by the Forth and Clyde Canal, the local woods at Callendar Park and the old village of Redding. It is a peaceful development, full of children on bikes and dog walkers. When sitting in the sun in the garden it is difficult to remember that this area was the scene of the Redding pit disaster where 40 men died somewhere beneath us. I reckon most of the people have no idea that our streets are named after some of them.

On 25 September 1923, at Pit No.23, operated by a local family but leased by the Duke of Hamilton, water from the Union Canal gushed into one of the chambers. It was a similar situation to the fires at Cresswell, in the sense that the problem was the narrowness of being underground, the impossibility of getting out quickly when something went wrong. Most of the men in this instance drowned as the water flooded in, but 11 were trapped in a dry section of the mine. As always, relatives crowded around the pit head, anxious for news, as divers from the nearby naval base were sent down to rescue them. The divers attempted the 800 feet of mine workings, sometimes through water as deep as 20 feet, but they were unsuccessful.

It took 40 days to recover all 40 bodies. I have spent hours walking these streets, pushing Jessie in her pram to get her to sleep, and only recently realised the street signs are a roll call of the dead.

Forrestor Street for John, married with two children.

Cochrane Grove for James, single, 52, of Redding.

Porteus Place for David, married only a fortnight before the disaster.

McGarvie Drive for Frank, married with three children.

The name that pulls at me the most is James Jarvie, now immortalised in the main road that runs through the estate. Mr Jarvie was the night fireman on the shift when the water started rushing in. It is reported he had time to escape but instead wanted to warn the others about the danger of the flooding and went further down the pit. All of them became trapped. The flood water never reached the chamber they were in, but rescue proved impossible and they were suffocated. Mr Jarvie's, along with 10 other bodies, was one of the last to be recovered in the December, weeks after the disaster happened. When they found his body, they also found his time-book with a series of notes to his wife.

The first was written on the day of the accident: 'Tell my wife to keep up for the sake of her children, for I don't believe I will see her again.'

The second message is undated. 'I am still living yet, and have great hopes of being saved. Keep your heart, Maggie and look after the weans, and my two boys in America.'

James's last message read, 'Dearest Maggie, convey the news to our two sons. Tell Peggie, James, Lilly, Jeannie, and wee Maisie to keep up. It is a sore blow to you Maggie. Good-bye.'

I cannot drive this road, with its awkward speedbumps to slow the traffic and its brand-new houses, without thinking of James and his wife. Mrs Jarvie was left with five young children at home. James knew how much of a 'sore blow' it was to lose your husband, your only source of income. At least (if there is an 'at least' in this story), by the modern age of 1923, 'wee' Maisie would not by then have been forced to work in the same mine that her father died in.

4

Water

We could have picked a better day to visit Thirlmere. It is the May bank holiday, and after one of the driest Aprils on record the weather is making up for it. Rain slings itself down at the side of the car and washes weeks' worth of grime from roads. Not surprising really. The Lake District, and for me especially the area around Ambleside, is synonymous with water. As a teenager, I spent hours watching it fall, soaking the tourists traipsing around the villages as I worked in cafés, pubs and galleries.

Thirlmere, the lake we have come to explore, isn't a lake at all but a reservoir. Previously two small bodies of water, Wythburn Water and Leathes Water, the land and the lakes were purchased by Manchester's Waterworks Committee in 1879 to provide a clean water supply to the people of the city. It took over 3,000 men to build the tunnels and pipelines along the 100 miles to the city; 570 men alone were employed to build the dam at the head of the water. Some men brought their families; some men came on their own and lodged in the area. The idea of housing this many people, of cooking and providing for them, simply maintaining a community of that size for a number of years in a rural isolated area – one set up for a fraction of the population – amazes me. I have always wondered what the camps looked like; did they look like shanty towns with rows of wooden huts with washing hanging out between them? Or were they scattered about the woods like an army camp waiting for morning battle? Today, we are on the search for where it could have been. Paul from United Utilities, who looks after the reservoir and the surrounding area, said the forest on the west side of the water is called City and, due to the name of it, he imagined this is where most of the people lived. But, like most historic temporary accommodation, traces of it are hard to find. Records, if any were ever made, were limited and now more than likely lost to time.

We drive with the children on the single-track road on the west side of Thirlmere. The main road on the east side, the A591, is the more regular drive for us, offering a scenic route home to Scotland via the winding roads and valleys up to Penrith. I have never ventured on this side of the water. The road skims the reservoir and follows its inlets and bays. You get a better view of Helvellyn from here and the way it rises steeply to the east. Right beside us on the left, Armboth Fell, although smaller than the famous Helvellyn, still towers over the car. I open the window to get a better view of the passing woods. I'm hoping I'll see a clearing or an old wall that could have been part of a building, any clue to where they would have lived, but the rain and cold air rush in and the children complain in the back. The woods are filled with huge boulders of stone and wind-blown trees and the ground rises sharply and unevenly. There is hardly a single space flat enough to pitch our family tent, let alone settle hundreds of men after a day's digging.

Failing to find an obvious place for a settlement, we park at the northernmost section of the water and walk the short distance to the reservoir. The children run ahead in the rain. We are, in fact, walking on top of the dam, which doubles as a road. The walls are high, blocking the view to the reservoir at the children's height, and the road feels like any other, so it is difficult to imagine the incredible feat of engineering below our feet. The dam was built in two sections at either side of a huge rock. As soon as we walk out of the shelter of the mounds of rock, we want to get back within it. The wind whips Manchester's drinking water in our faces and the rain fills the reservoir like bath water. The kids hurry back to the car, but I stay to lean over the wall, my jacket hood pushed back by gusts of wind, and marvel at how the wall seems to slide into the water.

Dams are always awe inspiring, huge monoliths of brick or stone, engineered to withhold pressure like I couldn't imagine, but Thirlmere's dam proves to be a smaller affair. Apparently, it was one of the most 'effective and economical dams anywhere'. I take some pictures and look up to the hills on either side of the flat-bottomed valley. White rivers of water gushing down the sides. Thirlmere holds 40 million cubic metres of water, which travels down to Manchester, with the help of gravity, at a speed of two miles an hour. I love this fact and back at home tell Ellis, who feigns interest.

For all that people moan about it, the excess of rain is what makes the Glens of Scotland, the Welsh Valleys, the Yorkshire fells and here in Cumbria so beautiful. It is green and lush for a reason. The water in these places was chosen by the authorities for situating reservoirs for drinking water, not just for the surplus, but also for the quality. I can agree with that. Our drinking water on the estate came right off the hills. The water tank supplied three houses and was just a little way up the hill behind our home. The water often ran brown and a bit silty and visitors used to look a little nervous when pouring a glass of it. 'Just run it a bit,' Mum would say. It always cleared after a few minutes. It was, and still is to this day, the best water I have ever tasted from a tap.

With the boom in industry and population during the Industrial Revolution, more and more reservoirs were needed to provide a clean water supply to mushrooming cities. Up and down the country, land was being bought from local landowners and farmers.

But not everyone wanted reservoirs where they were proposed. It is now thought that Thirlmere Reservoir was the very beginnings of modern-day environmentalism. The Lake District had long been associated with writers and artists such as William Wordsworth and John Ruskin, and when Manchester Corporation Waterworks, part of Manchester Council, started buying sections of land in the area, a group of local people, including John Ruskin and Octavia Hill (who went on to help form the National Trust), set up the Thirlmere Defence Association (TDA). The argument raged for years in newspapers up and down the country and, I imagine, by firesides and against stone walls. The TDA argued that the landscape was a public asset and the building of the dam would destroy the area, but the waterworks department challenged this by saying in fact the reservoir would 'enhance its natural beauty'. They also claimed that building it would 'preserve Thirlmere from the depredations of tourism and ordinary commerce'. An interesting point of view that I would have liked to hear them argue in person.

The Manchester Corporation Waterworks won, on the basis that the working-class people of Manchester, who were living in unsanitary conditions, needed clean water.

Harriet Ritvo wrote in *The Dawn of Green*:

The deeper opposition to the Thirlmere Scheme rested on claims that were absolute, novel, and difficult to assess. It invoked a nebulous new sense of ownership – a sense that the citizens of a nation should have some say in the disposition of significant landscapes even if they held no formal title to the property in question.

It is this 'sense of ownership' that is so hard to pin down. When you live and work on the land, in so many ways it feels like it belongs to you. But it does not; not in title anyway. Tempers ran so high that John Ruskin was quoted as saying he wished Manchester 'should be put at the bottom of the Lake of Thirlmere'. Overall, there was an understandable reluctance to let 'urban incomers' change the landscape forever for the sake of improving some distant city that few of them would ever visit. This started a movement that would become essential to the protection of rural areas. Thirlmere is now recognised as the first example of people mobilising against the threat of industrialisation to the natural world.

It is well known that in the construction of these reservoirs, sometimes whole villages were submerged, their residents bought out and moved on. But what is often forgotten is the communities of men, and often their families, who moved into these rural, quiet areas to build them. It's a funny set of consequences: often the growth of the biggest cities required the mass movement of rural labourers. I have always wondered about the transient life of the people who created these reservoirs. The men were nicknamed 'navvies' after the original name of the canal system in England: navigations. After the decline of canal building, the name navvie became synonymous with the labourers who worked on big engineering projects in the Victorian era, such as the railways and reservoirs. They were incredibly hardy. Dick Sullivan writes:

Apart from living apart in their own communities, two things set navvies apart from labourers: extra strength, extra knowledge. Endurance was basic (it took a year to turn a flabby labourer into a man hard enough to work his shift in a muck-shovelling gang) but knowledge was almost as important.

You needed to know how 'to handle your body' – from the start of the shift to the end you hardly had a chance to stand up straight. But you also needed to understand the geology of the work, 'how best to pick, drill, blast, shovel all kinds of muck from rock to sand, clay to loam'.

They could shift up to 20 tonnes of muck and mud a day, lifting and throwing it up and out of the ditch over their heads. Life must have been tough, dangerous and – I know it's a ridiculous thing to think, but – so wet. Working in damp tunnels, or out in all weathers, lifting, moving, building. What was it that brought hundreds of families to these inaccessible areas to spend a few years toiling day in and day out for a temporary job?

Grandad Vic, a future Bevin Boy in the mines and my mum's dad, was born into this transient lifestyle. His father was a crane driver and, in 1926, was helping to build a reservoir in Ewden Valley, Sheffield. They lived in the heart of the moors with hundreds of other families. Grandad was born in hut number 10. He left when he was only five years old but still recalled the idyllic scenery and the once-a-month trip into Sheffield. Uncle Jim, who, conveniently for me, is a great family-history researcher, took Grandad back to the Ewden Valley a number of times.

'The first time we visited, probably in the 1980s, some of the huts were still occupied by the families of the workers from the 1920s. One chap came out to ask if he could help us and it turned out that he had been born in that hut. As soon as we mentioned [our family] name, Squires, he took us to the place where Hut 10 was.'

There is a photo of Grandad in front of one of the remaining huts. It is single-storey and looks entirely built with dark planked wood. Only the chimney looks brick. The building is semi-detached and from the outside, at least, I'm surprised at the quality. Some of the workers bought the huts off the waterworks department for a nominal amount and stayed there for the rest of their lives. It must have been a beautiful place to be. Finally, in the Nineties, the huts that were left were sold off and rebuilt, some clever people realising that a house already on a bit of land made it easier to gain planning permission for a bigger, better one. I don't blame them.

My grandad's family were no strangers to the rolling list of manual work and moving around the country in order to carry it out. The list of places his grandfather, Charles Squires, lived reads like a roll call of historic engineering. He lived in '38 Canal Huts' in Ince near Manchester, building the Manchester Ship Canal, then later at '37 Hut, Big Field, Runcorn' where he was a locomotive driver on another project. He took his family to each job and throughout their time together, his wife, Mary-Ann, had 13 children, five of whom died. In 1891, when the census was taken, it showed Charles and his wife living in 38 Canal Huts, then with only four children and, unbelievably, 11 lodgers. A few months after the census was taken Mary-Ann gave birth to a boy called James. As I write this, I am about the same number of months pregnant as she would have been when the census was taken. Right now, plagued with sickness, I am not in the mood to share my home with anyone, let alone 11 men working in awful, wet conditions daily. Imagine the washing, the meals, the lack of space. How Mary-Ann maintained such a big family plus that many lodgers is incredible. I think about what happened the day she gave birth and who was there to help. I lost so much blood with my second child I couldn't stand up for what felt like days. Could she rest? Did some of the lodgers help out? The next column in the document notes the death of baby James at only five months old. I think about the day he died and then stop myself from imagining anymore.

The taking in of lodgers wasn't unusual. If there was a bit of extra money to be earned, then this was an easy way to do it. Accommodation for single men could number up to 33 a hut, with beds constantly in use with shift work. Still, overcrowding was an impossible issue and men would often sleep in the ditches or sometimes in the tunnels they were digging. An extract from the book *Wythburn Mine and the Lead Miners of Helvellyn* describes the accommodation at Thirlmere:

*The huts themselves were bleak and bare, corrugated-tin roofs and
walls offering scant protection against the harsh Lakeland winters.
There is little doubt these settlements were squalid, insanitary and
detrimental in every way to the well-being of the inhabitants.*

The word 'squalid' comes up again and again. Ian Taylor, who wrote
about the Thirlmere Reservoir, noted that, 'They lived the best they
could in their cramped and squalid conditions but fine weather was
a boon and children would play in the woods and fields. Food came
by the way of local traders, butchers and bakers and produce was
sold by the famers, whilst tinkers and pedlars brought all manner
of household goods.'

It's a more rose-tinted view, and to be sure, when the weather is
warm and dry in rural areas this kind of living can be heavenly. In
fine weather we camped by the lake, climbed trees and swam in
the rivers. Even when it rained, we played outside. My brother and
I used to dig out the gravel in our backyard and make waterways
and dams for the pouring water. Mum would stand in the doorway
and shake her head at us, as we knelt in gravel and rainwater. We
may not have had central heating in the house, but at least we had
an open fire and spare clothes to change into. At least there weren't
the clothes of 30 men competing for drying space.

As basic living conditions were so 'squalid', diseases were not
uncommon. Added to that, the dangerous working conditions meant
dying in these camps was commonplace. It is rare to find a list of
people who died in these environments; they have either been lost
or, more likely, were never made at all. Sullivan writes that a navvy,
working on all kinds of engineering projects from railways, canals
to reservoirs, 'stood the same chance of being killed as an infantryman in the Boer War'. There was an assumption that 'every
million pounds' worth of contract would kill a hundred men'.

During the Thirlmere construction, there is just one small note
of burials, which lists the deaths of six men and one woman aged
between 18 and 65 years old, who were buried near to their accom-

modation. There is no information about how they died or where exactly their graves are. I wonder why these people in particular were noted down and have no doubt there would have been more.

There was also a hospital up at Thirlmere, as was often the case on these kinds of sites. I have been told that it is now United Utilities' deer larder and before we leave the dam that wet May bank holiday, I want to see it. We park near the offices and I tell the rest of the family to stay in the car. Having already been soaked through once, they happily comply. I follow Paul from United Utilities' instructions and walk up to the side of the hill to the building. It is obvious which one it is straight away. It's clearly old, a solid stone-built rectangle, the original door now filled in with local stone. Modern windows now run along the side of the building where a new doorway has also been installed. I take a few pictures but am wary of trespassing, despite being told I am allowed to be here. I walk up a little further, level with the windows, and see a light on and movement inside. Someone is lifting, almost wrestling, with something large. I assume it is a deer carcass. Maybe they are just about to hang it; maybe they are about to take it down. Ironically, the room where human bodies were once treated, having arrived mangled, now houses deer in similar conditions. I vividly remember the deer larder behind the house at Graythwaite and don't fancy either getting a whiff of the dead deer or explaining to the land manager why I am peering through his window in the rain. So I leave. I turn back down the hill and suddenly am faced with the huge rocky side of the fell opposite. The rain seems to instil more colours in the landscape, make the bracken redder, the rock a richer grey. You can't see the water of Thirlmere from here, though it's only round the bend of the valley. I think of all the men who were carried or limped their way up to the hospital after an accident, the women who lived here too, carrying sick children. They would have been stretchered up this path, in the rain or snow. No doubt, a tough life.

Back in the car, I shake my jacket off, the windows steam up again and we set off towards Scotland.

A few weekends later, we venture further north. I have heard of a navvies' graveyard in the Glencoe area and am keen to see it. Again, there is no list of those who died when building the Blackwater Reservoir, so a small graveyard with headstones and names of just some of the people who lived and worked there will have to do instead. Blackwater Reservoir, just over the moors from the infamous Glencoe mountain range, was built in 1908 but was not, as I had originally assumed, the water supply for any new industrialised city. It was built to produce hydropower for the aluminium plant in the village of Kinlochleven just down the glen. The graveyard is supposedly quite a sight to behold, isolated and rather eerie. But I have miscalculated. I have made the same mistake that used to make me roll my eyes when tourists came expecting certain things in rural areas. I remember working in a café in the village of Hawkshead and someone asking me where she could buy kids' underwear, after the winding roads made the children violently sick in the back of the car, Kendal, I replied. Or Barrow. They looked at me blankly. These towns were about an hour's drive away, back on the winding roads that had made the kids sick. She didn't believe me and probably spent the next half hour asking in every café.

I may not be looking for knickers in Kinlochleven (I don't think there were any to be found there either), but I have forgotten the sheer expanse of the hills and mountains. I have booked accommodation in the village and was hoping to walk to the reservoir. It's only when I start properly poring over the maps, pinpointing the graveyard just south of the dam, that I realise it's an 11-mile hike up a 550-metre mountain. I am five months pregnant and walking up the stairs makes my heart rate race. Determined to see how far I can actually get, Phil and I set off on the Saturday morning via the post office, which doubles as a small museum. It is suggested by the very helpful woman behind the counter that we walk the 'moderate route' up to the dam. There are also remnants of an old First World War prisoner-of-war camp on that route, which she says I might find interesting if I am 'into all that'. This, I think, seems doable.

We leave the kids in the village with my parents, who I have persuaded to come up and stay with us too, and Phil and I set off, rucksack filled with food. Within minutes we pass the former aluminium works, now a power station that produces enough 'clean green power' to provide electricity to a city the size of Inverness. The waters of the River Leven run fast and fresh. There are signs dotted along the riverbank that tell the story of salmon and how they lay their eggs here. The path gradually rises through woodlands and the views become longer and leaner. I walk slowly, Phil having to stop often for me to catch up. The sounds of all kinds of birds and especially the recognisable sound of a cuckoo keeps us company. After about an hour of gentle climbing, we reach a wooded area full of strips of silver birch trees. Within them we get our first sighting of buildings from a hundred years ago. There are concrete pillars now overgrown with moss, the solid iron nails still wedged into them. The birch trees, a pioneer species, have grown tall around this area. The trunks look like the pale ghosts of soldiers posted here to guard it. This wooded area on a slight hill is where the officers were based. Below this, a few hundred steps away, the ground levels out and more and more remnants of buildings and concrete slabs can be seen. We stop by a pile of old stones that might once have been the railway platform and I catch my breath. It is so peaceful, with networks of rivers and waterfalls running down on either side of the valley. I sit and listen to the birds and the forever falling water. Two mountain bikers bump past on the rocky path.

The space in front of us was built during the First World War and held around 1,000 men, including German and Belgian prisoners of war, as well as British conscientious objectors. The original plans showed that the prisoners were housed in 13 huts along with the ancillary buildings, laundry rooms, washrooms and latrines, kitchen, a theatre, workshops and a hospital. The guards and officers were housed in the separate area overlooking the general campsite that the birch trees now safeguard.

Before the First World War, 80 per cent of the world's aluminium came from Germany. As the war cut off supplies, demand in the UK soared, but the recently built Blackwater dam, the one I had originally come to see, did not hold enough reserves of water to make mass production possible. It was decided that water from the nearby Loch Eilde would be diverted into Blackwater Reservoir. The POWs were put to work, building the aqueduct for this within two years. They also built the road on the south side of Loch Leven to Glencoe. Each morning they were marched through the village to start work. The POWs had a theatre group and an orchestra and some were allowed to mix with the villagers if they were classed as 'trust-worthy'. Some of the inmates even made rings from sixpences for local girls, connections forming as the war years dragged on, despite the gaps in language and the matter of national hostility against the Central Powers.

In the end, I can't make it to the navvies' graveyard, but this quiet space in the green hills above the village is good consolation. It is where so many people from different backgrounds met and spent a few years working hard and socialising together. They traipsed up and down this glen, just as I have done, except, I imagine, they would have carried equipment, tools, food, maybe even musical instruments on their backs. It has such a peaceful atmosphere, a contrast to what is going on elsewhere in the world, or indeed to how the men a few miles up the mountain built the original dam and aqueduct. We walk a little further and eat our lunch looking down onto the old camp, then head back along the same path to the village.

If I had made it to the navvies' graveyard that day, the prospect as we ate our sandwiches would have been quite different. The 22 graves are situated on a mound, fenced off within the classic Glencoe scenery. Here, there is only the rough ground of the moors and very little shelter. The graves name some men on their stones, and one woman. Some gravestones have no names at all. It illustrates perfectly the bleakness and the isolation of working up here, more a monument to the collective experience than a true representation of the individuals who died. There would have been more deaths than were marked here with stones, and we will likely never know how they all came to die. A man who knows all about this desolate kind of place is Patrick MacGill, an Irish navvy who had come to work on the dam in Kinlochleven. When he was just 21, he wrote a semi-fictionalised account in *Children of the Dead End*. He wrote about the living conditions, the work and, poignantly, about their deaths too.

> *While looking after sheep a shepherd came on the corpse of a man that lay rotting in a thawing snowdrift. Around the remains, a large number of half-burnt matches were picked up and it was supposed that the poor fellow had tried to keep himself warm by their feeble flames in the last dreadful hours. Nobody identified him, but the paper stated he was presumably a navvy who lost his way on a journey to or from the big waterworks of Kinlochleven.*

There was one account of a man who tried to escape the Glasgow police by joining the navvies at Blackwater Reservoir. The police searched the camps but, finding nothing, started searching the hills. Not only did they find the body of the man they were looking for, but three more bodies of other men lost on their own journeys. As Patrick MacGill would have testified, men often died on the way back from the pub. They attempted to walk to Kingshouses, the next valley along at Glencoe. We drive through the iconic Glencoe mountains and I point it out to Phil. 'They just didn't care, did they?' Ellis says from the back. Whether he is talking about the men desperate for the warmth of the pub or the company that built the reservoir, it doesn't matter. He is right.

Navvies were well known for 'hard work all week' and a 'full drink on Saturday afternoon and Sunday', and the issue of men drinking, and more specifically where the men drank, was always a fraught one. The locals didn't particularly want them in their taverns, even if they provided useful extra income.

About 30 miles down the Thirlmere pipeline towards Manchester, there is a tale of 'riots' that has been handed down through the generations. The 'Battle of Lupton' happened around the village of Hutton Roof when three or four hundred men were based within 'drinking distance' of the nearby villages. The riot was reportedly started when an Irishman beat an Englishman in the Nook Tavern.

The English mounted a full-scale attack on The Plough (a mile away) where the Irish drank in a specially segregated taproom. The landlady tried to lock out the English, now armed with iron bars and staves, but when she failed she bolted the door into her main building then bolted herself. In a lane outside a hundred evenly divided men brawled and swayed. One man died after being smacked about the head with a spittoon.

Local and regional newspapers buzzed with the tales of riots, this incident and those like it doing nothing for the reputation of the navvies, and the hostilities between local people and the transient labourers brought to their homes.

The Battle of Lupton may have happened in 1890, but it isn't a thousand miles from what still feels common today. As an 18-year-old, my nearest village was Hawkshead. Four miles away from Hawkshead, over the tops of hills, was Coniston in the next valley. The young lads from each village didn't tend to drink in each other's backyards. If we all met in some anonymous village there seemed to be no trouble, but when a group arrived in each other's territory, a tension seeped in and seemed to put everyone on their guard. Much like the incoming labourers who posed a threat to the innocence of the local girls.

Each summer, the villages had their own county shows with horse riding, sheep showing, fell running and wrestling. They also all had beer tents. The tents were full all day with the young and old, wellies and boots, walking sticks and flat caps. By the evening, the showground became damp and cold, and everyone began to stagger into the village. One year, I was on crutches after an unfortunate incident with a mountain board – picture snowboarding without the snow and the top section of bone ripping off a knee – and by the time I'd hopped into the village square, I knew something was amiss.

I had previously gone out with a nice young boy in the village of Coniston where I went to school. I was now going out with an older guy in Hawkshead. My ex was a genuine gentleman, but I couldn't put all of his friends in that category. The pubs are so small in these areas – low ceilings and beams – the inside becomes a boiling pot. Within minutes of arriving in the pub, I was back outside in the village square, using one of my crutches to try to stop the Coniston lad from going for my current man. I hissed at him, 'Get out of my village.' The landlord of the pub, a man easily of six foot three, stepped in and defused the situation. There were four pubs in the village and, excitement over, the boys dispersed into the other three and I sat in the beer garden in both embarrassment and poorly concealed excitement that a fight *might* have been about me. Of course, it was more to do with territory. Every rural village has had its fair share of fights with neighbouring ones. It's what makes the county shows more exciting.

During the building of some reservoirs, the settlements were so large and so well organised that they supported an active social life all on their own. At the Catcleugh Reservoir, built just above Newcastle between 1901 and 1904, there were 700 workers based on either side of the River Rede. Tony Evans, a volunteer ranger with Northumberland National Park who has researched the families and their lifestyle, describes it as a beautiful, tranquil place. 'Originally just a few farms and a shooting lodge, the reservoir totally transformed that area.' The local school roll shot up from 10 children to 60 when the labourers arrived; the church that had only seen a handful of events on a yearly basis was suddenly occupied with baptisms, marriages and funerals that filled the calendar. Within the camp itself, there were 47 huts, a post office, a canteen and a billiard room. Tony tells me there were sports days, dances, musical evenings with fiddlers from the workforce and a drama group.

I tell Tony it sounds idyllic. 'Well, I guess it was,' he says. 'Compared with a lot of housing in the big cities, it was nice out in the fresh air.' There was no running water but each room in the huts had a coal fire to keep them warm. They were lit by paraffin lamps. They had a market every Saturday where they would buy supplies and local farmers did a roaring trade selling milk and goods. When the reservoir was finished, the camp disbanded. The farmers lost the local trade, but it is reported that there was less drunk and disorderly behaviour in the neighbourhood.

Sullivan writes that the navvies' 'impact on a tranquil rural population usually enlivened it, frequently debauched it, and always scandalised the ruling gentry'. He quotes one contractor who said, 'The females were corrupted and went away with the men, and lived amongst them in habits that civilised language will scarcely allow a description of.'

It must have been rather exciting, the influx of a new breed of men to the isolated, buttoned-up villages of the Victorian era. At Catcleugh there is one hut left standing now, restored to its original condition. The reservoir, which feeds water to Newcastle and Gateshead, is surrounded by native as well as conifer woodland, and otters, red squirrels, ospreys and even the occasional golden eagle have been spotted there. It sounds like a wonderful place to spend a few years. I wonder if the families missed it when they left.

Back at home, I receive a phone call from a John Butcher, who Paul from United Utilities put me in touch with. I tell him about our trip to Thirlmere and how I struggled to find the site where the camps had been.

'Well,' he replies in a Northern accent I miss, 'the forest called City wouldn't have been the forest as you see it now.' Before the dam was even imagined, a group of lead miners lived on the site of the current reservoir. I suddenly remember visiting the Pencil Museum in Keswick as a child, only 7 miles away from Thirlmere. At the time, I hadn't been all that interested in where lead came from, but now I wish I could remember something of the visit to Derwent Pencil Factory, otherwise known as the 'home of the first pencil'.

John tells me that when the land was bought for the building of the reservoir, the miners stayed on as they had a lot of expertise. 'The "City" you're thinking of refers to that original settlement of miners and is now under the water of Thirlmere.' Of course, the flattest place for a camp is the bottom of the reservoir. And once again, I'm reminded how amazing it is that history runs in layers, one on top of the other, creating the land we see today.

After our conversation, John kindly sends me more information from books now out of print or near impossible to buy. I read that there were six sites for the huts around the reservoir. At Lakefoot, the text notes, there were 163 men and 74 women and children with 15 huts to house them. At a site called Raise there were 69 people on the workforce and 33 women and children, but there were only five huts. The total number of people housed 'in the northern section on one year alone was 681'. In only 44 huts.

I had imagined huge, sprawling, loosely constructed towns, hut after hut after hut with tools leaning up against the doorways and communal washing areas. But it was nothing like this. There were a handful of buildings standing apart in isolated areas, none substantial enough to protect much against the winter, let alone survive a hundred years later. Dozens of people – families *and* lodgers – were squeezed, cheek by jowl, inside. The men worked in shifts so the beds were slept in day and night. When there were no available beds, they spilled out onto the fells, the roads, the tunnels and ditches in the surrounding area. In such cramped conditions, with so many people and nowhere to move or spread out, much of life must have been spent outdoors.

Next time we drive past Thirlmere, the weather has not been like it was that May bank holiday. It has been dry all summer and more than just the edges of the reservoir are on show. The water has been so low for so long, the earth has a parched look, and I can almost fancy how the men dug at the ground and scraped it away. I cross my fingers and hope for the regular rain I remember from my childhood.

5

Food

The radio dips in and out of signal as the road winds and twists. I am driving a route I don't know very well, despite growing up round here and having friends still in the area. It's not a road many people know very well. Dad once worked with someone who hated the Lake District. There were too many people, too many cars on the bends, he said. Then he drove over this road and changed his mind completely. This feels like the proper Lake District. The views as you top the bumps are stunning: miles of fields that grow into the mountain ridges of Hardknott Pass and Scafell Pike. You can even see the coast: a high view of the Irish Sea and the cluster of elegant white wind turbines far out in the water.

I'm a little nervous, heading back to a farmhouse we used to have parties at as teenagers. Our school friend Roger lived in a small village between the muddy coast and the mountains where his parents ran a dairy farm. It's been years since I've seen them, and I hope they don't hold too many grudges about what we might have been up to in their home as drunk teenagers.

Doreen and Dick, Roger's parents, have lived here for 30 years. At the huge kitchen table (reclaimed for £25 when the local pub shut down, I am told) Dor places photos in front of me of what the kitchen used to look like. 'It was the roof,' she says, 'it was falling in.' I look at the pictures of it, bowed with slates slipping clean off. 'Well, it started as a new roof, but we needed this whole section redone in the end. He was very good to us, the new land-lord. Why did no one tell me how bad the kitchen was before? It was horrible!' I say how lovely it is now, looking through photos and trying to put it together with the vague memories in my head.

Dor and Dick's first farm was near Preston. They took on a short lease tenancy from Dick's uncle as a young married couple, knowing that it was only six months. The farm and the surrounding area had been bought by the Council Commission for the New Towns and was pencilled in to be knocked down to make way for new houses. 'It gave us a chance to look for a new farm,' Dick says calmly. In the end it took 11 years of consistently renewing the six-month tenancy before they had to move on. During that time, they were often applying for farms. 'We came second a lot,' Dor says. 'It's a competitive business.' But they were successful with this one, in the South Lakes: 110 cows, the dairy based at the top of the pretty village. It's a peaceful but bustling community with a view of the bay from the kitchen window.

In 2016, they had the chance to buy it. I had looked it up online at home before coming to see them. 'A traditional investment farm in a picturesque village on the southern boundary of the Lake District National Park. For sale by formal tender as a whole.' One hundred acres. It sounded a lovely prospect. I think about how many people would queue to own a place like this and how many people would actually be able to buy it. Then I think of Dick and Dor. This was their life for sale. Someone could buy the farm, but *they* came with the land. Their tenancy was single succession, which meant they had it for life with only one generation. They could live and work here until Dick died but their children would be unable to take it on. The chance of owning the land you had worked on for 30 years must have been an exciting prospect, security for old age, finally independent and able to make decisions that suited what *they* knew about the business and the land.

'Oh, yes, we got all the finances sorted, took money out of the pensions. Dick has always wanted a farm of his own.' But it wasn't to be. A very wealthy local man had his eye on the land. 'He didn't want any new developments round here,' Dor says. He outbid them, quite easily, and the farm is now his. They seem resigned to the fact now. It's just the way things go. 'He's a good landlord. He hasn't put the rent up.'

Farm tenancies are complicated. The rules seem to have changed repeatedly over the years and it depends on who you rent from as to the conditions. You could rent from a landowner, the council or the National Trust. The old tenancies, originally given in the Eighties and before, could be three generations long. Some are just one generation, some last 15 years, some just five. The length of tenancy depends on so many different things. And these rules apply just in England and Wales. Ireland has no specific agricultural tenancy legislation (and during the Land Purchase Acts of 1903 and 1906 most Irish tenant farmers became owner-occupiers).

Farming tenancies in Scotland are different again, and then added to that, Scotland has a whole raft of complicated crofting laws. Whichever country or laws you farm under, it's safe to say that tenant farming is a vulnerable lifestyle. At a meeting in 1883 on the Isle of Skye, one crofter stated, 'I want the assurance that I will not be evicted for I cannot bear evidence to the distress of my people without bearing evidence to the oppression and high-handedness of the landlord and his factor.' A promise that the farmer could keep his home would be a fine thing indeed.

I am reluctant to ask Dick about retirement. It feels like a sensitive subject, where they might go and how they might get by. I sidestep it by talking about other farmers who have had to leave their farms, and Dick picks up on what I'm saying immediately. 'My grandfather was a tenant farmer and had to move out of the farm when he couldn't work anymore. He was like a fish out of water, living in the town.'

I tell him my parents have lived on estates all their lives with fields and woods all around them, and now find themselves in a terraced house in town. The view out of the attic window at Mum and Dad's is like something from *Mary Poppins*, roof after roof after roof. A forester in a sprawl of brick and concrete. A fish out of water.

Doreen turns to her husband, weighing in. 'I don't want you to be like those farmers who can hardly walk, though.' Dick smiles. He's 65 this year and has no plan to retire any time soon. He gets up at 4.45 every morning to milk the cows, like he's done every day for over 40 years.

'We go on holiday for one week a year to Cornwall to my sister's, but that's it,' Dor says. 'I'm tired of it. I'm tired of feeding all these men' – she meant the men who worked on the farm. 'Men come in at all hours, wanting to be fed.'

'There's always enough in the freezer,' Dick says with another smile. I feel they've had this conversation before. In the couple of hours I'm chatting to them, two different men stride into the kitchen, dressed in jumpers streaked with mud and whatever else you might find on a dairy farm, and make themselves a cup of tea. To me, their kitchen is a farming cliché, a shelter from the outside and a place to settle until the next job. It needs a big, solid pub table to handle all the thoroughfare traffic, and it is, to my eyes, lovely. But I've not had to feed 'all these men' for years on end.

'My dad was a farmer,' Dor says. 'I've been tied to cows my whole life.'

The phone rings and she rushes into the next room to answer it.

'We've basically been told the house is ours. We're not to worry.' Dick seems calm about everything; the measured way he talks, how he sits at the table, still, without any sudden movements. I notice, though, that he looks up at the clock. 'Do you have to milk the cows soon?' I ask.

'Twenty to four, we'll start milking them again.' It is three-fifteen.

It turns out that the new landlord is keen on rewilding – he doesn't really like the concept of a dairy farm. Dick shrugs when telling me this, the concept beyond him. 'So when you retire, it'll be fine', I say, 'you'll have a place to live.' I pause in the silence across the kitchen table. 'But you're not ready to retire yet, are you?' He shakes his head and smiles his slow smile again.

Dor takes me round the house. I tell her I remember the living room well, the back dining table and fireplace. It now has toys for their grandchildren on the deep windowsill behind the dining table. 'Well, this is where you had the parties,' she says proudly. There are photos of Roger on the wall, on the sideboard, grinning. He looks happy. When we were 18, Roger died of a brain tumour. It was a shock to a group of teenagers who had nothing but partying on their minds. Roger was always the tallest in the class, even from a young age; he topped the queue into the dinner hall, or into the classroom. He was also handsome, incredibly bright and funny. The day we all found out he'd died we were at sixth-form college. I can't remember who told us or how I felt when I heard the news, but I know we left straight away. We all got into my little red Corsa, and I drove a group of us back to Coniston where we went to my boyfriend's house. Since I was driving, I couldn't cry, not really, and I didn't know what to say. I pressed play on the CD player and songs came on that didn't fit; happy songs about beautiful days. I turned it off and we must have driven home in silence, each of us watching our own section of the hills pass through the window.

I think about the nights we crammed into the small living room, raiding Dor's fridge in the middle of the night. 'Did you not mind us having parties here?' I ask her. 'No, not at all. You were all sensible, really.' We stand in Roger's old bedroom and talk about the people we're still in touch with, what they're doing now, what their kids are called.

In the farmyard, as I leave to get in the car, she wishes me luck with the baby. She has bought me a toy rabbit as a present. I look around the farmyard and tell her about a memory I have of a bunch of us sitting in my car right there in front of the barn, giggling at something silly. I say we were just giggling, rather than admitting that we were passing around a joint, the girls in the front of the car, the boys in the back. 'Oh, he had a good set of friends, Roger did,' she says as I get in. I put the toy rabbit on the back seat.

Dick and Dor held a tenancy first with the council and then a local landowner, but it is the National Trust that is one of the nation's largest farm owners, with 250,000 hectares of land, renting to more than 1,500 tenant farmers all across the country. Set up in 1895 by Octavia Hill, Sir Robert Hunter and Canon Hardwicke Rawnsley, the National Trust's aim was to preserve the natural environment and invest in the nation's heritage. Both John Ruskin and Beatrix Potter, two names synonymous with the Lake District, had a hand in the founding of the National Trust. Ruskin is said to have 'inspired' the establishment of the National Trust and introduced his friend, the housing reformer Octavia Hill, to Canon Rawnsley. Potter was a good friend of Rawnsley and when she died in 1943 she left 4,000 acres of land and 14 farms to the National Trust.

Both writers took up the cause for conservation with passion, and the things they campaigned for are still relevant today, including town and country planning.

As a child growing up in the Lake District, in the shadow of these reformers, I couldn't care less about their books, their teachings or preserving the land. My secondary school was even called John Ruskin School and was split into two houses, one of which was Brantwood, my house, and where Ruskin had lived on the other side of the lake. But I remember nothing of his work, his writing, his art. It is not a reflection on the school; I imagine they tried to teach us something of use about our local history, our heritage, but it was lost within the more important issues of discos, ouija boards in the music rooms and art lessons with the radio on.

The same fate for Beatrix Potter. In every town around the lakes of Coniston, Esthwaite, Windermere, we were bombarded with images of Peter Rabbit, Jemima Puddle-Duck and Jeremy Fisher. We had copies of the books at home, but I don't remember reading them. We avoided the Potter-heavy villages and areas that the tourists flocked to.

My brother and I had never even stepped foot into Hill Top, where Beatrix wrote her books up in the village of Sawrey, until the day the BBC called looking for a wild-looking, tame rabbit to play the part of Peter for a new adaptation of the books. The production team had asked a local farmer if he knew of any Peter Rabbit lookalikes and, having been to our house the day before and seen my brother and I playing with our rabbit, Sherbet, he gave them our number. It still baffles me that they didn't source a suitable rabbit before they pitched up with all their filming equipment and lighting, but we were chuffed. Sherbet was excellent in the role and was paid £80 a day, given to us in a little brown paper envelope; and Tom and I each had a day off school to watch the filming. We've still not been back to Hill Top.

The tenancies of National Trust farms come up rarely and, as Doreen says, it's a competitive business. I look at the website and, as I write, there is a 77-acre farm with a three-bedroom house in Wales. It notes in the particulars, 'This is a stock-rearing farm, which we envisage being run in a nature-friendly manner to build on and deliver better habitats and opportunity for wildlife to thrive as a result.' Understandably, delivery of better habitats for wildlife is a driving force for the National Trust. And at least this one comes with a house. Not all do.

Rose and her husband run an organic beef and sheep farm near the coast in the southwest area. They are National Trust tenants and took on their first farm in 1983 as a lifetime tenancy. When another farm came available, they were asked by the National Trust to take on the land for that one too – although no property was offered. (The farmhouse that should have been with that offer of land is rented privately and is now run as a bed and breakfast.) Rose and her husband run 420 acres on their farm. I call her one day and ask whether this is a common thing, farmers being asked to take on more land and farms getting bigger, but the house on the land being used for other purposes. 'Yes,' she says resolutely. 'They used to let them to local families, but things have changed.' This doesn't surprise me, really. We all know there is more money in self-catering and holiday lets – and the booming Airbnb market – than in renting a farmhouse to farmers. Rose tells me that when the tenancy came up six years ago, they asked for another 15 years. No, they were told, without negotiation. They could have another five.

'It makes it very difficult for long-term business plans. You don't know where you're going to be.' She worries that the National Trust are leaning towards shorter tenancies and have lost their way, their spirit of supporting and preserving the countryside – which launched the trust in the first place – waning. They simply don't look out for the communities as much as they should anymore. 'Things that were agreed on years ago were agreed on a handshake. But staff have changed. There are no records now. And there is a frequent change in policy.'

I ask her if it's been worth it, all the worry, the work.

'I don't know whether it's been worth it,' she says after a pause. I imagine her in her farmhouse kitchen, standing by the sink, looking out onto the farmyard. 'My partner has had mental health issues, my brother-in-law is single [he runs the farm too], neither of them have a good social life.' There is another pause. 'I feel like it's worth it, but I married into it, so I think I have a better balance.' I recall Doreen saying she was looking forward to her nephew's twenty-first birthday party and then sighing, saying they can't stay over. 'We have to come back for the cows.'

Chewing it over further, Rose tells me that there is always worry and insecurity, but that they live in a lovely place. 'Put it this way, we haven't been on a family holiday for twelve years, my son has never been abroad, but I was out on my paddle board this morning.'

'What about your son?' I ask. 'Would your husband try to steer him away from a life in farming?' 'Yes,' she replies definitely. 'He'd say don't go into farming. There's no money and lots of stress. But you need to be happy. You just need to keep learning and doing what makes you happy.'

I have never lived on a farm, but in my first few years of life we lived in North Yorkshire, often visiting friends and their 1,200 Swaledale sheep. We lived on an estate in a tied house on the outskirts of a small village, the back garden of which looked out onto the moors. Dad worked as a forester for the landowner and Mum stayed at home looking after me. They became very good friends with a local farmer, Chris, and his wife, Margaret, who lived deep in the moors. Mum was only 21 and on her own a lot of the time, her family a long way away. When they moved to the area, Margaret was the first person to knock on the door and ask Mum if she'd like to join the Women's Institute. Mum laughs when she tells me this. Wasn't it full of old women? 'Not round there,' she said.

Their farm felt as far flung as you can get. There were four cattlegrids on the single-track road that you had to unlock, open and shut again every time you drove to the village and back again. The house was an extensive stone building, formerly a shooting lodge. It was two storeys high, very simply built but grand in presence, with many wide windows on the upper level to look out at the landscape. They didn't live in the whole building, though. Margaret, Chris and their two daughters lived in a small section – a few bedrooms, the kitchen and a small living room. The rest was reserved and kept primed and ready for when the landowner wanted to throw shooting parties.

I can remember walking into the house, through the huge front door into a cavernous hallway with a box of walking sticks, a coat stand overloaded with thick jackets and a spiral staircase. There was a heavy wooden door to the right and a similar one to the left. We were only ever permitted to turn right into the farm kitchen; the left was a locked door into the west wing that was not for us and which would only be opened two or three times a year.

On the other hand, the kitchen was the most lived-in room you could imagine and everything a farm kitchen should be, with a tatty Belfast sink, a huge solid-wood farmhouse table and an enormous range where the faded farmer's chair sat snug against it. Behind the kitchen was a small living room and then upstairs, via a small back staircase, were the bedrooms. This was one long corridor with doors lined up each side, like a murder-mystery film. They were all shut – locked, most likely – so it was dark, and the wind rattled around the chimney in every room. I stayed in the bedroom of the Manchester United-mad daughter, and we fell asleep listening to the sheep, or the rain on the glass panes. The house is now a boutique holiday home to rent, with roll-top baths and luxury bedding, sleeping up to 17 guests at nearly £500 a night. The farm sheds and barns are also converted to self-catering. It's tempting to go back one day and pay to stay in the parts of the house I was not allowed to go into and remember how I used to sleep on the floor under the watchful gaze of Eric Cantona.

There are many photos of us feeding lambs and playing with puppy sheepdogs in their farmyard. Mum and Dad look younger than I have ever felt as a parent. Fresh-faced and very happy. I phone Margaret up one day and ask about her time on the farm. 'It was a calling, farming there; you just worked all hours,' she says. She talks very fast, her sentences full of words that rise and fall in the North Yorkshire accent. I struggle to keep up making notes. 'Oh, it was remote, but we loved it.' She tells me her two daughters went to ballet, Guides, gymnastics, all kinds of activities. I'm impressed at the organisation that must have taken on top of everything else, arranging where the children needed to be, dropping them off and picking them up, making tea for their return. And then you add the remoteness. I picture her daughters getting in and out of the car at the edge of every field in the driving rain, opening and shutting the gates. That is the price you pay to live in a beautiful place. And, mostly, it's worth it. Margaret goes on: 'We had all sorts of parties there. The landlord liked us to be part of the community – choirs in the barn, that kind of thing.' After Chris died, the main buildings were renovated into holiday lets, which Margaret helped decorate and design. The farm, and a new farming family, are still there with the Swaledale sheep scattered about the moors, though on a far smaller scale. I ask where she lives now. 'Well, Chris and I had bought a little house. We felt pressured into it, for our retirement. But he always said I'll never live there. He used to say, "When I leave here I'll be brought out in a box." Well, we never thought he would. But there you go.' They ended up selling that house but luckily, she had 'kept up with' the life insurance policy and, after Chris died, this enabled her to buy the bar in Tenerife. I stall. 'You bought a bar in Tenerife?' 'Oh yes,' she laughs, 'the bar was mine.' I knew she had left the farm and spent some time in Spain, but I had no idea as to her business acumen. She did this with another farmer's wife who had recently become divorced: they clubbed together and bought a business abroad. I'm amazed. It's such a contrast to how I remember her, baking in the kitchen, clearing the table for tea. 'You can never go away as a farmer so after we [her and her friend] were on our own, we just did it!'

They don't own the business in Tenerife anymore as Covid made things difficult. But she still goes to Spain often to enjoy the life. 'I was born on a farm, worked my whole life on a farm and now I'm laid on a sofa drinking gin,' she laughs. I picture her in the old house I knew, in the old living-room, laid out on the sofa, a lady of luxury, with all those bedrooms above her and acres and acres of land outside the living room window. But in reality, she's in a one-bedroom flat in the village down the road. Her view now is probably more houses, roads, maybe the moors in the distance. And, it seems, she's never been happier. 'It's close to the grandchildren, it's small. I love it!' she laughs again.

I chatted to another farmer's wife based in Yorkshire. Christine was holed up with a broken foot so had all the time in the world to chat to me from her living room. She married a tenant farmer; her husband's grandad was the first one there in the early 1940s renting off a private estate. They had a three-generation tenancy, which was still available before the Eighties. Now they don't exist. 'Back then, it was as good as your own,' she says. 'It meant you could invest a little bit.' Three generations feels like a long time but it goes much more quickly than you'd think, and when another farm on the estate became available to rent with the caveat that the old tenancy had to be handed in, they took up that offer. 'Ours was the last generation and we don't have children to pass the business on to. Friends and neighbours who do have another generation left on the tenancy were obviously reluctant to do that in order to safeguard their children.' In those cases, she says, 'Well, the whole thing becomes a different animal.'

She talks about how the structure of farming is changing. 'It's the biggest change in sixty years.' Speaking to Christine, herself on the verge of a huge life change of retirement, it feels everything is shifting. The way we have produced food over the last few generations won't work anymore. Politics, trade deals and the weather are more varied. This is only the tip of the iceberg. She doesn't seem worried, quite the opposite, but she seems to be standing ready for whatever is to come.

'We got enough for a deposit and bought a house,' she goes on to say. When they can no longer work and live in the house, they will retire to the nearest market town. Here it is again, the fish out of water. It seems so topsy-turvy. Most people talk about retiring to the countryside, to rural areas, where the pace of life is 'slower', where the views are endless. For people living in tied housing, the opposite is true; they are forced to retire into a town where, hopefully, housing prices are more affordable. But even then, this isn't always the case.

For Christine, she felt much happier when they bought the 'little' house as they felt more secure. She knew where they were going to end up. It's her husband she worries about, the dynamic not unlike Margaret and Chris's. 'This place is his home. It will be strange to move. There are fantastic views here; there's no price on those views. It's in a lovely situation looking across the hills. And we'll be moving to an end-of-terrace.' I can hear the sadness in her voice. The apprehension.

It then turns to frustration. Despite good words about their landlord earlier on in the conversation, she is disappointed at the state of the farmhouse that has been their home since she was a young married woman. Now, as a landlord herself, their little house in the town is being rented out and, in the meantime, she is well aware of the high standards they need to keep it in. Whereas the farmhouse was 'built under less regulation – no damp course, resulting in the wallpaper starting to peel off as soon as you put it on', their house in the town has to be kept to the highest standard. She says of the farmhouse, 'Oh, the essentials are all there. But the whole place will likely get gutted with a new tenancy and an increased rent. There needs to be a change in mindset.'

I guess everyone needs an exit plan as a tenant, if you have the resources to pull one together. And you need it formulated in plenty of time.

It's often said how difficult it is for young farmers to even get on the tenancy ladder, let alone buy something. Matt is a young farmer I spoke to one day over the phone. I didn't know he was sitting in his tractor cab until the very end of the conversation, but he'd been on the job the whole time, bumping along, spraying the fields ready to plant wheat. When I was young, tractors drowned out all conversation, the roar and mechanics of them going at full speed, but all I can hear when talking to Matt is a distant whirr of something and, every few minutes, a beep.

Matt is currently looking for a farm tenancy. He has applied for four so far and thought, 'naively', that that was a lot. It seems he was wrong. It can take years to be successful and each application will take a different format. 'When we did the first one, we were clueless. We have a bit of a template now, but still each one varies enormously. There is a lot of research into how the farm enterprises work; different terrains, different parts of the country. It's hours of work. And then you get the crushing disappointment of not getting it and just have to start again.'

Matt is living in a tied house just now with his wife. They are still young, Matt not even 30 yet. He has big plans, much he wants to do, but finds that working full time on someone else's farm makes it difficult to find the time to farm your own, no matter how small. They currently have 100 sheep, 59 breeding ewes and all kinds of other animals, including ducks, chickens and a pig. They rent parcels of land for the animals, which are scattered about, some miles apart. He has to trailer food, water, equipment between each field. It sounds like a real pain. 'We are still very much a dog-and-stick small farm. We can't afford a quad bike yet.'

Matt and his wife have lived in tied houses, working on various farms, since they got together at 19 and 21. They are ready to take on a tenancy, but the competition is fierce. 'At open days at farms, you can get twenty or thirty people coming to view it.' He's heard of some with 50 or 60 applicants. It's a long game. And now, with tenancies getting shorter and shorter, I wonder about the security of them. Is it really worth it for a tenancy of just five years? He thinks so. And buying land or buying a whole farm is simply not a possibility.

There is one part of farming tenancies I've not touched on: the system of crofting in Scotland. Speaking to one person about crofting, she jokes that it takes 30 years to understand the ins and outs of the laws around it and I well believe this.

However, the concept is simple. According to the Crofting Federation based in Inverness: 'A croft is a small agricultural unit in the Scottish Highlands and Islands. Each croft has a share in common or hill grazings. These common grazings are managed collectively by all crofters in the township.'

And a crofter is usually:

the tenant of the croft, paying annual rent to the landlord who owns the crofting estate. Rents are only for the bare land on the croft. The crofter provides the croft house and agricultural infrastructure. In 1976, crofters gained the right to acquire title to the croft, becoming an owner-occupying crofter. Crofters are required to live on or near their crofts and to work them.

It is this clause – 'In 1976, crofters gained the right to acquire title to the croft, becoming an owner-occupying crofter' – which interests me. It seems like a great clause, a real revolution. During the Highland Clearances, landlords forcibly evicted thousands of crofters to create areas devoted to extensive sheep farming. It was the beginning of rural depopulation, a trend that still continues today in many areas. The clause of 1976 gives people who work and live on the land the chance to buy their stake in it. You can be your own landlord, a landowner. And what's more, the purchase price of your croft is capped at 15 times your annual rent. Rent on crofts is usually low. It has all the makings of a good idea, but as often with these things, problems have arisen in the long run.

The act might have done much to protect the rights of crofters, but it has its harms. 'The crofting system of the Highlands', notes the writer John McPhee, 'is borne forward ever more incongruously toward the twentieth century, perfectly protecting people from the terrors of the eighteenth century while isolating them from the twentieth.' It is the new ways of the twentieth century that make the crofting laws unsustainable. For instance, if you own your croft, you can sell it. And over the last 50 years, many of them have been bought as second homes. I am reluctant to say sold as second homes. No one wants to sell their home of decades to be someone else's summer hideaway, visited or rented out for profit, but sometimes they don't have a choice. Circumstances force your hand, and you accept the highest bidder, who is often an incomer who made their money elsewhere – and will, for the most part, stay elsewhere. This ability to sell the croft and for it to become a second home means the population of small villages in rural areas is, once again, under threat.

And it's not easy to make a living as a crofter – the average size of a croft is about 5 hectares; some are smaller, while a few extend to more than 50 hectares. Most crofts cannot support a family or give full-time employment, so crofters diversify into small-scale tourism, while often taking another job such as postmen or policemen. Crofting is not only a full-time job; it's a whole lifestyle that only a few can hack.

It may be a tough life, but there's no denying that when a community like this gets together, they can achieve almost anything. In the 1990s, a group of forward-thinking – some at the time said 'audacious' – crofters, changed history. The hundred or so crofters on Assynt, in the far northwestern corner of Scotland, didn't want to buy their own crofts separately as the 1976 act allowed them; they wanted to buy the land as a whole. They wanted to be in control of their own future.

In 1989, Lord Vestey, whose fortune was second only to that of the Queen, sold 21,000 acres to a Swedish land speculator for just over a million pounds. Within a few years, they had gone bust, and the land was back up for sale again, instead this time in several lots with no concern being shown for the impact of this process on the crofting activity of the inhabitants. At a public meeting of the crofters a proposal was made. Someone said, 'Why don't we buy the land ourselves?' I can just imagine the atmosphere in the room, the sheer improbability of it, but then the exhilaration of what if? Why not? Could we really? The buzz that spilled out of the building after this was suggested. Within days, most crofters in the area were keen. Within a few meetings, the original venue of the local library was not big enough and they moved to the primary school, and even then people had to sit on the window ledges.

Within six months, the Assynt Crofters' Trust had raised enough money, helped by donations from around the world, to buy the 21,000 acres. The crofters still rented their crofts, but, instead of paying an absentee landlord who didn't understand or care about their needs, their traditions, their history, they paid the rent to the trust they created. Given the crofters collectively made up the trust, this meant that the land now belonged to everyone. Not only did this idea at the original public meeting change their *own* way of life; it set some mighty wheels in motion. It enabled other rural communities to challenge landlords and take control of where they lived and worked. By the year 2000, 144,000 acres of land were in community ownership, bought by trusts set up by the people who lived there. By 2010, community-owned land had grown to 420,000. At their 25-year anniversary, Ray Mackay, vice-chairman of the Assynt Crofters' Trust, said, 'The big thing that we have done is survived – nobody thought we could.' Today the estate has around 187 tenanted crofts. It took a long time for them to pay off their debts and they only built an estate office in 2012, but they have done it. They have a successful hydro-electric project that generates electricity, and they also provide income by stalking and fishing.

Reading the speeches celebrating their twenty-fifth anniversary on their website, I can't help but feel a real thrill for every person involved and every crofter who lives there now. Inaugural vice-chairman of the Assynt Crofters' Trust John McKenzie's opening speech starts with the line, 'I think that it can be fairly said that the pattern of land ownership throughout the Highlands was, until then, almost exclusively that of landowner and tenant and each knew their place in society.' They certainly changed that. He goes on to say that after the takeover, a BBC commentator said, 'Landlords were rattled.' And it seems landlords have been rattled ever since. For crofters, some of whose family had been working on the same patch of land for generations, these changes were ground-breaking.

Like most people, my closest connection to a working farm today arrives when I'm stood in front of a supermarket shelf, looking at the sausages, milk, cheese, bread. The older I become, the more I try to buy from farm shops and more sustainable local outlets, but I'm keenly aware – from years when affording that would have been impossible – that this is an option for only a certain type of person.

I watch the tractors and the combine harvesters line the fields in the late summer sun and feel a mixture of both envy and relief. To have that calling, to be so invested in the rhythms of the year and to produce food for the people they see driving slowly behind them on the road, getting more impatient at every bend. To do it with the barest profits and without ownership of their own farm. To do it with the knowledge that, when they can no longer phys-ically work, they will likely be turfed out of their home into a town, an environment that is foreign to them.

Farmers often get a bad reputation and I have never understood why. Like foresters, people think they are destroying the land for their own profit. But this is so far from the truth. You cannot work on the land without loving the cycle of it: the soil; the plants; the birds; the unpredictable, annoying weather – every bit. Farming is changing. Open a newspaper just once a week and you'll find a story about the difficulties of farming: the droughts, floods, soil conditions, the price of milk, the cost of fertiliser. Turn on the TV and you'll happen upon a programme about a farmer's way of life, romanticised no doubt, but they are there all the same. All you need to do is drive the country roads and see them working at night, floodlights on the tractor, just to get the job done before the rain comes. But we still don't seem to understand them. We need to help farmers too. They can't change the way they farm unless we change the way we demand food and see them. They are not the enemy. They work harder than anyone I know and I envy their connection to the land they live on, whether they own it or not.

6

Slate

It is the start of the summer holidays and I am restless; my son is away with his dad for a week. I have booked a small room in a bed and breakfast on Easdale Island, a tiny mile-wide patch of metamorphic rock for myself, my friend Jen and Jessie. I have wanted to visit Easdale Island, just south of Oban on the west coast of Scotland, for a long time. The pictures I've seen look like something from an old film, with rows of cute cottages and deep pits filled with water now used by wild swimmers. There is no road – it's too small – and no cars. Despite its size, Easdale was once at the very heart of Scotland's slate industry. The island looks over to Mull and, beyond that, the North Atlantic Ocean to America.

We have never been away together, all three of us. We chuck our swimming stuff in the boot and snack on grapes and crisps and drive west with the windows down. Gradually the roads become thinner, and eventually, with around 30 minutes on the sat nav to go, the road becomes single-track. We reach Ellenabiach, the small village on the mainland opposite Easdale, and squeeze the car behind a neat row of houses with old ale barrels for water butts.

Looking at the great cliff of grass and rock that rises above, I can't believe it. I have been here before. I have been desperate to come to Easdale for months, looking up accommodation, trying to arrange a time that suited everyone, and now I recognise the grey rocks, the shape of the land, the car park in which, last time I was here, I was trying to change into a wetsuit that didn't really fit me. We had been coasteering, a day trip from Oban on a mixed-sex stag do where you clambered across the rocks and jumped into the sea. I was so hungover, I clearly didn't take in the name of the place, let alone the journey there. I didn't last long in the water; I am generally skinny and my wetsuit didn't hug as it should have, the cold Atlantic finding its way into my bones. I couldn't swim for shivering and wound up warming myself in the pub as the rest of the party continued up the coast in the water.

Today feels very different: I am six months pregnant with my three-year-old in tow; I want to know about the island's history, about the people that lived here in the small, whitewashed cottages that lined the paths. We head straight for the ferry, a wee motorboat that could seat around eight people. Jessie clings on to me as we skip across the small stretch of water. They host the World Stone Skimming Championship here on Easdale and I fancy we bounce across the sea like the slates they skim each September. As the boat motors into the harbour, I can't believe the amount of slate. It is everywhere you look, making up the walls, the steps, the harbour floor underneath the boat. Great stacks of it across the sea floor make the water clear and inviting. It is every shade of grey.

A multi-coloured selection of wheelbarrows lie upside down on the grass near the harbour, for the residents to cart shopping and large items around the island.

We walk around the small harbour looking for 'the house with the flag' where we have booked to stay. It was the former quarry master's house and was at one time one of the biggest houses on the Island. We find it by the edge of the harbour, a Scotland flag flying in the breeze. Too early to check in, we walk past the front door, keen to explore.

Past the main section of the village are the quarries. The whole place has an untouched, abandoned feel. Huge heaps of slate lie cut and sliced in unwanted mounds. It seems improbable that it was all done by the hand of man. The miners sized up the slates, working out which ones were suitable, and the rest were flung away, creating metre-deep peaks of slate.

It is difficult to know where to look and which path to take. The sea that spins up the coast towards Oban shines in the late-afternoon sunlight. The slate underneath our feet chimes and clatters. It feels a little like walking on eggshells, except none of the slate ever shatters or splits. The edges seem to rub off each other, making an odd musical tone. We come across a ruin of an old house that is almost camouflaged against the slate backdrop. I am told later that the building materials for these houses have been part of numerous houses over the years, moving from one site to another, the same stones reused again and again – not unlike my son making and destroying his Lego houses.

A little further and we reach the first pool. The island is pockmarked with these quarries. Some are shaped like Olympic-size swimming pools, 50 metres across but a dizzying 80 metres deep. Some are smaller and rounded, like large fairy pools. I feel jittery looking down onto the quarry floor, clear as the glass at the bottom

of a gin bottle. The water looks like the highest-quality volcanic drinking water you could buy. The colours are spectacular, the sun reflecting off the shades of grey/blue rock. We are barely off the west coast of Scotland, but it's like something lifted from a Caribbean holiday brochure.

The pits of Easdale are all man-made, carved out of the rock over years of hard, back-breaking work. First, the men relied on natural resources and what they had to hand: the tides and the sea water. The practice was to insert wooden wedges into natural cracks in the slate. As the tide rose, the wood swelled and the cracks widened. Gradually the slate was cut away. The pits became deeper and deeper.

When gunpowder was introduced, everything became easier and quicker. Bags of gunpowder, favoured over dynamite as the latter was too powerful, would be inserted into fissures and then lit. Blasting was done at certain times of the day, and in the bigger quarries, there were shelters where the men would retreat until the dust had settled. At Easdale, not only did the men need to secure the pits they were working in from rockfall and collapse, but they also had to defend them from the sea. To do this they dug a barrier – effectively, a smaller pit – between them and the water. When the tide came in, the first pit filled with sea water, which shielded the bigger quarry where the men were working. In typical fashion, the sea could be helpful and destructive by turns.

Jen is desperate to get in the water and swim. I am reluctant. As I know already, I don't deal with cold water so well and, being pregnant, it worries me. A couple who took the ferry with us are already in the big pool and so, reluctant to share the space, we wander on.

The next pool is filled with young people in wetsuits jumping off huge rocks into the still water. I wonder if they are local. They certainly seem to know the pools well. On the north side of the island, we see our spot. This pool is a rough rectangle shape, like the others, but slightly smaller. The water rests neatly within the gunpowder-blown stone and the walls rise to meet the North

Atlantic. A small area in the corner is easy enough to walk down and act as a beach. The water is shallow at the edge but then descends into a sudden drop where it deepens along with the colours.

'What about sharks and crocodiles?' Jessie says as I help her into her swimming costume. 'Nothing in here but stone, darling.'

Jen is in the water within minutes, my daughter following suit. I stay on the rocks, dangling my feet in, marvelling at the man-made but natural swimming pool on the edge of the sea.

Easdale Island and its fellow mines and islands in the area are said to have 'roofed the world'. Its slate has been mined steadily from the twelfth century and then, predictably, the Industrial Revolution saw its production ramped up to incredible levels. In 1772, there was a permanent workforce, which was exporting 2.5 million slates annually. By the mid-1900s, 19 million slates were being exported annually to places as far afield as New Zealand, Australia, the West Indies and the United States.

In the mid-1800s, Easdale was a bustling, successful community of around 500 people where mining was, as always, a family affair. Like in other places, the profit of the mine didn't translate into living conditions. The dimensions of the island, the lack of infrastructure, added to the challenges. Women and children carried the slate on their backs or in wheelbarrows to be put on board the ships. There was no soil on the stony island, so growing food didn't come naturally. To begin growing vegetables, the community had to ask ships from Ireland to bring soil as ballast and swap it for the slate they took away.

When the 5th Earl of Breadalbane took over in 1843, he created a railway track to carry the slate, freeing time for the children to start going to school and the women to step back from the manual labour. He also ordered improvements in the cottages. Before, they consisted of one or two rooms and were thatched using reed or heather. There was no proper chimney, just a vent in the roof that would sit above the cooking fire. Mary Withall, writer and current resident of the island, wrote of the changes in dwellings: 'The roof space, although hardly high enough for a man to stand upright at the centre, was used as a sleeping place for children. A skylight made of isinglass lit the attic, while small panes of glass were introduced in the ordinary windows to provide natural lighting.' The residents paid a rent that reflected the existing success of the mines. When the quarry closed, Breadalbane Estates offered the houses to their tenants for sale 'at the cost of a year's rent'. Mary notes that some of these houses have been handed down through the generations and are still in the hands of direct descendants of quarry workers.

By all accounts, it was a tough life. Children at the school had to bring a piece of coal or peat every day for the fire. If you couldn't afford to bring your piece, you were told to sit at the back of the class, furthest from the warmth. The miners created dugouts for themselves, small pits sometimes covered in canvas, to protect themselves from the wind and rain as they worked. You can still see these as you wander around the island. The reality is captured in Mary's accounts: 'In this crude shelter, the men, often seated in the water which collected around them as they worked, split and shaped the slates throughout the hours of daylight. It is little wonder that the most prevalent diseases amongst the quarrymen were rheumatism and arthritis.'

In 1881, there was a storm like none they'd seen before. Described as a 'tidal wave that swamped most of the quarries', it must have been terrifying. The island is so small, it must have felt like it would break free and be swept out towards America. The small slate houses are close to the water's edge – everything is close to the water's edge – and the waves will have crashed over them, the families inside frightened of the fury of the sea.

Unbelievably, no one died, although it must have been a huge shock to the population. Most of the pits had to close production but they continued to mine the slate on a much smaller scale. Finally, the quarry closed in 1911, unable to keep up with competition from bigger slate quarries in places such as Wales.

Watching Jen and my daughter playing in the water, I realise I was wrong: there is more than stone in the pools. Tiny fish have started to appear around the edges of the water.

'It's a bit salty,' Jen shouts over. 'It tastes like both rainwater and sea water!'

When I look closely at the rock around me, I notice tufts of green and tiny splashes of colour. Small plants are clinging on between the cracks in the rock. I recognise some of them – lichen, moss and definitely heather – but have to look up the rest at home. Mary Withall lists alpine plants such as wild thyme and stone crop as well as angelica, wild carrot, pig nut and sea plantain as all growing on Easdale. She writes, 'As you wander in the wild areas of these beautiful islands, step lightly on the growing plants. It has taken a hundred years to attain the growth which now softens and disguises the man-made scars of an obsolete industry.'

The sun has warmed up the slates around me. I can hear the gentle waves of the sea just a few feet behind us. I think about the force and the terror of the storm in 1881. The way the water could easily breach these walls or the walls of a cottage. I splash my feet in the shallows. The baby in my growing bump seems to be asleep so I inch myself carefully into the water as it gradually cools my skin.

Like the children who live on Easdale Island, I grew up surrounded with slate. This magical, grey, metamorphic rock is bedded into the bones of the Lake District, making up the hills, the houses and the dry-stone walls. Our secondary school stood in the shadow of a series of slate mines, hidden within the heart of the Old Man of Coniston. The Old Man is one of the highest fells in the area and a popular walking and climbing route. Not only did they mine slate here, but copper too, which geologically went hand in hand. Since we were little, Dad has tried to explain geological concepts to us. I ask him again, on one walk near Coniston in the summer, why the Lake District hills and mountains look like they do. He thinks a moment and then says, 'Africa bumped into Europe 440 million years ago. The first shock waves created the alps, huge spiky mountains, then by the time the shock waves reached the Lake District they were smaller and created these mounds that the Old Man is part of.'

I repeat it back to Ellis, forging the information in my memory even more. He looks amazed. Dad explains further that the slate was made by compressing and compacting mud repeatedly at very high temperatures. And the copper was made when the heat of the volcano created fissures in the rocks, and minerals such as copper and tin were deposited into the cracks. I ask where the volcano is now. 'It's under our feet, it's underground,' Dad says. 'It's difficult to really comprehend the full scale of it all,' he shrugs. Rocks acting like waves on a beach, land moving over millions of years: truly mind boggling. It was only when we started to understand what was beneath our feet and how useful the UK's particular geology was that we started to mine coal, lead, copper, iron, tin and slate. And Coniston, like so many other small rural farming communities, was transformed into what we see today.

Our teachers took full advantage of this rich outdoor classroom, creating lessons where we studied the effects of the weather and geology. One summer our whole year group tramped up the side of the fell to study the water course that ran past the former copper mines. Pens and paper in sweaty hands, we probably should have been noting down comments about the way the river flows, or the type of rocks in the water. But it was a hot day and nearing the end of term and we must have been like caged animals, released into the sun. We begged to jump in the river, Church Beck, which ran fast and clear down the steeper part of the fell, creating white foam like champagne bubbles over the rocks. After the small slate bridge that crossed onto the other side of the fell, the river levelled out to create a slower, deeper water course. Along this stretch, we found small waterfalls, where the rock was as smooth as a flume in a swimming pool. We slid down them into the pools, splashing, shrieking, our lessons forgotten.

I took a wander up here last time we were in Coniston. They now do organised ghyll scrambles here, wetsuited and helmeted. Herdwick sheep roam about in the bracken on the side of the fell and along the paths. They look like sturdy dogs, with thick, close wool and friendly, fat faces. We walked past Miners Bridge to where the landscape levels out and the river slows. There were huge mounds of slag left over from the copper mining, rubbish tipped away and abandoned. On the same geography field trip, we had also climbed to the top of these mini mountains of spoil and run down them, shards of coloured slag moving and rushing down the mounds. Later, at home, I read that 153 kinds of lichen, some of them rare and threatened, had been found on these spoil heaps alone. As in Easdale, it takes a long time for nature to return to these bleached, often metal-rich areas, but it does, eventually. I felt immediately guilty that we had trampled on what might have been the difficult start of plant life, 25 years ago.

This was also the spot where we had to cross the river during the annual school fell race in October. Every year, the whole school of around 250 pupils ran up the side of the fell and back down the other side to the school in the village. I always hated crossing the river, as your trainers got wet and your feet got cold. Not much fun in the driving rain, but there was no skiving the fell race. If you didn't run it, you weren't allowed to go to the school disco, which was always a few nights after. And the disco was always worth it.

Just above Church Beck and the old spoil heaps stands a strip of former copper miners' houses called Irish Row. These buildings are iconic now, having been on many painters' canvases and walkers' photographs.

Irish Row – we assume so-called after the influx of Irish miners that came to find work in the early 1800s – has the usual one- or two-roomed dwellings with an open fire and a grand view. The man who ran the mine was a Mr John Barratt who owned the Big House of the village, Holywath. Mr Barratt was, by all accounts, rather a character, self-claiming the title of 'mines adventurer' rather than manager. He was the named partner in the mines lease and transformed the copper mines into something both profitable and also, compared to other employers at the time, a decent place to work. He gave out winter clothing to his workers, and during a particularly severe winter in 1865, he paid for a quarter of a ton coal 'for each poor person'. As the mine's success grew, overcrowding became an issue. In 1841, reports note that there were 134 people living in 'Forge Cottages', a row of 20 houses. Ten years later, the census records nearly double that in the same row. Barratt and the mine company rented extra accommodation in the village, but also built some rows of cottages. By 1875 the company owned 41 houses and 13 leasehold cottages and were advertising jobs in newspapers promising 'good cottages with gardens attached'.

Many of these are now small self-catering cottages, billed as a 'chance to explore the fascination of the fells, enjoy the clear mountain air and watch the quietly grazing Herdwick sheep, beneath a stunning panorama of mountain peaks'. It certainly is out of the way and peaceful up here. If you don't mind the regular line of people walking up the Old Man. Or the groups of people ghyll jumping in the river. Although slate is still mined in the area and farming will always be important, the main employer in Coniston now is tourism. When I come back to see friends who live here, we arrange our day around what we call 'the visitors'. We organise coffee in cafés early to miss the arrival of people or meet in other out-of-the-way places. This time we meet at our friend Lyndsay's house, where there is a block of slate the size of a pavement as her mantelpiece. She has baked a cake and our slices are gone in seconds as we catch up, our children playing on the living-room floor.

It is summer and I ask what the village is like now. 'So busy,' Lyndsay says. 'It was so quiet during lockdown. You could see how many self-catering and second homes there are – some streets had only one house with a car outside. It's so busy now, I don't really bother taking the kids to the park.'

We reminisce about the fell race, the school discos and what other people are doing now. None of us realised how lucky we were going to school here, taking boats out on the lake for PE lessons, wandering the village in the rain. Lyndsay's children will go to the same school, and I wonder if they'll have to run up the Old Man for the fell race in October and have geography lessons in Church Beck. When we leave near lunchtime, the pavements are full of walkers and the roads are filled with campervans and big cars.

There are numerous things the village of Coniston is famous for: John Ruskin, the writer, poet and artist who lived in Brantwood, the huge Arts and Crafts house on the other side of the lake. Donald Campbell, who broke the water and land speed record in the 1950s and 60s. He died attempting to break his own water-speed record on the water of Coniston in 1967 in his boat *Bluebird*. The grainy old film footage of his boat tipping up and then smashing into nothing is harrowing. They only found his body in 2001.

And Arthur Ransome, author of the classic children's story

Swallows and Amazons, who set the story of the daring young kids camping out on the lake island here on the shores of the village.

But there is something else Coniston is famous for that many locals would rather forget. In the late 1980s and early 90s, as clubs and bars exploded in big cities, sleepy little Coniston witnessed a literal underground dance movement that put it on the map – the rave caves.

It was 1988, and a local boy, Steely D, and his mates were riding their motorbikes across the fells, around the entrances of the former mines, over years' worth of discarded slate, when they had an idea. Music must sound great in these old caves, the walls catching and reverberating every sound. In an interview for *VICE* magazine, Steely D said, 'It started with a dozen of us, then out of nowhere it went absolutely mental. It was just a handful of us, then around 200 the next week, then thousands after that.'

I was too young for the heyday of the raves but having been in the caves since, the idea of thousands of young people crammed in there, drunk or high on something in the dead of night, makes me shiver. I think, even if I had known about them and been old enough, I wouldn't have gone. I was more than happy to get served in a pub with solid walls.

'A house at the bottom of the road realised how many people were going through and set up a café in their garden serving breakfast,' Steely D recalls. 'People were skinny dipping in the lake. Someone was doing little tours around the local village in his car, picking people up and taking them round at five miles per hour, pointing out local attractions – all high on ecstasy.' I love the idea of someone tripping out, delivering short introductions to John Ruskin's views on socialism.

When you search for memories online about the raves, they talk about the dancing, the music, but also the sunsets, sunrises and the scenery around the caves. One comment, made by 'Moon', seemingly one of the organisers, talks about how they set up the parties. 'We needed some light so we could see the sheep – they used the cave in bad weather, bless them.' He lists some of the equipment they brought: 'a few terra strobes, roboscans & some other bits & bobs, including uv's'. He describes how they 'had a right carry on trying to get them all up in the cave roof, balancing on oil drums, bits o'slate & trees'.

Most of the older locals weren't keen on the situation, knowing how dangerous the mines were without the added issue of drunk and high youths, so, threatened with police action over and over again; the raves mostly faded away, with one-offs popping up every few years. I chatted to some of my friends who used to go, including one of my ex-boyfriends. By the time he was going, they were rare, with lads from Liverpool and Manchester organising them. They would travel up with their equipment, the local people only finding out near to the day because someone would spot the arrival of newcomers setting everything up.

'There would be DJs, a bottle bar of sorts. Yeah, they were dangerous. It was often damp and lots of drugs were consumed.'

It didn't take much to get stories of antics flowing. On the phone to a friend one night, she volunteered that her husband and a group of other local lads crept out one night to scythe a huge smiley face in the bracken on the fell just below the mines. I could hear him in the background, laughing and explaining how they did it in the dead of night, a test run first, then the real thing the next evening. The memory comes rushing back of a massive circle around 20 metres in width, a child's drawing of a smiley face that stuck out like a sore thumb in the rusty bracken. You could see it from the school bus. My friend said there was something in the local paper, and even in the church service that weekend, about the happy face on the hill. I feared she was going to say they were reprimanded but they weren't. Apparently the smile coincided with some sad deaths in the local community. The vicar reportedly said how nice the face was, smiling down on them.

Raves might be rare now in former slate mines, but the landscape still provides tourists with its share of controlled danger. Zip lines, rope walks, canyoning and caving are regular sights in these former blasting zones, adventurous hobbies that actually emulate the profoundly dangerous mining practices of years gone by – albeit with much-improved health-and-safety measures. Back then, men climbed rock faces with nothing but a chain wrapped around one leg, or sometimes a rope wrapped around their waist in case they fell. Before electricity, holes for explosive charges were drilled by hand and repeatedly beaten into the rock. When activated, they would blow a chunk of the rockface free. On Easdale in 1980, a bag of live fuses was discovered in the loft of one of the cottages. It had remained undisturbed for 70 years and required a bomb-disposal unit to travel to the island.

Geology dictates the approach with slate mining. The aim is always the same: the most efficient, most bountiful extraction of slate. But the landscape provides different challenges. Where Easdale had open pits where the men won the slate from relatively near the surface, the mines around Coniston created galleries and caves, where slate had to be dug out. Some mines had men working at the seam of slate right on the hillside high above everyone else. The job of the rockmen was to drive a rod into the stone to prepare for blasting. These rockmen were incredibly talented; they needed to know exactly where to drive this rod in and exactly where to split it so it was blasted apart in the correct way to ensure they won as much usable slate as possible. When the slate was extracted, it then needed to be split. This was the ultimate show of skill. The men would rest the slate on their legs or on a bench and simply tap or gently hammer it on the 'natural but invisible grain'. It took years to learn how to do this, to hit the correct section in the right way. We invented machines to split slate, but they were invariably failures, so hand splitting has been the technique for over 200 years.

The amount of pay was governed by how much usable slate the men produced each month, so the knowledge they had of the geology and the make-up of the rocks was unparalleled and, clearly, very necessary. They had to understand the way the rocks were formed and how to get it out as their livelihood *and* their lives depended on it. Anthony Coulls in his book *The Slate Industry* notes that 'experience could not be taught in a college and father passed that intuition to son and so on for generations'. This can be said of so many rural industries.

Like Easdale in Scotland, Wales also claims to have 'roofed the world', the title for which I think can be given to both, since each played their part in the industry. By 1898, when Easdale was winding down in production, Wales was ramping it up. There was a work force of 17,000 men that produced half a million tons of slate from this small, rocky country. Slate was its dominant industry.

Phil and I took a trip south to Dinorwig Quarry, in the north-west of Wales, now home to the National Slate Mining Museum. Only two days before our visit, this area had been granted World Heritage Site status and I could see why. Like Coniston, the valley sits beneath the mountain, which has shaped it geologically and economically. Snowdonia is a former volcano, which was formed in the Ordovician period, 450 million years ago. The view from the bottom of the valley, where the former quarry workshops and buildings are, makes the mountain look formidable. Every side is cloaked with discarded slate that looks like it could slide down at any minute. Slopes of slate full of different colour variations, green to grey and blue and even a deep, rich red, tint the hillside. We drove 20 minutes up the mountain to the top of the valley and there the piles of slate were even more impressive. Incredibly, up to 90 per cent of the rock extracted in these kinds of quarries were usually classed as waste and chucked away.

We parked at the foot of one slate mound. Up close, you could see flora and fauna taking root, finding spaces between the rock. The plants created patches of colour: heather purple, rose bay, willow pink. A little walk further up the quarry and the sheer scale of the old operation was apparent. Down in the valley we could see small black holes in the hillside, which we figured were mine entrances. Halfway down the mountain, a strip of houses called the barracks now stood in ruins, only the shape of them remaining. An information board tells us that men came as far as Anglesey to work here, setting off at 3 a.m. on a Monday morning. It involved a ferry ride, a 10-mile walk and then a climb up the rock face. The miners stayed in these barracks during the week, which were simple two-roomed huts made of slate with four men in each. The wind could be piercing up here on the hillside, and at the row at Aberdaron, almost 650 metres above sea level, it was christened 'Ireland View'.

Back down in the valley, the National Slate Museum displays a strip of houses decorated to portray a different era in slate-mining history. Each house is as you expect: tiny rooms, low-ceilinged, with huge slate slabs like gravestones on the ground. The scent of wood and coal smoke is strong inside and it feels like the wives of the miners have just stepped outside to fetch another bucket of coal.

These houses are now museum exhibits but were once real cottages in the near village of Blaenau Ffestiniog. They were due to be demolished in the 1990s and, reluctant to lose an important part of Welsh history, historians painstakingly labelled every slate and brick, brought them here to the museum and rebuilt them exactly.

There was a man who worked for the museum standing outside the houses. We asked him how they kept them dry and free from rot, since no one lives in them. 'We light the fires,' he said, matter-of-factly. 'It's a fierce heat; you won't go cold in there.'

Not far from there, where those cottages originally came from in Blaenau Ffestiniog, lies the Manod mine – a place where the mine itself became a kind of museum.

Winston Churchill had many things to worry about when German bombs started raining down at the start of the Second World War. Among his concerns were the priceless paintings in the National Gallery in Central London. Initially they were evacuated to Penrhyn Castle and the university colleges of Aberystwyth, but as war raged, it became clear the risk of air strike was still high there. The decision was made to move them into the disused quarry on Manod, which became classed as Top Secret. The entire enterprise was no small feat. First, they had to use explosives to enlarge the entrance to the mine. Then they were forced to build houses or small bungalows within the caverns to protect from differing humidity. Each had its own air-conditioning system, which ensured four changes of air an hour, and a constant atmosphere of 65°F. For the first time, the paintings were catalogued properly, and art experts were able to actually study and record their condition in a stable environment. The paintings were kept under armed guard and bunk beds were set up for the guards to sleep alongside Van Goghs, Da Vincis and Gainsboroughs. Two thousand works of art stayed there for the duration of the war. The National Gallery was bombed nine times between October 1940 and April 1941; one bomb totally destroyed the room where, only months before, a Raphael had hung. The mine was such a useful asset that it was only after the Cold War that the government decided it no longer needed the space for hiding priceless artworks.

Back on Easdale, we are having breakfast in the Quarry Master's house. Ruth and Dougal, the owners of the bed and breakfast, tell us they won't be taking many more residents as they are moving. They have sold the house and are building a new one in the garden of this one. Land is so limited here, they reckon it'll be one of the last houses ever to be built on Easdale. We ask how they'll build it – will the wood, the roof, the windows come on the wee eight-seater ferry? 'We'll helicopter it,' Ruth says with delight. I'd like to be here when that happens.

We are sitting in their kitchen at an old wooden table in front of the range where Dougal is frying up bacon and eggs. We talk about the island and its past, the men who worked here.

'You were an old man at thirty-two,' he said, serving the bacon onto plates. 'The bell went at 3.45 a.m. to start work and [you] finished at 9 p.m.' Dougal volunteers at the small museum on the island, which is currently closed. It is one of those odd strokes of luck that we are staying in his house.

I ask about the system of payment. 'At the start they used to pay people in alcohol here. That didn't go well,' he said. 'And when they were paid with money, they were only paid twice a year.'

It's the same story as most of the other slate-mining quarries. The men were paid twice yearly and often only on how many slates they mined, or the weight of them. They didn't know how much in advance they would be paid as they didn't know how much of the slate would be accepted. There was no system of support, no back-up, and the miners often found themselves in debt to the local shops, buying things on credit regularly, as one pay cheque never lasted as long as six months.

'Easdale Slate went round the world,' Dougal says proudly. 'Do you know how to tell it's from here? The gold in it. The iron pyrites.' I have seen the slates glittering in the sun and wondered about it.

Tiny flecks of fool's gold, worthless but a marker of its origin. And very pretty. The work of an ancient volcano.

After we pack and Dougal has washed up, he puts on his boots and takes us to an empty terraced cottage just off the main square of the village, one of the few still in its semi-original state. We clamber over a thick layer of slate in the back garden and in through the rear door. It's tiny and reminds me of my old slug-filled cottage. The kitchen is floored with huge slabs of slate and, you can tell by the faded colours and style, has not been touched for maybe 50 years. The windows let in almost no light. We step into the living room through a doorway almost a metre thick. The fireplace straddles most of the wall. The previous residents have built wooden shelves all around the room to house their books. Most of the spines are old and faded but I recognise some modern titles, such as Graeme Macrae Burnet's *His Bloody Project*. The house is neither modern nor completely stuck in the past, but it isn't what we would call a comfortable home. The people who had once lived here were not miners, but I think it is fair to say that nothing much has changed since the miners were here.

At its busiest, there were 500 people living on the tiny island of Easdale and I ask Dougal how many people live on the island now. 'About one hundred,' he says. 'But most are second homes.' He locks the door behind him with a shrug.

On the way back over the water, there is a rush of excitement. The two ferrymen saw dolphins a few minutes ago, so, instead of the regular straight line back to the mainland harbour, they motor the boat a little way out into the bay and turn off the engine. It is quiet, just us and another couple watching the sea's surface. Suddenly, there they are. One, two, three fins are seen 100 metres or so away, moving through the water as if in slow motion. We all half shout in excitement. Even the ferrymen stand up and take videos. We motor about the bay for a little while, our overnight bags by our feet, as the dolphins follow us, pushing through the water like silk. The ferrymen also have a business taking tourists out on wildlife boat trips. They'll put the video up on Facebook, they say.

I wonder if the next set of passengers on the mainland waiting for the ferry mind that we are taking longer than the normal five minutes to get across. I look over at the group of people standing on the edge of the slate harbour wall, but they don't seem to care. They are taking pictures and watching the dolphins too.

7

Textiles

Jessie runs around the neat streets, cobbled and clean, in her bright-orange jacket. Her hood has little orange fox ears. It is threatening rain. We are spending the morning at New Lanark, a former cotton mill, hidden somewhat in the lowlands of Scotland. Things haven't yet opened up properly since the pandemic and it is quiet here. A few people wander around the buildings like us, but the doors are shut to the public. The play park has one other youngster in it; the swing and climbing frame sit back within the trees. A small stream runs down to the main river in between the factory buildings and the tenements. There is a pretty wooden bridge crossing the stream and Jessie leans over it to watch the water. I like places when they are quiet. Even before the pandemic, I rarely chose to go somewhere where I knew there would be a lot of people. I had heard huge busloads of tourists came to New Lanark when things were normal. They must have filled the streets, the corridors and the former mill rooms with their waterproof jackets and leaflets. But for now, the streets are almost deserted.

The scale of this place, the design of it, is quite something. The buildings are clean and imposing, all with many windows, regularly spaced. The shared gardens of the rows of tenements have neat grass with empty washing lines strung across them. Part of the old mill is a museum; part of it is lived in. The residents have a beautiful space when the busloads of tourists leave, when the woods and the streams are their own again. The whole place reeks of organisation, which is not a bad thing, though a far cry from what it must have been like at the height of its production, when the water wheels and the women and children worked from daybreak to dark.

New Lanark was classed as a UNESCO World Heritage Site in 2001. It was founded in 1785 by David Dale, a Glasgow banker and entrepreneur who chose the isolated spot to take advantage of the water of the River Clyde. The waterfalls that ran down the glens here could be used to power the water wheels in the cotton mill below. And there was enough space in the woods and on the hillside to build a whole village for the workers. This is what makes New Lanark different. The village that was built was designed *for* the workers to live a (relatively for the time) decent life. It put the workers' welfare forefront. New Lanark is now seen as a 'milestone' as it combined planning and architecture with a genuine concern for the working classes. It sounds like the start of something wonderful.

During the Industrial Revolution cotton was big business. In 1769, Richard Arkwright had invented the water-frame wheel for spinning cotton. The design of it meant that, powered by the natural waterfalls, it could be operated in the factory by unskilled workers and cotton could be produced on a large scale. All the workers needed to do was constantly feed the machines with raw cotton, change the bobbins when they were empty and pick up any pieces that had broken off from the floor. The result of this system was a continuous supply of strong yarn that could be then made into cotton. Then, in 1779, Samuel Crompton invented the spinning mule and, again, production vastly increased. Instead of using water-power, the spinning mule used steam, in the system invented by James Watt. Incredibly, by 1850, Britain was producing half of the world's cotton and we didn't even grow the stuff here.

In the rural areas of Scotland, where Arkwright's water frame was used, cotton mills were built at places where there was a steady supply of water flowing, such as Loch Katrine, Deanston, Balfron, Stanley and New Lanark. A whole new workforce was needed for these factories, and this consisted of hundreds of women and children. Men were, unusually, redundant in these mills as physical strength was unnecessary. And besides, men didn't want to work in these conditions. Historian T. C. Smout notes, 'Factory work demanded submission to a work discipline of a wholly new and unfamiliar kind.' Even labourers who tended to work in the fields had always worked at their own pace and enjoyed different tasks depending on the season. They were, and not surprisingly, reluctant to earn money in these new 'work-houses'. This was also around the time of the Highland Clearances. Some men did ask for work in the lowland mills, but Highland men weren't the first choice of workers for the mill owners. Smout notes, 'Employers found they proved restless, refractory and unreliable, more trouble than they're worth.' At Katrine it was said of the Highland recruit: 'He never sits at ease at a loom, it is like putting a deer in the plough.' I don't blame them. The contrast between the great expanse of the Highlands and a noisy factory full of people would have been stark.

It was the women and children who were called upon to do most of the jobs. And they were paid less too. Mills would publicly ask for widows and their children to come and work for them. Children were especially sought after. T. C. Smout notes:

If caught young they could be bent like saplings and without question whatever was required at work, and (with any luck) they would eventually become themselves the parents of a new generation of operatives to whom the factory was neither alien nor a particularly unpleasant environment.

Employing children was also advantageous as their size meant they could crawl under the machines and clear away the dust and the cotton. Children were often beaten and, given the proximity to dangerous machinery, the chance of accidents was incredibly high. Fingers and limbs could be caught in the gearing or their clothes could be dragged into parts of the machinery. On top of this, the long hours meant the children were exhausted and therefore even more prone to accidents.

It is said that Dale emptied the orphanages in Glasgow to bulk out his workforce at New Lanark. He built barracks capable of housing 500 children, but, contrary to what might be happening in other factories, he attempted to care for the welfare of the children, a fact he was proud of and known for far and wide. In the 1780s at New Lanark the children rose at 6 a.m. and worked for 13 hours, with an hour and a half off for meals. They then attended the factory school for two hours. Visitors from all corners of the country came to witness his successful system. Dale's admiring guests noted that the children slept 'in well aired rooms, three in a bed with straw mattresses', and the dormitories were scrubbed weekly and lime-washed twice a year. One visitor wrote, 'What number of people are here made happy and comfortable who would, many of them, have been cut off by disease, or, wallowing in the dirt, been ruined by indolence.' Like the cotton the children would have been breathing in at the mill, these facts, these opinions, lodge in the throat slightly.

Within a few years, Robert Owen, Dale's son-in-law, took over the management and ownership of New Lanark and improved more so on the conditions. It is Owen to whom we now give the accolade as the social reformer and the 'founder of utopian socialism'. So much so that a movement called Owenism sprung up, which focused on radical reform in society and is considered a forerunner of the cooperative movement.

Under Owen, the children's working day was reduced to (only) 12 hours, and those under the age of 10 were not called to work at all. Instead, they attended the day school. He funded a doctor and an infirmary and opened a shop at the heart of the village, where workers could buy fruit and veg at near-wholesale prices. These new practices, which Owen clearly believed in wholeheartedly, made his workers, of all ages, as healthy and literate as possible at the time. It also ensured they were a (relatively) happy and dedicated workforce – which, of course, generated ample profits for Owen over the years.

We peer into some of the buildings that are closed to us. The former school, the village store and the post office are true museum pieces: stalled, silent, dusty. The waters of the River Clyde rush on, loud and demanding. It starts to rain as we walk alongside it, and Jessie runs through the puddles.

It feels odd to think that my grandad, the one born in a dam-builders' hut in 1926, who worked in the mines as a Bevin Boy during the war, *also* worked in a mill like this one. Maybe it is not so odd. Maybe these connections are as commonplace as these industries once were, and the crossovers likely when people from certain areas and of a certain class only had certain employment options. My grandad's mill was in Nottinghamshire, and Grandad was deter-mined to work his way up.

After spending the war stuck working in the mine, Grandad Vic did all he could not to go back underground. He put himself through night school while labouring, earning qualifications in engineering, including electrics, welding, heating and plumbing. With these to his name, he was offered a job as a contractor, building the Bairnswear Factory in Worksop. After the factory was built, he was offered work inside it on the maintenance side. Bairnswear produced all kinds of garments, including cardigans, jumpers, baby mittens and pram suits from cotton, wool and nylon. Over the years, Grandad Vic worked his way up to become factory engineer and by the 1970s, he had 400 'girls' working underneath him and four apprentices. The machines kept going all night and the factory was powered by steam. Grandad maintained the machines that kept the whole factory alive. Uncle Jim remembers how Grandad and his team 'had to move heaven and earth to get the machines back going again – any problems in machinery meant they were losing production'. He also recalls going in on a Saturday morning as a kid and walking through the mill rooms. 'They were very hot, steam everywhere, very noisy and crowded, with an overwhelming smell of either cotton or nasty chemicals for the nylon production.' He tells me he vividly recalls them being 'like a sweat shop'.

It made sense that the company wanted managers like Grandad close by. Bairnswear built a cul-de-sac of houses for its supervisors – smaller houses at the bottom of the street, the biggest at the top. Eventually all the senior managers earned enough to buy their own house, outwith this street, miles away from the factory floor, but this was not an option for Grandad Vic. He happily accepted the tied house and since the senior execs no longer needed theirs, he was offered the biggest house at the top of the road. With four young children, this was very welcome indeed.

The house was just opposite the factory. Mum, when I spoke to her on the phone one night, called it 'posh' with a big garden and plenty of rooms, although she still shared a bedroom with her sister Catherine, inseparable then as they are now. Mum tells me how they used to gather in the kitchen and they – she and her brothers and sisters – would sit on the coke stove while Gran did 'everything', preparing the meals, baking, scrubbing. She says it was a nice place to be; the stove heated the radiators and it was always a toasty, central part of the kitchen. We still do this now, although there is no stove to sit on. We lean on the sink or the wall, while Mum is cooking tea, talking, telling her what's going on with work, friends, the kids. Talking *at* her, really. Like a psychiatrist's couch. I hope I can fulfil this service for my own children one day.

Bairnswear did well for Grandad, not least because he also managed to secure jobs for all kinds of relatives and friends. Gran worked in the pressing department, manipulating fabric across huge ironing boards to disappear creases and crumpling before clothes went out to be sold. Mum remembers her working in the evenings and then, later on, managing her own 'line of girls'.

Grandad got a job for his father, driving lorries and coaches of girls to other factories. (He had never taken his driving test, but this didn't seem to matter much.) And finally, when Mum turned 18, she took a job in the office. There weren't many options available to girls like her in the 1970s. She left school and went to a nearby college where she studied typing before working at Bairnswear. 'It was that or nursing,' she said. 'And I didn't want to do nursing.'

She was calculating the wages for the hundreds of staff as they clocked in and out each day and night. I asked if she thought Grandad specifically requested a job in that department for her. 'Oh yes, it was much better than the mill floor.' She recalls her time there fondly, as do many of the people who worked there, whether it was on the factory floor or not. There was a canteen where everyone had lunch, Christmas trips, summer trips and circuses for the kids of the workers. And it was always an exciting time when the buyers from Marks & Spencer came to view the products. 'Everyone was on their best behaviour.'

There was also a shop where you could buy 'the seconds': all the clothes that hadn't made it out to the shops. I think of the jumble sales we went to as children in the village hall. Trestle tables piled high with musty, faded clothes. We skidded from one side of the room to the other under these thin-legged tables, playing games and hiding from each other as the grown-ups cherry-picked jeans, jumpers and shirts. I don't remember a beloved item of clothing from a jumble sale – though plenty of what I wore must have been bought there – but I do remember a boy giving me a small, chipped ring, made of white pottery, which I kept for years after.

Mum was at Bairnswear for two years. She had met Dad when she was 16 and by the age of 20 they were married 'from the house at Bairnswear' and went to live in another tied house on a nearby country estate. And so the cycle continued.

As for Grandad, the spanner in the works appeared in the mid-1970s. The phone in the hallway would ring at all hours, even 3 a.m. Grandad would jump out of bed and head into the factory to fix whatever the problem was. Around the time Mum left home to start her married life, Grandad had his second heart attack. He was 55. He had carried on working after his first one, brushing it aside, still answering the phone at all hours and servicing the huge machines that kept the factory burning. After his second heart attack, the doctor told him he had two choices: either go back to work and your third heart attack will kill you, or retire now.

Discussions between the managers and Grandad went on for some time. They didn't want to lose his experience, his unwavering loyalty. They threatened eviction, thinking this would keep him in his place, but before they had the chance to implement it, Grandad and the rest of the family left. Some weeks before, the moment he had made his decision to leave, he had phoned the council and asked to be added to the list for a newly built council house. They were granted an end-of-terrace house with three small bedrooms and a thin garden. With only two children left at home – Jim and Mum had already married – this was plenty spacious enough for the family. They made the tough choice to move for his health, an early retirement at just 55. It would have been a nice retirement, alongside Gran, who was

10 years younger than him, but unfortunately she died only a few years later of cancer. Maybe it was a good thing that Grandad had retired early as it enabled him to look after Gran when she needed it most. He never got over her death. He never remarried, always saying she was the only woman for him. Grandad Vic, who lived numerous different lives – reservoir builder, coal miner, mill worker – might have been forced into retirement at 55, some might say because of the ferocity of work his body was put through in those years, but, unbelievably, he lived until the grand old age of 95. He was difficult to pin down in some senses: sometimes solitary, sometimes brilliantly sociable. Whenever he came to visit us in Cumbria, the barmaids in his regular pub requested he fill in a holiday form so they knew how long he'd be away. Like many people who realise too late that their grandparents won't be around forever, I wish I'd asked him more about his life before me.

An hour and a half north of Worksop's Bairnswear factory is the pretty village of Todmorden in North Yorkshire. A friend from university, Helen, lives in a former mill worker's cottage here. I have visited her before, when she lived in a different part of town. When we park outside her address, I swear it's the same house, or at least the same street. 'They all look the same,' she laughs later on. In this area, it is quite difficult *not* to live in a former mill worker's cottage. Not just the valley floor, but every space on the hillside is commandeered by strips of houses that lodged the huge workforce needed for the local mills. The villages have a cluttered but cosy feel to them.

Helen's house is on a hill, made up of two cottages knocked into one, the bulk of the work done before they owned it. Both the living room and the kitchen have huge, enviable fireplaces. 'It's cold, though,' Helen says. 'There isn't much insulation, and the floorboards just sit on the ground.' But the view is lovely over to the other side of the valley, where you can see other rows of houses and a few farmsteads and the weather rolling in.

We go for a walk before tea and her son takes us on the path they completed every day on their daily walk during lockdown. It rises steeply up behind the main houses and onto the old packhorse road that looks out over the fells. I walk slowly – I'm seven months pregnant now, so it gives me a chance to take in the scenery. The packhorse trails over the moors are ancient, windswept paths that date back to Roman times when salt from Cheshire was brought over the moors. The convoys of ponies could reach up to 1,000 in number and carry all kinds of goods, including cloth. Helen often runs on the thin stone paths made for the trains of horses and their cargo. The landscape is broad and quiet with just the wind whistling and the distant bleat of the sheep. The Brontës lived not far from here. I almost feel we're going to bump into them.

Anywhere I walk takes time and involves a lot of heavy breathing. These hills are constant. We visit the small village of Heptonstall, just above Hebden Bridge, and I think often about the women who lived and worked in these cobbled streets. Roofs jut out over the paths at strange angles. The houses are mostly black, the original beige sandstone stained by years of factory smoke from the town below. It gives them a kind of patchwork quality. In the windows of some of the houses are small blue plaques. One says, *Mary Elizbeth Collinge, cotton weaver in 1916*. I wonder how many children she had, what her husband did. I wonder if her back ached at night.

In rural areas, before the mills became the large employer, weaving was a very decent way to earn a living. There was a boom in the industry that started in the 1780s, but by the 1830s it was over. During this time, rows of weavers' cottages were built around the countryside. Sometimes commissioned by cloth manufacturers to house their workers, sometimes constructed by builders acting of their own volition, the weavers' cottages were notable by the long strip of windows in the top floor where the hand loom would be situated to provide as much light as possible for working. The living quarters were below. There is a belt of these houses just above Heptonstall; their slightly wonky appearance sits at odds with the landscape behind it, which is all rolling hills, drystone walls and green fields against the black of the stone of the houses.

In a village near Stonehaven in Scotland, weavers lived a traditional life where 'every householder in the village had a workshop and a loom, rented a large garden and a croft of land from two to four acres and kept a cow'. Weavers enjoyed huge prosperity; they enjoyed pastimes such as golf, curling and fishing, and formed clubs and societies to enjoy literacy and debating. Men and women worked in a relatively relaxed manner; they could take breaks when they wanted and produce as much material as they needed. Weavers, in some areas, could make a good living in this way, enjoying a three-day weekend in some cases. But the golden age didn't last. By the late 1700s, when Arkwright invented the water wheel and then Crompton invented the spinning mule, the cottage industry of weavers simply couldn't compete. Cotton was mass-produced. And it was in the north of England, especially the 50 miles around Manchester, where the growth was most apparent. By 1850, this area produced 40 per cent of the world's cotton output. The rural weavers had had their day.

Walking the cobbled streets where so much cloth was produced, I think about the people working in the mills. As the majority of them were women and children, it figures that a percentage of the workforce were, at some point, pregnant. Although some factory owners insisted that female workers leave their work when they were married, most did not. Mary Woodhouse, a midwife at Manchester's 'lying-in' (maternity) hospital, was interviewed in 1833 for a parliamentary report that sought the opinions of a broad swathe of people, including young girls and boys who had worked in factories for years. These conversations sound as clear as the day they were written down. Here is part of midwife Mary's interview.

Have you much business among the factory classes? – *Yes, a great deal. I deliver some hundreds [of babies] in the course of a year.*

At what age are the women belonging to the factory classes generally delivered of their first child? – *Sometimes, but seldom, at sixteen; very often at eighteen; generally before twenty.*

Are the factory women often pregnant before marriage? – *Too often.*

Are the unmarried women often deserted by their seducers? – *Often.*

Do the factory women take good care of their houses, and make good housewives? – *Why, they are kept so long at the factory work, that they have not often inclination for such things.*

Do they make their husbands' shirts and mend their clothes? – *I cannot positively speak to that.*

Do the factory women often miscarry? – *Often.*

Do the factory women miscarry more frequently than the other classes who you attend? – *Why, I cannot speak positively, but, however, it does happen that the factory women do miscarry, but the others, sometimes.*

The information is there online, on the television, in documentaries, on film, provided by charities. It doesn't make for restful reading.

The numbers attached to the fashion industry are shocking. They are worse than the numbers in Britain 200 years ago. In some countries 'garment workers are often forced to work 14 to 16 hours a day, 7 days a week. During peak season, they may work until 2 or 3 a.m. to meet the fashion brand's deadline.'

There is more. In the factories there is often 'no ventilation' and the workers are 'breathing in toxic substances, inhaling fibre dust or blasted sand in unsafe buildings'.

It is reported that 168 million children around the world are forced to work as 'low-skilled labour'. In South India, girls work under a scheme in which they 'work in a textile factory for three or five years in exchange for a basic wage and a lump sum payment at the end to pay for their dowry. Girls are overworked and live in appalling conditions that can be classified as modern slavery.'

I want to cry. It could have been written about Yorkshire or the south of Scotland 200 years ago. The bags full of children's clothes behind me, the clothes I am wearing, are all wrong. While writing about the conditions in the mills in the 1800s, I had thought about where the cotton material had ended up, how it was made into the dresses that swished about the balls in Jane Austen novels. But I had forgotten to think about where it had come from in the same way I do now. The middle-class women of the 1800s had an excuse; they had no real way to find out where the textiles came from. But we do now.

We go back to New Lanark when it is properly open. I want to see inside the buildings, to get more of a feel for it. The streets are much busier this time. It is the summer holidays and they are encouraging families and children to visit with huge models of dinosaurs – raptors, a stegosaurus – around the grounds, which lends it an odd, almost out-of-sync feel. We walk on the cobbles between the tenement buildings and Ellis states that he doesn't like it. I had thought he would. 'It's too organised,' he says. 'It's like everything is really controlled here.' I don't say anything. Without even meaning to, he has boiled the essence of a planned workers' village down to a sentence.

We visit the school room the children went to after work every day and learn about a little girl who worked here called Annie McLeod. The room with the spinning machine, just above the café and the gift shop, is hot and smells strongly of chemicals. They still make their own yarn here, spun on a historic nineteenth-century spinning machine that was salvaged from a mill in Selkirk in the Scottish Borders. I tell Ellis a few facts, knowing fairly well he'll not like the idea that, at age 11, he would have had to work 12 hours a day. It's difficult for him to comprehend. You can see him processing it, almost thinking, 'Why? Why would they do that? Why would they make the children work? Why didn't the children just refuse?' I don't tell him what I've learned about modern factories abroad.

'We'll have to bring your Gran here. She worked in a factory a bit like this. In the office, though.'

'Really?'

'Yeah. And your Great Grandad Vic used to fix the spinning machines like this.' I look at the huge contraption in front of us, constantly rising up and down, still making yarn. It looks dangerous. It is dangerous.

Jessie runs up and down the long rooms, skidding slightly on the floor. I am hot, the baby is kicking my insides and I want to sit down.

'Come on, let's get some ice cream.'

We sit outside the old school room eating our cones as the streets of New Lanark fill up with tourists.

8

Tourism

The square in Hawkshead, Cumbria, has a classic English-village feel to it. I love it best early in the morning, before the breakfast shift, when there is no one else about and the only sound is the jackdaws. The stone-built, slightly wonky Town Hall sits at the top of the village and ivy-covered buildings, housing various cafés and shops, line the sides. I worked in the pub that sits at the bottom of the square and have come back to speak to Ed, my old boss.

Everything seemed to happen in this square. As school children we danced on the flagstones during the Rose Queen Gala, the celebration every June when the whole village seemed to come together to support the primary school. One New Year, at midnight, all the pubs in the village emptied and the drinkers congregated here, grabbing hands and singing 'Auld Lang Syne'. In the summer, after the washing-up had been done in greasy kitchens, groups of staff and locals sat on the ground in the gloaming of the evening, our drinks staining the grey slate black.

Ed has run the Kings Arms for 30 years, but this, my mum has already warned me, might not be the case for much longer.

It is mid-summer today and the wooden bar tables on the flag-stones are full with customers. I look for familiar faces; people I knew, served or drank with. People who sat next to me in my car after a shift, smoking and laughing, listening to music. People I kissed. But the only person I vaguely recognise is a woman serving food in the café behind the pub and she isn't someone I knew all that well.

I started working at the Kings Arms when I was 16. Since the age of 13 I had worked every weekend in cafés and, at one point, a crystal and gem shop. But it was pub work I loved the best. Every shift offered something different, whether it was time to think during the washing-up, the challenge of waitressing and running the room or the certain kind of power you feel standing behind the bar. It was 'serving' customers, yes, but you were the host, the giver of drinks. In this tiny bar area – and it *was* tiny; only two people could fit behind it – you ruled this land and no one else could step foot on it.

Ed is in the office, a cubby hole under the stairs. The building is sixteenth century, a former coach house, so the wooden beams are low, the rooms are small and everything is a tight fit. Ed is six foot three and he looks like a giant unfolding himself from under the stairs to greet me, both of us heading to the bar for a lime and soda. He was a good boss, mostly part of the team, drinking and socialising with us, but he also had the seamless ability to take charge. He wasn't shy about chucking people out (sometimes physically) if they were causing trouble. He was fair, and when the customers were not, he always had our backs.

The pub looks exactly the same as it did when I worked here 20 years ago, and I say so. There are still the same tankards on the shelves and brass horseshoes lining the beams. It's all dark wood and low ceilings (the number of bumped heads we saw ...). Old photos line the walls and red velvet lines the bar stools.

'That's the magic of it,' Ed says. 'It just doesn't change.' Ed has been at the Kings Arms more than half his life. His mum, Lee, took on the lease in 1979 and, as a teenager, he used to wash up in the evenings. It was a smaller business then. The staff they employed were either locals or lived upstairs in the rooms above the pub.

Providing a room for someone who worked in a pub or a hotel

is a common thing in rural areas. Often chefs or bar managers come from far away, and a business that runs almost 24 hours a day, from breakfast to last orders, needs people on site all the time. If, however, there was no room inside the pub, staff were accommodated in a separate house. I've heard of caravans being used for staff housing, barns with doors that don't quite shut, damp tents. Whereas Ed's staff lived above the bar back in the Eighties, another pub in the village, the Red Lion, had a house for their staff.

'East View [a three-bedroom cottage just off the road out of the village] was the staff house for the Red Lion back then,' Ed says. 'The guy who owned it turned up one day and it was a mess. He was furious at the state of it. They just didn't look after it.'

Incredibly the man asked Ed's mum to buy it off him. He was sick of the hassle of it and wanted it off his hands. '*You* put your staff in it,' he said. Lee was reluctant – she didn't know if *she* wanted the bother of a staff house in the village either – but she was persuaded, and the Kings Arms staff have stayed in it ever since. I went to a few parties in it, although I don't remember much. This exchange of property feels like a rare occurrence but somehow seems to happen more in rural areas. Some people are in the right place at the right time and are offered land or property that otherwise would never be available. Luck. Knowing the right people. Providence. The opportunity doesn't happen often enough.

Having a new, separate staff house gave Lee and Ed the chance to make the rooms above the bar available for customers. They fitted out eight bedrooms in the low-beamed, wonky rooms. The business grew, as did the staff turnover.

'We had staff coming from afar – a few undesirables worked here, sometimes people in trouble with the police, that kind of thing. Then one day a minibus pulled up outside and these Aussies all fall out.' He has a lovely way with words I never noticed before and I get a clear image of the Australians I knew working here, laughing, dragging bags from the back doors of a bus. They were looking for work and Ed gave them a chance pulling pints and washing up. 'They were bright, intelligent, happy, and all had experience in places like this. They told me about the magazine *TNT* and as soon as I started advertising in that, they never stopped coming over.'

Ed talks about this time for the pub with a glow that matches my memories. I was just starting out waitressing, local myself but pulling pints alongside a young, glamorous couple from Canada. She always wore, in my 16-year-old mind, outrageous clothes: slinky cotton dresses down to her ankles, oversized jumpers that still looked cool. Utterly unsuitable for serving meals in. She had all the confidence in the world and I was fascinated by her. Not long after she left we were given a uniform: dark blue polo shirts with the Kings Arms logo on the left breast. My brother, who also worked there after me, gave his hard-wearing polo shirts to Dad, who still wears them today working in the woods. I remember a South African couple, Jenny and Kenny, who gave me a colourful beaded necklace when they left. I still have it now and my daughter loves to wear it. I remember Belinda, a slight Australian girl with strawberry-blonde hair, who always seemed to be the centre of the party. It was a melting pot of people; young travellers looking for fun, mixing with the locals.

'Then the next wave of workers arrived,' Ed says. 'The Eastern Europeans. They were making more money pulling a pint than they were at home being a doctor, a teacher.' He shakes his head and tells me they were fiercely loyal, dedicated workers.

'Last summer, when everything was shut, I was burning old paperwork and I found a sheet of paper you'd written. You'd listed all the names of the people who had worked here in twelve months. I couldn't believe how many there were.'

I don't remember this at all, but it does sound like the kind of thing I'd do. Listing and noting. Wanting to remember. My old diaries are full of lists like this.

So, what changed? What happened? Lots. Brexit was one factor. And when Covid hit and things closed down they didn't need as many staff. Some went home (to Poland, Romania, Bulgaria) and others were kept on, painting, cleaning, just keeping the pub going as much as they could.

'Now there is a serious shortage of staff.' The ones who left haven't come back. Even if they wanted to, they are unable as there are new rules about working abroad. 'Covid has masked the situation that Brexit is now causing,' Ed tells me. The village has grown busy again, but the Kings Arms is the only one still serving food during the day. There used to be four pubs open every day for lunch and dinner, providing work for people, serving the thousands of tourists that visit every week. But it's a different place now. There are simply not enough staff to serve lunches to the tourists. It feels like such a wasted opportunity.

'Staff can name their price,' Ed says. 'I know one hotel who lost a chef as he was offered fifty pence an hour more with another job. Just upped and walked out.'

It feels like this is a tipping point, where the village is on the edge of losing its balance. Of becoming something different.

'Where are the teenagers like me, the young people who want to earn money?'

'There's hardly anyone left. There are very few locals who live in the village anymore.' Ed shrugs. More and more houses have become second homes or Airbnbs in Hawkshead. It's a story being repeated in many pretty, rural villages across the country.

The latest figures available, which are shockingly out of date at 20 years old, state that 17 per cent of existing housing stock in the Lake District National Park is made up of second homes and/or holiday homes. The same figures state that 'in Coniston 51 per cent of the existing housing stock is either used as a second home and/or holiday home'. The phenomenon of Airbnb incredibly only started in 2008 when two guys from San Francisco came up with the bright idea of renting out their air beds to tourists when all the hotels in the city were full. It gave tourists a place to stay and gave people the chance to earn money from their spare rooms. Millions of people have used Airbnb over the last 15 years, and of course I have too. But that tipping point has been reached. In some places around the UK, such as the Isle of Skye, one in four properties is now an Airbnb. In the slate-mining town of Dinorwig in Wales I visited (we stayed in the youth hostel, as that was all there was available, and yes, I looked on Airbnb), one family was kicked out of their home, their landlady admitting they get four times the money doing Airbnb. Locals in Cornwall have been complaining about over-tourism for many years now. The number of listings on Airbnb are well over 250,000 and, ironically, many sell themselves on their past rural industry, which has a decidedly 'cosier' feel to it. You can rent a slate miner's cottage in Dinorwig or Coniston, a weaver's house or a mill house in Yorkshire, forest lodges in the Lakes, a coalminer's house with 'gorgeous wood-burning stove'. You name it, you can stay in it. The romanticised rural idyll of past industry is good business.

The combined efforts of Airbnb and second-homers have changed the very fabric of rural areas, but it wasn't always like this. One friend who grew up on the small island of Bute on the west coast of Scotland told me how every year they looked forward to the second-homers. They brought in money to spend in the pubs, at the horse-riding school, in the cafés. But there are just too many now and the community fades away. An Airbnb or a second home might bring in some money for the local shop, but it won't bring more children to the school. It means those houses are full of people effectively passing by. They won't be on the fundraising committee for the pantomime or the summer dance, they won't be part of the church congregation or able to organise the local ceilidhs. I think this is what I find most ironic. The reason the tourists loved the area so much was the feel of the place; not just the views but the community too – the full pubs, the events, the markets, the country shows, the things that make a small community, an actual commu-nity. I can understand why people want a slice of that. *I* want a slice of that. But by buying a house to experience that for a few weeks, or even a few months of the year, they have gradually suffocated that life forever. Throughout these villages, UK wide, country shows are being cancelled, pubs are closing down, hotels can't get the staff and schools are shutting. Some areas might have even passed the tipping point now.

It's why it is so quiet in the pub, why there are no faces I recognise sitting outside. There used to be a set of people who came in regularly, leaning on the wooden bar, chatting to the staff and to each other about God knows what. There is no one left.

'I felt like it was time to go,' Ed says when I ask if it's true he's leaving. The lease came up for renewal and he took his time signing it. There were new clauses in it, things he wasn't quite comfortable with. And then Covid hit.

'It gave me time to really think about what I wanted to do.' He spent that first spring of lockdowns and restrictions sorting paperwork, tidying, painting. And thinking.

'What will happen to the pub?' I ask.

'It'll go to a pub co. And it'll lose all this.' He gestures around at the bar. He means a chain will buy it. It will lose its individuality, its cosiness, its character.

'And what will you do?'

'Something will come up. If I stayed, it wouldn't. If I leave, it will.' It's a brave attitude. Leaving it up to the universe. I think he's right, though. Nothing changes if you don't change. His wife, Vanessa, a New Zealander who came over here to work years ago, now runs a bed and breakfast near by. She also rents a bit of land where she set up a shepherd's hut. 'Would you believe people will pay more to sleep in a shepherd's hut, basically a wooden shed, than they do to stay upstairs in a room here?'

Hawkshead is one of the prettiest villages in the Lake District, which, unsurprisingly, also makes it one of the busiest. In Coniston, Ambleside and Grasmere too – places steeped in both beauty and history – visitor numbers have risen exponentially since the first wave of tourists started coming to these areas in the eighteenth century. These tourists refer to their guidebooks, more than likely online now, just as they did almost 300 years ago, finding the best places to stay, eat and walk. At the very dawn of tourism as we know it now, there was a certain type of tourist for whom travelling was *the* thing to do. The working classes couldn't afford to go on holiday and probably had little time to anyway. The upper classes were embarking on 'Grand Tours' to Europe, experiencing the Acropolis of Athens, the Colosseum in Rome and Notre Dame in Paris. The more limited means of the middle classes meant they couldn't quite stretch to months away in a hotel on the Continent, so they started travelling in their own country. A new, highly romanticised version of Britain's landscape was born. Samuel Johnson and James Boswell had already published their accounts of travelling in Scotland. The Lakes, more accessible than the Highlands, were written about in numerous guidebooks, including William Wordsworth's own *Guide to the Lakes*. Rural areas, especially the mountains were suddenly the fashionable places to go.

Writer Anna Pavord notes in her book *Landskipping*, 'The Lakes. The Highlands, Snowdonia. Those were the three must-dos for those who travelled for pleasure in the eighteenth century. A "correct" taste in landscape was now an accomplishment to be learned, as you might learn the piano.'

You ticked off these areas and boasted about staying there in the same way our generation does on Instagram. Back then, there was even a type of filter photographers used when taking photos of a lake or the mountains, a tinted glass screen to make the colours pop or to enhance the sunrise or sunset. Nothing changes, it seems.

This element of 'a correct taste' points towards class and education, and defined what kind of person should experience what. Poet William Wordsworth certainly had a strong idea of what a tourist should be, where they should go and even *how* they should enjoy the landscape. His guidebook, written in 1820, wanted to encourage 'persons of pure taste' to appreciate the fells, the waterfalls and the lakes properly. He saw the Lake District as 'a sort of national property, in which every man has a right and interest who has an eye to perceive and a heart to enjoy'.

If you did not have the 'eye to perceive' and 'heart to enjoy' then you were maybe less welcome. In 1844, the railway from Kendal was proposed to extend to the small town of Windermere. Wordsworth was one of the strongest objectors, believing it would spoil the peace of the area. He wrote letters to the press and even penned a sonnet. He may have seen the Lakes as 'national property', but he didn't want the whole nation to descend on it.

'Go to a pantomime, a farce, or a puppet-show, if you want noisy pleasure,' he said in one of the letters. 'But may those who have given proof that they prefer other gratifications continue to be safe from the molestation of cheap trains pouring out their hundreds at a time along the margin of Windermere.'

Working in cafés and pubs, it did sometimes feel as if the whole nation *had* poured into the villages. Getting stuck driving behind a tourist on a windy road, I could almost agree with Wordsworth – there were too many of them. But when you love the beauty of where you live, it's hard to blame others for wanting to come and see it. Who doesn't want to go tramping up the hills and to a pub lunch afterwards? After all, as we were always keenly aware, they paid our wages.

Wordsworth lost the fight and the railway line to Windermere was opened in 1847. It's an essential connection to the bigger town of Kendal. My friend's daughter takes the train from Windermere to school every day, and today 15.8 million people visit the Lake District every year.

Like me and Tom, Wordsworth went to primary school in Hawkshead. I imagine him wandering the streets – they really have not changed much at all – walking across the flagstones of the square under the gaze of the Town Hall. If he was here today, I don't think he would believe the number of tourists trailing in the village and up the hills. And I don't think he'd take kindly at all to the chalk board at the back of the Kings Arms pub, which states, 'I wandered lonely as a cloud, then thought sod it, I'll have a pint instead,' though the Instagrammers certainly do.

The onset of the railways spreading around the country gave the working-class person much more opportunity to travel, and this clash between the middle-class tourist and the working-class one is rather delightfully played out in the pages of visitor books. Just below Snowdonia sits the Pen-y-Gwryd, a former farmhouse that was converted into a hotel in the Victorian era to accommodate the ever-growing mountaineering crowd. The Climbers' Club was founded in Pen-y-Gwryd in 1898. It was also the training base for the team that would reach the summit of Everest in 1953.

Most of the visitors' books from this period have not survived and this is true at Pen-y-Gwryd too. But what makes this establishment stand out is the fact that a special, separate book was bought in 1884, as one regular guest was so fed up with the poor quality of the entries. This book wouldn't be for just any 'sort of nonsense scribbled by the passer-by', it would be for the elite climber, botanist, geologist and 'other members of the professional middle class'. It would also be kept under lock and key, protected from the scrawls of the unworthy.

This practice of keeping a separate book for the different classes was, thankfully, rare. Alan McNee, who researched Victorian visitors' books, says, 'In some ways, they can be seen as a precursor to modern social media, combining the memorialising function of Facebook or Twitter with the democratic ability to post reviews offered by TripAdvisor.' You could rip a sheet out or scribble over a bad review, but essentially there they are: unedited views from a wide spectrum of society, all sharing the same page.

During this boom for tourism, hotels popped up in the most unlikely places – the highest mountain in the UK, for instance, Ben Nevis. The Observatory Hotel (which also had a visitors' book – 'three hours from Fort William Pier to see nothing but mist, tho' I enjoyed a good luncheon') opened in July 1885 amid 'drizzling rain and a stiff breeze'. The *Scotsman* newspaper reported that a party of 17 gentlemen ascended the mountain to see the grand opening of the hotel, which had four bedrooms, and cost 10 shillings a night including dinner and breakfast. Surely a candidate for one of the most remote hotels in the UK, it needed live-in staff. Two ladies were reportedly responsible for running the whole thing. I would have liked to have met them. Preparing meals on rather limited ingredients, cooking, cleaning up there. It will have been quite an unusual existence.

The hotel, which had been built by a savvy hotelier from Fort William, was really just an annexe to the Ben Nevis Observatory, which was built for scientific research and to record the weather. The original weather observatory was made with granite blocks and had thick walls to protect it from the elements. The hotel, however, was a little flimsier. It was a single-storey wooden building that only took a few weeks to build. I'm surprised it wasn't blown away.

The weather observatory had four meteorologists living in it all year round. Horses brought up supplies for the scientists, including nine months' worth of tinned food, paraffin for the fire, letters and a fresh supply of water for the warmer months. Winter, when the snowstorms didn't prevent the men from opening the main door, meant they could go skiing and tobogganing. In such a challenging place, I imagine the meteorologists would have been pretty pleased when the hotel opened. They would have enjoyed more company and maybe something different for dinner, prepared by the two ladies. I would love to see a diary of the women who ran the hotel, the kinds of things they saw, the things they put up with, the weather, the isolation, the customers. But we are left only to imagine.

The weather observatory closed down in 1904 due to lack of funding and the hotel closed in 1916, unable to carry on a decent business during the First World War. You'll find nothing but the wind and, if you're lucky, the view at the summit of Ben Nevis today.

*

The mountains have always been one of the greatest pulls for people since tourism blossomed in the mid-eighteenth century. Popular routes are so busy now, often there are streams of walkers lining the paths. On warm, sunny days, walkers sometimes have to queue to reach the summit of Snowdonia or Ben Nevis.

One of the first literary accounts of climbing a mountain appeared in Wordsworth's *Guide to the Lakes*. The climb up Scafell Pike was originally attributed to William, but was actually undertaken and written by his sister, Dorothy.

Dorothy, who lived with William most of her life at Grasmere, was a keen walker. She walked miles every day and didn't seem to care at all that the simple act of a woman walking alone was frowned upon in this era. So in 1818, when Dorothy and her friend Mary Baker set out on a day of walking up Scafell, I wonder how they felt. I wonder what their guide thought of them. Guides were common when climbing mountains in these areas – mountains were, and still are, very dangerous places. The weather can turn quickly and injuries can be fatal. Dorothy describes 'the calm confidence, yet submissiveness, of our wise Man of the Mountains, who certainly had more knowledge of the clouds than we'.

They had planned only to go so far but when they saw the summit of Scafell, 'apparently very near to us, we shaped our course towards it'. Although, she admits, it was much further than they realised, as most summits are.

Dorothy's account doesn't just reflect on the views, but also on the smaller details of the mountain, such as what can be found between the rocks if you look carefully. She conjures up the feel of the place too. She writes, 'On the summit of the Pike, there was not a breath of air to stir even the papers containing our refreshments, as they lay spread out upon a rock.' This act of noticing tends to anticipate writers such as Nan Shepherd, whose relationship with the mountains is something quite different to the more commonly read-about male perspective. There was no 'conquering' the summit, rather a meeting of it.

I loved walking the hills and the fields around my house, but I didn't do it to study the plants or the wildlife. I didn't know I was even 'experiencing' the mountain at all. I was simply bored. I was a teenager and needed time on my own away from everything else. I probably thought about boys, friends, school. I usually just wandered, sometimes down to the lake, or to the river and the ruined building, but occasionally I had a destination in mind.

From the other side of Windermere, you could quite clearly see the hill behind our house. It was mostly covered in a green sweep of trees, mainly the dark green of larch. But there was a blot among the green firs, just below the ridge of the hill, which looked mysterious. It was an almost vertical slab of basalt rock that nothing grew on. This patch of rock was like a black hole. I wanted to find it, to see what it was, to be on it.

It took a few weeks of exploring the woods, finding my bearings and getting lost. I went too far into the hill once and nearly fell down a crevice of rock so deep I would surely have died if I had broken something.

Eventually, a route started to make itself clear. The place to go off the path and in among the trees from was our water tank. From there, I joined deer paths, found parts of old crumbling walls, remnants of enclosed spaces for sheep. I met deer, buzzards, carcasses of rabbits and birds.

Almost at the top of the hill, I could see more light flooding through the trees. I crawled on my hands and knees under spiky fir trees and then there it was, the edge of the big rock. Up a bit further, under the boughs of trees that hadn't been touched by humans for 30 years or so, the very tip of the big rock lay in front of me. I sat on it, legs dangling over the precipice of about 10 feet. I could see the stretch of Windermere, from Newby Bridge to Ambleside, and the range of hills behind it. From then on, I spent hours up there on this ridge, watching the weather. Tom and his best friend, Adam, were the only other ones to join me once.

I occasionally went further up to the plateau at the top of the hill. There was no real summit there, but from some spots you had a 360-degree view of the landscape. The Old Man of Coniston, Ambleside and Langdale, and further south, as far as Barrow too. Of all the times I was up there, I saw one other person, the gamekeeper's lad. We just nodded hi and went on our way. The hill wasn't something to conquer. It was something to explore, as it was, I suppose, for Dorothy and Nan. But I was too young to appreciate it like they did. I don't remember the flowers or the moss. I remember the quiet and the air. I miss that empty hillside now.

Our hills and mountains, usually so full of walkers and climbers, all of a sudden emptied during the first lockdown of the pandemic. The hospitality business was one of the main sectors to be hit by closures. Hotel bedrooms lay empty, cafés were deserted and pubs shut up shop. The way the staff were dealt with told you a lot about the owners. Some hotels kept all their staff on and invited them to stay in the hotel to sit out the lockdown, essentially creating a temporary family. People from all over the world – chefs, waitresses, bar managers – cooked for each other, played games and explored the area on their daily walks. They had the run of the hotel *and* of the surrounding countryside, which was also devoid of visitors. Staff, who couldn't dream of being a tourist, suddenly had the chance to act like them, having the time to walk up hills, swim in lochs, eat in the restaurants, the chef cooking for a smaller, more familial group. It must have been like living a borrowed life, like looking after the Big House when the landowners were away. Rags to riches. Then back again.

This wasn't the case for most people. One hotel in the Highlands, run by a chain, sent a letter out to their staff. It stated: 'Taking the latest government advice, this letter is to confirm that with effect from

19 March 2020, your employment has been terminated and your services are no longer required. You are asked to vacate the hotel accommodation immediately, returning any company property.'

Most of the staff were from Europe – Latvia, Poland, Spain. They lived and worked in the hotel and in one moment had lost their home *and* their means of making a living. Newspaper reports showed photos of former staff sitting on the side of the road within a picturesque mountain landscape, surrounded by bags of belongings, stuck in this country now, the travel corridors to their family shut.

Claudia, who cleaned in a hotel in the Lake District, was made redundant at 20 weeks pregnant when the pandemic hit. She is from Romania and had been in the UK for a few years. She lived in a house, owned by the hotel, in the busy village of Ambleside with four other girls.

'It was £210 a month, including bills, which I thought was really cheap,' she tells me in perfect English. 'I had my own bathroom, we had a big kitchen, we were really happy to be together. Like a family. When they told me I didn't have a job anymore, I thought, "What am I going to do?"'

The hotel owners let all five of the girls stay until they found somewhere else. 'I was the last one there. They were very nice. I kept applying for housing association places, but everyone wants to live here [in the Lakes.] So I applied for a place in Carlisle and they rung in a week with a place for us.'

Her baby starts to cry. She settles him and I ask about the other girls. 'Some went home [to Romania], some got other jobs. I want to stay. I like it here. It is hard now, though,' she says. 'It is hard for people to work here.' She has all her papers already sorted so she can work when the baby is older. 'Life is not good in Romania when you are there a long time.' I visited Transylvania, where Claudia is from, when I was a student. The landscape was beautiful. Everywhere seemed to be stained in deep green, the hills covered with ancient woodland. But the poverty was hard to miss. I think of sending her Ed's way to the Kings Arms in Hawkshead, but then I remember he's leaving. And I couldn't vouch for the next boss.

I am due in two weeks. I am uncomfortable and admittedly very grumpy. I am keen to go north for a day as it always releases something as we drive further up the country. The temperature drops from a mild September day at 20 degrees Celsius to 17 degrees within just a few miles. The trees are bigger here and the roads have more personality than the straight motorways and huge roundabouts where we live. The clouds are lower too, as if the road has climbed up into them. I often find September, although beautiful as the leaves start to turn, has the claggy feel of a hangover, without the fun of the night before. It is always fresher further north.

I have booked lunch at a boutique hotel; one we can't afford to stay in, but which has been recommended by friends in the area. For some reason I think it only takes 40 minutes to get here but I have forgotten the 6-mile section of single-track road and it actually takes nearly double that. The road has occasional passing places, but the woods rise steeply on one side and the loch hugs the verge on the other. We pause repeatedly for vehicles coming the other way. But it's a beautiful drive. The grey loch stretches out into the distance, banked both sides by mountains. We once camped here, on the stony edge of the loch, before the rules changed and it became a Management Camping Zone, only allowing camping in certain areas at certain times, despite Scotland's 'right to roam' law. I'm amazed by how many cars there are now on this stretch. It's a dead end, only the hotel and a farm at the end of it, but there are paddle boarders and swimmers out in the water, despite the low drizzle. Jessie complains about a sore tummy and I tell her to open the window and look for red squirrels.

I'm hoping to catch the owner of the hotel, whose family bought this place as a farm and, step by step, made it into a successful, expansive business. They now run another hotel just off the main road and branded shops in the nearest town selling their speciality bread and fish, and even put on yearly music festivals. It is more of an empire now. We went to one of their first festivals, which had a horse box full of straw where kids played, acrobats in the woods, and oysters and champagne for the adults. Today it is quiet. There are just a few expensive cars in the car park. The tables outside are shiny with rainwater.

The owner is nowhere to be seen. He has said he will be milling about today, but with so many businesses bubbling away he is hard to pin down. The meal is delicious and looks like it should be on the front of a cookbook, with all the colourful trimmings of flowers and splashes of sauces. In other words, it is 'fancy' – the word we use to describe anything we consider a bit posh. Or, possibly, something we aren't used to.

Over dessert, I can't help but pry and ask a member of staff what it's like working here. It's such a beautiful place, I say. Do you enjoy it? She pauses.

'It takes a certain kind of person to live here,' she says slowly. I'm surprised. I thought the answer would be the one I'd give: It's wonderful, I love it.

'You really need to get on with each other.' She talks about how nowadays there is often a generational divide. You need Wi-Fi in a place like this; there is no phone signal so without Wi-Fi younger people don't want to work there.

I say I had forgotten how far the single-track road is to get here. 'That's nothing,' she said. 'I worked near Oban and that had a 16-mile single-track road to nowhere. That was a long way. No food deliveries,' she laughs. She stayed in a caravan while working at that hotel and, during a bad winter, had no power or heating. 'We had to lean out the window with the kettle and pour hot water over the gas cylinder to unfreeze it.' She ended up in the city for a number of years after that but has been back out in this rural hotel for a month.

She points out the staff accommodation, which is just two minutes away from the main hotel, a wooden building that blends into the side of the hill quite naturally.

'It's beautiful here and you save a lot of money while working as you have your meals paid for, but it's not for everyone. You need to drive. Staff turn up thinking what an idyllic place it is to live, but if you don't have a car, you're stuck.'

I nod. No buses, no trains, no taxis. Lifts from colleagues the only way out. I love the roads, I love the view. But I know if I worked in the hotel, my feelings on it would change daily, like the weather.

After lunch we visit Joanne, a friend on the other side of the loch. She is also pregnant, and I want to drop off some maternity clothes that don't fit me anymore. This is Joanne's second pregnancy. Her first baby was delivered at 26 weeks, dangerously early for the baby, and the same number of weeks she is now in this pregnancy. I wonder if she is on high alert, waiting for this one to come too early again. She laughs. 'A little, but what can you do?'

Last time, when she went into early labour, she figured there was no point in waiting for an ambulance – it would take twice as long as driving to the hospital herself, so that's what she did. By the time she reached the motorway, her contractions were so strong she couldn't drive any further and her sister had to pick her up at the side of the road.

The baby was born at a tiny 2lbs and was in neonatal for months.

'Would you ever move?' I ask. 'Somewhere closer to things, like the hospital.' 'I couldn't do it,' Joanne says. 'We love it here too much.' Jessie sits backwards on the sofa and looks out onto the field behind Joanne's house. They rent part of an old stable block, which used to house the workers of the Big House just a few hundred yards away. Joanne's horse potters about in the field, and in the woods above this she points out a family of red squirrels. Jess watches them play until it's time to leave.

Another girl I know, due in a few months, lives on Arran. There are no maternity facilities on the island and, two weeks before she's due, she's packing up and staying at her aunt's in Glasgow. These extra layers of stress, being so far away from medical care, must be frightening. But neither of them would ever dream about moving closer to the city or the big towns.

On the way home, I weigh up our 15-minute drive to the hospital – the one we'll be doing in a few weeks – with what I can see out of my car window. Trees laden with wet branches hang over the loch and the road curves beside the busy river. The scenery hurries by as we head back south into the central belt. The temperature edges up to 20 degrees again.

9

Development

The baby is 18 days old, and I finally have the strength to push the buggy through the woods. We have called him Rory, but it's difficult to think of him as anything other than the baby yet. The path is thick with damp November leaves and every so often I dig out a block of mud and needles wedged between the wheel and its arch. It's not really the right kind of buggy for the woods and he is bumping away on the uneven surface. I worry that he's being jolted around too much, but I push on anyway.

It's a Sunday. I have tried to persuade everyone out of the house for some fresh air but gave up after an hour. The hassle of cajoling Jessie out of her pyjamas, away from her colouring in and the TV, is not worth it. Phil and I are still in the newborn haze anyway, taking stages of sleep like relay runners. Phil was up at 5.45 a.m. for his shift looking after the baby and I slept for a few hours. He went back to bed at 8.30 a.m. I feed Rory on the sofa, the pain of feeding still not completely abated. Out on the street, I can see patches of blue sky as the clouds skid past. The window frames a view of the other houses on the street, brick and roof tiles, but the portion of sky I can see is too thin. I want to see more of it. I want to see leaves and the spidery frame of trees at the edge of autumn. I have so much to do: so much washing; the breakfast dishes are abandoned on the side; there are small pools of milk on the coffee table from breakfast; the living-room floor is scattered with pens, toys and cushions – stepping stones for when the floor was lava.

I leave the other children still half-dressed, wrap up Rory in blankets and settle him in the buggy. I walk through the estate, down Jarvie Road, faster than I have done in months. I have been waiting for this, ambling around the streets and woods to get the baby to sleep. I remember doing it with Jessie. I like the wandering, the aimlessness of it: it settles my mind. We live on a housing development, which is about 10 years old. There are 600 houses here on old farmland. I used to see this muddy patch of ground from the train as it shot past on the way to Edinburgh when I worked in the city. The waves of new housing have been bubbling up, stretching further out for decades now. It's turned into prime commuter belt. I push the buggy past the smaller semi-detached houses at the bottom of our street, then cross over and into a more expensive area. The houses are bigger here, the cars fancier, the trees more established.

I think about how this development has many of the same characteristics as the estate I grew up on and the model villages of the past. George Cadbury built Bournville with his chocolate fortune, and William Levers built Port Sunlight for his soap-factory workers. They were both designed as attractive places to live with access to natural areas, highly planned streets, different styles of houses for families of different means, green spaces for children to play in. Some even have grand-looking walls at the foot of their gardens, borders which proclaim territory.

But, of course, the main difference is ownership. Most people who live here own their homes. We are not tenants in houses tied to a job or a landowner. There is no one employer who all residents work for or pay rent to. We do not fear losing our house if we lose our jobs. (Unless, of course, we cannot find another job to pay the mortgage.) So, what of the community? Does it still exist if there is not one industry or purpose bringing us all together? Can it ever be similar?

During the first lockdown in summer 2020, when our lives reduced to a strict 5-mile radius, communities across the country reinvented themselves. There were chalk drawings, hopscotch and artwork on the pavements. People didn't go anywhere, unless they were key workers. Kids rode their bikes up and down the streets, the lack of cars a blessing. Here, the couple across from our house, a policeman and a paramedic, brought out deck chairs and caught the last of the summer sun when they weren't on shift. We drank beer at a distance and watched the children play. The outside space, usually so marked off, so linear, was suddenly shared in a different way. The guy next door washed his car (again) and a gaggle of kids dared him to spray them. The shrieks brought out more children and more wet clothes to hang on washing lines.

Rory and I leave our development and reach the edge of the wood. I wait a few minutes for the road to clear, something I never had to do during lockdown, and then cross it, entering the old country estate, which sits at the heart of this area. It's the kind of estate from my childhood. A big wall, in some spots in a state of collapse, skims the edge of the wood. Last summer, I found a den snug up against this wall, made with larch branches and muddy tarpaulin. There were makeshift seats and a small fire burning in the stone ring. I could smell wet, burning logs and the tell-tale scent of a joint. A couple of teenagers were hunched over the flames in hoodies. I smiled as I walked past, and they smiled sheepishly back. The next time I walked on this route, the den had been destroyed, the branches used for the roof discarded on the ground, the fireplace wet with rainwater. It could have collapsed by itself, but it looked deliberate. Maybe it was done by another group of teenagers, maybe by the council, I'm not sure. This was during the time when people were banned from mixing, when teenagers were locked up in their bedrooms, prohibited from socialising. I was outraged for them. At least they had been outside.

I push the buggy underneath the huge larch trees and the beeches with almost no leaves left. I see a few dog walkers, a runner, and hear a train on its way to Stirling and beyond. Rory is sleeping. I walk slowly and finally my mind settles. I lost my temper with Phil, shouted at him for not helping enough, not helping everyone get out of the house. Now I am glad no one else came.

I think about my mum walking around the estate just like this with me and my brother. Every day, she tells me, she took us out, whatever the weather. I believe this, as it is what I do. It is what I have to do. I need to escape the stuffed atmosphere of home and get outside. I look at Rory wrapped up tight in his blankets and think about babies, about the trauma of having them. During labour, perversely, as I bit hard on the gas and air, I remember thinking about women labouring generations ago in candlelight. The pain of pain with no pain relief. The thought of just hot water and towels. What to do with the mess that comes with childbirth. And God, is it a mess. I think of my great-grandmother who had 13 children. The thought makes me want to cry. During the night, when I'm sitting up in bed, my phone light on to feed Rory, I think, 'How did they do that in cold bedrooms?' Did they need to light a candle to feed and change the nappy? The nappies! The damp that must have leaked, every night, through the bed sheets. The constant washing. The fear when the baby starts to cry that he'll wake up the other kids. I feel guilty when I wake up and he's still beside me in bed. Today, they tell you not to sleep with the baby, not to bring him into your bed, as it increases the chance of sudden infant death syndrome (SIDS). Every time I put him back in his Moses basket and place my hand on his chest to settle him, I think of the overcrowding in the reservoir builders' huts, the slate cottages, the mill workers' houses. The cold. There was no choice but to cuddle the baby all night. There were not enough beds for everyone.

Out of the woods and back on the modern estate, the pavement is smooth. Rory sleeps on. I push him slowly up the hill to our front door. My womb is still not fully recovered; something still feels loose in there. It might spill open if I do too much. Every time I do this walk, through the new estate and into the woods of the old one, I am glad we are here and not further away from this bit of nature. I park the buggy in the hall, take my boots off and sit down heavily on the sofa. Everyone is upstairs and it is quiet. The living room is as I left it, milk pools on the table and cushions over the floor. Rory stirs, grumbles and then starts to cry.

The issue of land, who owns what and what they do with it, has always been a complicated one. The question of current land ownership is covered comprehensively in two books, *Who Owns England?* by Guy Shrubsole and *The Poor Had No Lawyers* by Andy Wightman. Their extensive research shows that, even in 2021, we do not know who owns all our land. Some of it is in the hands of companies that seem to have no faces attached to them, names that are hard to pin down and therefore cannot be held accountable. Much of the country's land has been handed down through generations and has never been sold, making it impossible to fill in the gaps. Andy Wightman believes that half of Scotland's rural land is owned by only 432 landowners – a number that has remained largely unchanged in decades.

In England, Guy Shrubsole reckons that the aristocracy and gentry still own roughly 30 per cent of England today. The rest is owned by various sectors, including companies such as Tesco and BT (18 per cent), the Crown (1.4 per cent) and charities (2 per cent). Only 5 per cent of England is owned by homeowners, despite a rise in homeownership in the last 30 years. Shrubsole states that his investigations 'have led me to conclude that an elite of less than 1 per cent of the population owns half of England. A few thousand dukes, baronets and City bankers own far more land than all of Middle England put together.'

Although this doesn't surprise me, personally this fact has never troubled me. As a child, I lived on that 30 per cent and saw it as my own. I never believed I was gentry – I could see the clear line between them and us – but we were allowed to use the private beach by the lake, lugging our picnics down there. At one point we had a small red dinghy, which we sailed in the muddy bay on Windermere. When cousins came to stay, and later on boyfriends and girlfriends, we lit fires by the lake's edge and watched the tourist boats on the water. I spent hours exploring on my own, walking across the hills to the lake, up the fells and through woods in which they fattened up the baby pheasants. And I never saw another soul. It was private land. We didn't own it, but by living on it, it felt like it was ours. We were allowed to wander where we wanted. The general public wasn't. This now feels like an injustice – to everyone who doesn't have this kind of access, but also, mainly, selfishly, because I don't have it now.

Today I live in Scotland, where you *can* wander where you want, within reason. The 'right to roam' was established in the Land Reform Act 2003, which means anyone has access to anywhere unless, of course, it is a private garden or land where crops are growing. You can walk up fells, play by the loch and walk in the grounds of many country estates here in Scotland. It is different in England. Only around 8 per cent of England is under a law similar to the 'right to roam'. In the year 2000, the Countryside and Rights of Way Act (CROW Act) gave people legal access over mountains, moors, commons and coastlines, but the land we can wander here is very limited. There are still many more 'Private Land, No Access' signs scattered about the countryside in England than there are in Scotland. And since the Kinder Trespass in 1932, when 400 walkers ascended the Kinder Scout moor in Derbyshire to protest against the lack of access to the countryside, the 'mass trespass' has had a revival. More and more groups of people are meeting and walking on private land, highlighting how little access there really is in England.

Access and, some would say, the harmless act of walking on the land is one thing, but actually building a house is an entirely different matter. 'Planning' – the concept of controlling development and deciding where and how buildings are constructed – has been in existence in some form or another since Roman times. Towns such as Salisbury and Stratford-upon-Avon were planned by the Romans, with street grids and plots for shops. During the seventeenth century, if you built a house in London without a licence, you could be imprisoned. For centuries, the authorities did not want the capital stretching out beyond the original city boundary. Over the centuries, though, various rules have come and gone. Thatched roofs were banned, brick was required, street widths have been regulated. A lot of this had to do with safety, preventing the spread of fire and disease.

During the Industrial Revolution, however, overcrowding in cities led to the idea of the Garden City. Urban planner Ebenezer Howard wrote how we could combine the advantages of both the country and the city to create 'the Garden City', in the process eliminating the disadvantages of both. He notes the country to have a 'lack of society' but 'beauty of nature' and the city the opposite, where he believed people were 'closed out of nature' but had more social opportunity.

Garden cities were all-new developments and highly planned, with much more space around them than the city could ever imagine. They had big gardens and parks for children to play in – they had the benefit of both worlds. Letchworth Garden City in Hertfordshire was the first to be built in 1903 and at the celebration of the community's opening, it was said that:

> *The fortunate community living on this estate will rejoice in the knowledge that the unearned increment which may result from the rents of a population of 30,000 souls will not go to enrich an individual landowner, but will be spent in such a way as will tend to refine the lives, ennoble the characters and exalt the minds of all who reside on the estate.*

Most of the town, now much expanded, is owned by the Letchworth Garden City Heritage Foundation and rents still go towards investing in the area.

Prior to the idea of the Garden City, the 1866 Labouring Classes Dwelling Act gave local authorities the chance to borrow money to build houses for workers in their area. That same year, the first 'council houses' were built in Liverpool, and more were built in Glasgow a few years later. Rural areas also benefited from the building of council houses, though not nearly as much as urban areas did. The first rural council houses were in Ixworth in Suffolk, where eight homes were built in 1894, the result of the local priest's efforts, who found the conditions of the houses for local labourers simply not good enough.

Then, in the 1920s and 30s an average of 300,000 houses were built every year, many of these council houses. This seems a remarkable number. Jen, who came to Easdale with me, lives in a council house in the small town of Bo'ness along the River Forth. The block of four flats was built in 1925. She has a large living room, two bedrooms and a huge garden. It's the garden that feels like the gem in the crown. 'We're so lucky with it,' she says. Since moving in she has planted vegetables and sweet peas, and dug in a pond at the end of the long strip of green grass. There is enough room for a huge paddling pool as well as the biggest trampoline you can buy. Her daughter's friend, who lives in a much more expensive postcode only a few miles away, can't believe the size of her friend's garden. Her parents' house is worth half a million, but she prefers their council-house garden.

In rural areas, the 1936 Housing Act gave local councils the chance to build agricultural cottages for labourers by subsidising the costs, and so council houses became more widespread in the countryside. Only three years later, there were 159,000 council houses providing homes for people who worked in rural industry in England alone. I guess providing homes in the countryside was seen as a benefit to society back then.

In 2022, there are new developments in most parts of the UK, with the bulk of new house building in already populated areas such as

London, the Southeast and the West Midlands. Part of the Conservative Party's manifesto in 2019 was to build 300,000 houses a year. The numbers were below that in 2020, at only 216,000 new homes (including conversions and change of use from shop to flat). Understandably, Covid caused issues, slowing things down, and costs are still high, but this figure is still too low for the millions of people waiting for a home.

One study suggested we should be building 340,000 new homes in England alone, and 145,000 of those should be affordable. Whatever the true stats are, it seems we are nowhere near the peak of house building in 1968 when 350,000 homes were built in one year. In 2010, they hit their lowest yet at only 106,000 houses built in a year due to the last recession. We cannot begin to imagine what the next slump in economy will do to house building, but we know there are more people in need of a home than in 2010.

Not far from me is a big new development near Edinburgh called Calderwood. It is a five-year project with planning for 2,300 houses and is almost at the end of one of the building phases when Phil takes me to visit it one day in 2020. Phil is a land buyer for a house builder, an irony that is not lost on me. When I first met him, I was a single mum with a one-year-old kid and he was a master's student working in a call centre. (There is an almost-generational six years between us; he grew up with a mobile phone, whereas I was nearly driving by the time they were commonplace.)

I met Phil on a night when my son was at his dad's. At that time, I would walk the short distance to the pub where Jen, the one with the council house, worked behind the bar. It was a Tuesday, quiz night, and I was in with a group of other mum friends. Phil and I kept catching each other's eyes. I thought he looked kind; I liked his eyes and the way he spoke softly when chatting to his friends. He didn't flinch at all when I said I had a one-year-old son. He was studying sustainable community design at university and told me about a study into blue-green algae. I had heard about the particular toxic species before – it must have been my dad talking about it – and it turned out I could hold a conversation on the matter, surprising us both. Ten years later (after three house moves and two more children), his job is to buy land for his company to build houses on. This is not as easy as it sounds. There is more to it than circling a field and saying, 'Let's build houses there.' Despite what people think, landscape and environment are always thought about, as well as transport, energy, biodiversity, links for the community, schools, doctors. As house builders, they need to understand the geology of the area, any previous mining, any possible contamination, any nesting birds, any ancient areas that need to be protected. They factor in all of this when buying a site. I see Phil go through every stage. As with any business, there will be good examples of practice and bad ones. I know Phil tries his best to make any land purchase work for future generations. But no matter how hard you work at the early stages, no matter how much the company is aware of the environmental impact, getting approval from the council and, more importantly, from the local people is the hardest part of all. If the local council, made up of members elected by local residents, don't want houses in a particular area, those houses don't get built.

The house builder Phil works for bought some land at the huge site at Calderwood and he told me one day about its community-based approach and the eco-friendly credentials. I like the idea of this but am unconvinced, thinking of our own street, built by the same house builder, which is, in my opinion, rather lacking in trees and wild, natural spaces. But I am keen to look at it. Phil has always tried to push more sustainable ideas forward in his job, but this doesn't always add up commercially (studying sustainable community design gave him a good base for this). The company behind Calderwood is led by a farmer and businessman who has an ambitious vision for this place. He has sold off sections of the site to seven different developers, but his company still acts as the factor, overseeing the shared spaces of the site and maintaining them. The whole development is billed as 'a new, established village, where a vibrant community thrives'. The website boasts 'scenic beauty and opportunities to connect with nature'. A tough call, I thought, in a development with thousands of houses. I was keen to take a look.

We drive into the estate. The houses at this entrance are not built yet. I look at the foundations of the homes from the car window – black squares of mud and concrete – amazed that such a small space can fit a three- or four-bedroom home in it. Further down the road, some of the plots have their timber frames assembled (most new housing developments in Scotland use timber frame – it stores carbon for longer and can insulate well; Phil tells me how Scottish building regulations are more stringent than in England – they do use timber frame in England but not as often). Some plots have their grey concrete walls constructed. It's a cold day and the black holes of the windows make me shiver. We drive further into the development, where the houses are fully built, with cars on the driveway and families settled in. It is not like our estate. The streets do not feel like straitjacket arms that jab out in different directions. They curve round again and again, which, from the road anyway, gives a view of something more natural. The houses are built in a variety of styles, using various building materials. I don't like seeing the same house type repeated up a street like the green miniature ones on a Monopoly board. These are a mixture, some built with red brick, some grey. Some have wooden panels on the front giving them a beach-hut look. There are very few straight lines.

'It's so … higgledy-piggledy,' I say.

'I'm not sure that's what they were going for exactly.' He sounds a little offended.

'It's a good thing,' I say. 'It's cosier. It's less planned.'

We circle around in a cul-de-sac as Phil tells me there are no pavements. I hadn't even noticed. 'Pedestrians have priority here. It makes the drivers automatically slow down.' This seems counter-intuitive, but it's been proven to work.

The newly built nursery and primary school sit at the edge of the development, a series of fields behind them. When a developer asks for planning permission for houses, the council sometimes says yes, but only on the provision that they build a school or new roads too. This one was built from scratch and its roll now sits at 430 kids.

'All the kids must walk to school,' I state. I was never able to walk to school, our house being too far away from the village.

We park in the school car park and look at the spread of homes from the front of the school. I imagine kids meeting up outside each other's front doors, backpacks on, kicking a football down the road just before the bell. It seems like something from an old film.

Just along from the school is the transport hub. Phil points to an electric car parked on the side of the road. 'You can hire it for the day. It means people don't have to buy a car if they don't want to.' There are also electric bikes to rent. We park outside the café at the centre of the development. I run over and order coffee and an ice cream for Jessie. Next to the payment machine is a basket of blank wooden baubles for children to decorate so they can put them on the community Christmas tree. 'That's nice,' I comment to the girl serving the coffee. 'Must be a nice place to live.'

'I don't live here actually,' she says, 'but I bring my dog for a walk here all the time. Lots of good walks round here.'

New sites like Calderwood need a certain percentage of affordable housing, usually 25 per cent. This means that a quarter of all the homes here were built for the local council or for a social landlord so people can rent them as council houses. This is a decent percentage and in 2020, 52,000 affordable homes were built in England. But it is still not enough. In England alone more than 1.6 million people are on the list for social housing. Margaret Thatcher's Right to Buy, which enabled a sitting tenant in a council house to buy their home for well below the market value, meant that between 1980 and 2015, more than 2.8 million dwellings were sold off. Many of those sold off are now in the hands of private landlords. By building 42,000 a year, we are still only chipping away at the problem – we haven't even begun to build as many homes as were sold.

Despite this much-reported need for new houses, social and private, there are often many reasons why people are against new developments and it usually boils down to location. There are current proposals to extend Calderwood further towards a neighbouring old country estate, and these proposals are being met with anger. Over the field, further up the hill, is the walled open-air art museum Jupiter Artland. It is a fascinating and unusual place. It invites various sculptors to create art pieces within nature around its grounds. Ellis had a school trip there once. Edinburgh City Council has proposed more houses, an extension of Calderwood, bordering the grounds of the estate, but the museum is against this. For them, the idea of building on this 'green belt' of fields so close to their doorstep is a step too far. (I always thought 'green belt' meant an area of nature surrounding a town. This would hopefully be the case now, but initially it was coined 'to check the unrestricted sprawl of large built-up areas' or to act as a 'buffer zone' between one settlement and the next. Essentially it was to stop growth, not to save nature. I would hope it extends its aims to protect nature in today's climate.)

A number of prominent artists have spoken out against the further development on behalf of the museum. One artist, Nathan Coley, said that Jupiter Artland is, 'preserved for the people of Scotland, for the people who visit Jupiter from elsewhere, for the children from local schools that call it theirs. Jupiter Artland's air and tranquillity needs to be preserved, and importantly the idea that such a place can exist needs to be preserved.' I'm not sure how building homes will affect the 'air and tranquillity' of a place. Sir Antony Gormley said, 'We should not be building in the countryside: the future of our species depends on high-density housing on inner-city brownfield sites.'

I find myself torn. I understand the passion to stop concrete and brick filling green spaces, especially in close proximity to something precious. But can we really expect all new houses to be built in the city or the immediate outskirts of them? Can we really cordon off the countryside so no one can live there? Is it OK for one wealthy person to build a house with acres around it in a rural area, but not OK for a developer to build houses that might do for local people? Of course, brownfield sites – land that has previously had developments on it in some form or another – should be built on, but if we don't ever build anew in rural or semi-rural areas, what happens to the communities?

Inevitably, the open land around a city or a town has become a destination for wealthier homeowners. They can enjoy the benefits of the country, open air and nature, as well as the short distance to the city where they travel into work and make their money. People who bought their houses in the last wave of development in these semi-rural places are now finding that the next wave of houses are being planned for the fields around their settlement. And they are the people shouting loudest about how they do not want the new development.

I imagine the people who buy these homes have no objection to the development. They will be happy that their children can walk to school and have a garden to play in, where they can grow flowers, and maybe some vegetables. They will enjoy walking their dog by the nearby river. They will be happy to live somewhere nice.

I admit, I wince when we drive past a field and Phil says it has planning permission for a new development: I don't like to see huge developments where fields used to be either, but if people are forced out of the countryside, how will we ever learn to understand it, to love it?

Of course, housing issues in semi-rural places are different to the issues in remote rural areas. (Semi-rural is defined as living on the outskirts but close to both the city and the countryside, and remote rural is defined as a population of fewer than 3,000 people and more than half an hour's drive from a large population.) One thing which connects them all, however, is a lack of decent and affordable housing. And the land to build them on. Back in Hawkshead in Cumbria, I visit an old friend, a girl I went to primary school with. I wouldn't describe Hawkshead as 'remote rural' – it's certainly not difficult to get there compared to villages in the Highlands and Islands, but it does take more than half an hour to get to any kind of small town.

Evonne now lives in what used to be our former playgroup. A huge Victorian building, it was converted into flats about 10 years ago with four more houses built on the small bit of land alongside it. Evonne lives here with her husband and two children. She has lived within 3 miles of this house her whole life. She doesn't own it but rents it through a housing association, which has a local occupancy clause on it. She thinks she was lucky to get this. Councils around the UK have various other schemes, but the local occupancy clause is the one mainly used in the Lake District and often in the Yorkshire Dales. The aim is to sell or rent houses to people with an 'established connection to the local area', which should prevent the property being used as a second home or a holiday home. On the face of it, this is a great idea, but it doesn't always work as it should.

It is pouring down. We have stacked our wet coats on the table in the kitchen and Evonne and I are waiting for the kettle to boil as Mum, who wanted to come and see her too, plays in the living room with Jessie and Evonne's girls. Rory is asleep in my arms.

The conversion from a huge Victorian hall to a two-bedroom flat has been done well and the kitchen window looks north, over the old yard where we used to play in the sand and up towards the hills.

'I love the view from here,' Evonne says. 'In autumn, Latterbarrow is lit up when the sun sets. It's bright orange. Cos of the bracken.' She hands me my tea and I take a quick look out of the window. Today you can't see Latterbarrow, the biggest hill behind Hawkshead. It is shrouded in cloud.

Evonne spent many years applying for houses in Hawkshead.

She has lived in housing owned by the Co-op and a house owned by the National Trust, but says this was the hardest one to get.

'I'd rung up, cos they'd started building new houses up Vicarage Lane. They literally said to me, "Why do you want an application form?" Cos I want one of the houses. "Well, how many of you is there?" I said there's just me and my fiancé. "Have you not got any kids?" No, I said, but I thought there were some two-bedroom houses coming up. "Well, are you going to have kids?" I hope so, but I live in a flat, and there is no way I can get a pushchair down these steps. It's not even an option.'

It's a points-based system. When Evonne first applied, she was category E, but when she had her first daughter this 'bumped her up to a category C'.

'We were a couple with a kid and a dog, and they said to us we'll have to toss a coin with a friend who was a single person and a toddler to see who got the bigger house. The guy actually said, "Let's go back to the office and toss a coin."'

It feels like a gameshow where points make houses. Heads or tails, who gets the biggest prize? Another friend was denied a house in the village she grew up in as she had already moved away to the bigger town, despite her parents still living in that area. She wasn't 'local' anymore. It doesn't make sense. The parameters can be so complicated, it blocks out the people it should be welcoming.

In the end, the slightly bigger flat in the old playgroup was given to Evonne – whether they did actually toss the coin in the office or not, she doesn't know. Her girls share their bedroom. ('We couldn't have the three-bedroom as we only had one kid at the time.' And even though now they have two girls, the authorities said that they still only needed two bedrooms – the girls 'can share forever'.)

What about buying? I ask. Is that ever a possibility? 'The private rentals or National Trust rents are so high it makes saving for a deposit impossible. Unless I win the lottery the chances of buying in Hawkshead are slim. I could move out of the area but while the kids are at school, we'll stay.'

Evonne works as the dinner lady at the primary school. She cooks for the 45-strong school roll, which fluctuates over the years. It is currently a little less than when we were there in the Eighties, which isn't bad considering that the number of second homes in the area has shot up.

Mum was also a dinner lady at the school. 'But I was only the helper,' she says when we talk about it. There were three dinner ladies back then; now Evonne runs the kitchen on her own.

I'm glad they converted the old playgroup building. I know the names of most of the residents along that stretch of new houses and flats, and it's good to know that some places were built with local people in mind. A community might be desperate for new homes, but if the land isn't available, what do you do? Helen MacDonald, who runs the Ulva Ferry Housing Partnership partnered by Mull & Iona Community Trust, literally asks for it. 'We've written to every landowner on Mull, saying would you be willing to release land for housing or crofting? One landowner replied and was pretty indignant at being asked. Some reply saying we don't have any suitable land. But mostly it's just been silence from them.' This is disappointing to say the least.

However, in the last 10 years they have managed to build six new homes, four of which have families in now, and one of them a single person who works as a fisherman. The last house is up for let now. 'There were fifteen applications, for a two-bedroom house,' Helen says. 'Thirteen of the applicants were already living on Mull in houses that aren't suitable. Some were sharing friends' houses or still living with family in cramped accommodation.' She tells me only two applicants were lifestyle choices rather than 'need', the meaning of which you can infer yourself.

This land for the houses came from a local farmer who sold them the first plot. He then donated another plot. Helen explains how Mull has masses of land, but that making it usable and available, and connecting the houses up with electricity and water, is the difficult part. Even just getting building materials there can pose a problem due to it being so geographically isolated.

I start to tell her about growing up in a tied house and she immediately explains how, on Mull, 'there used to be two police houses and two teachers' flats, a house for the coastguard officer, the BT guy, the hydro guy. All our essential services came with council houses. They were good family-size houses. And now they've all been sold off.' I remember how Mum told me there was a nurse's house in Hawkshead once but it had been bought and sold and is now a holiday cottage. Maybe tied houses should be brought back to ensure communities do have a teacher, a police officer and a nurse. But, I guess, communities don't need teachers, police officers or nurses if those communities don't exist anymore.

10

Business

I am on a ferry with three-month-old Rory. It feels like an adventure, bringing him this far away from home on my own, and so far he seems happy watching the sun on the sea and feeling the rock of the boat. I have come to Arran, an island just off the west coast of Scotland, to visit Brodick Castle. It's one of the most accessible islands in Scotland, a 40-minute drive from Glasgow and

a 55-minute ferry ride. It is owned by the National Trust for Scotland (NTS) and there are staff that live on site all year round, some actually in the castle itself. It is closed to the public in winter, but they have said I can come and meet some of the people who are currently living there, maintaining the house, the grounds and even the biggest mountain on Arran, Goatfell, which also falls under the NTS's stewardship.

I drive through the gates, past the lodge house and up along the winding road towards the Big House. I have been directed to veer right, away from the castle and towards the park rangers' hut, which is situated behind a row of old cottages beneath the sharp tip of Goatfell. There are a few cars parked here but I can hear nothing but birds. I breathe in the air. It feels like I'm coming home.

John, the gardener, appears between two old cottages. I had expected an older man, someone near retirement, gruff and quietly spoken – a stereotype of a Mr McGregor figure, I suppose. John was quite the opposite. He had a bounce to him. His hair was thick with dark curls and his beard was long and unkept.

'I thought I'd show you around the gardens!' he announces.

I push Rory in his buggy as John tells me the history of the castle and its grounds. A house of some kind has been on this site since the fifth century, initially as a fortress. It has been added to and improved over the centuries and has changed its look from a castle to an opulent stately home. The garden, John tells me, is famous for its many types of rhododendron, brought from around the world. The famous plant hunters George Forrest and Frank Kingdon-Ward travelled the world in search of new plants in the early twentieth century. (Forrest, I learn later, was from Falkirk, where I live now. He collected 1,200 plant species in his life, including buddleia and alliums, and has been dubbed the 'Indiana Jones of Plant Collecting'.) Lady Mary Louise Hamilton, who owned Brodick at the time, bought shares in plant-hunting expeditions, like many estate owners did. Even on this still January morning, the gardens are lush with a variety of colours, textures and scents, like a super-size version of my old estate. The trees are taller here, their trunks thicker. The gardens are thick with rhododendrons, their deep-green leaves dwarfing the ones I knew at home. One of them is in flower now, a bright pink that shocks against the grey winter sky. The climate on the west coast is more temperate than the rest of Scotland – it creates an environment that enables plants to grow bigger. As we walk, I mention that my dad was the forester on our estate and John suddenly veers off the main path onto a smaller, thinner one. I follow, the buggy only just fitting on the thin strip of gravel. I duck under a couple of huge tree ferns – *Dicksonia antarctica*, John tells me later. They look like palm trees, and I say how much I like them. 'Oh, them, they're just weeds here.'

He stops and says, 'Here, I wanted to show you this.' He points to a corner of a brick structure, stuck deep in the soil. Huge rhododendron bushes that look more like trees rise out from where the building would have been once upon a time.

'This is the old forester's house. You said your dad was a forester – I thought you might like to see it. He would have planted all these trees.' The silver fir trees a few metres away from the old house are so massive they overshadow everything else around them. A beck – a burn here in Scotland, of course – bubbles away under the ferns. I think how lovely it would have been to listen to the burn every night while going to sleep in the cottage.

We continue around the gardens, John taking us off-route every now and then to see a tree, the summer house or a sprawling bush with bright-yellow flowers. 'In the summer you just get a waft of this as you walk past,' he says. His enthusiasm for the garden is infectious.

We stop at the top of a hill. I can see the ferry port below and the village of Brodick, the biggest village on the island. The sea looks calm and the sun is making its way through the clouds every now and then, flooding the bay with flashes of light. The weather is meant to worsen later and I am a little worried the ferry will not sail. I mention this to John. He checks his weather app and tells me to try the earlier ferry. I can chance my luck in the standby queue. 'And if you get stuck, you can always come back. It happens all the time!' The bay looks so peaceful now, I can't imagine the weather turning on us in just a few hours.

From here I can see a seal flopping about on the rocks below and I point it out excitedly like the tourist I am. 'They're always here.' He shrugs a bit. 'And otters. We've got loads of them. I had an otter nesting in my garden last year!'

John lives on site in one of the cottages that has no central heating. His cottage is typical of its time. It was built in the mid-1800s and has thick stone walls, tiny windows and a slate roof that once was thatched. It is very damp and cold. 'I get dressed to go to bed in winter,' he laughs. As he tells me this, he zips open his fleece and shows me a woollen jumper. 'Worn this the last few days.'

I ask him if he likes living here. He looks at me as if I'm crazy. 'Course. I step outside my door and have seventy-four acres of this. I'll never afford a house, not on this wage. But why do I want to when I've got this?'

I am due to meet the manager who actually lives inside the castle itself and, as I leave John, I realise that I have hardly looked at the grand house since I arrived. I walk Rory round the backyard to the staff entrance and watch the wind whipping up the steam from the boiler room. The manager is running late and I keep looking at my watch. I check my weather app and see the forecast has not changed. Still due to be 40-mph winds at 4 p.m., the time my ferry is due to board. I text the manager with my apologies and leave, hoping to fit on the earlier ferry, suddenly desperate to get home to Jessie and Ellis.

As I drive away, I know I am not that fussed about missing out on the inside of the castle. It was better to spend the time talking to John and finding out how he sees things, and the castle would have been like most other grand estate houses on the inside. There would be rows of books up to the ceiling in the library, huge portraits of stern-looking earls or what have you, silverware, suits of armour maybe. The accumulation of wealth, here at Brodick especially, is tainted with a part of history we are finally forcing ourselves to remember.

I have heard people talk of the three 'Ms' of a successful estate: mining, management and marriage. But one word has been conveniently forgotten and that is slavery.

I talked in the first chapter about how the National Trust has been researching the links their stately homes have to slavery. The report names 93 properties so far and Brodick Castle is one of them. The links are plenty. In the late seventeenth century, Anne, 3rd Duchess of Hamilton at Brodick, was reported to have 'one of the fashionable Negro footmen, known to his colleagues as John Timothy the Black'. Anne's youngest son, Lord Archibald Hamilton, later went on to be appointed Governor of Jamaica. Many British landowners held titles and roles such as this in Jamaica.

And in 1844, Alexander, 10th Duke of Hamilton, married Susan Euphemia Beckford, who went on to inherit her father William Beckford's fortune. The Beckfords were one of the first families to obtain sugar plantations in Jamaica; they owned 13 plantations and an estimated 3,000 slaves – an unbelievable number. Brodick Castle, like so many other estates around the UK, is full of artwork, silverware and furniture bought with the profits of the slave trade.

This clear link to the slave trade for so many wealthy families is dreadful, but what appals me most is the injection of wealth the stately homes were given following the payouts from the slave compensation scheme.

After the Slavery Abolition Act in 1833, the Slave Compensation Act 1837 followed. Those who had owned slaves could claim reimbursement from the government for their financial loss. Of course, it did not compensate the enslaved. The British government borrowed £20 million to compensate the planation and slave owners, which has been estimated as the equivalent of around £17 billion today. That debt was only paid off by the British taxpayer in 2015. And it was this injection of money which enabled many estates to be lavishly enhanced, their gardens and grounds improved, artwork acquired and heirlooms increased.

At Penrhyn Castle in Wales, the landowners, the Pennants, received £14,683 17s. 2d. (around £1.3 million today) for the freeing of 764 enslaved people in Jamaica. The Pennant family had links to Jamaica for decades, and by the time Richard Pennant, 1st Baron Penrhyn, took over, they owned over 1,000 slaves. Richard Pennant, however, never visited Jamaica; he was an absent landlord who controlled their properties by letter. He describes the slaves as 'chattels', not as people, on the basis that the cattle and the human slaves were considered his possessions and were all classed under the same term. Unsurprisingly, Pennant was against the abolition of slavery. But despite these views, he is known as 'Richard Pennant the Improver' as he invested the compensation money in his North Wales estate. Money from Jamaica paid for Welsh roads, railways, houses and schools. He also invested his money in Penrhyn Quarry, once the largest slate quarry in the world, which employed 3,000 men.

So, not only are the stately homes, their art collections inside and their gardens a result of colonial conquests, but the local communities are the result of this money too. Homes, businesses, schools, roads, the very heart of communities were built with profits and compensation from the slave trade. Did many more small villages owned by estates benefit from this? They must have done. It feels we are only at the beginning of understanding how our country was really built.

There is one more story from Brodick Castle that I wanted to find out more about. The last person to own the castle, before the National Trust for Scotland took over, was Lady Jean Fforde. In her earlier life, she holidayed with the royal family from Monaco and hosted politicians as powerful as former prime minister Harold Macmillan at Brodick. During the Second World War, she worked as a code breaker at Bletchley Park, although this time of her life, she comments, 'was excessively boring. It was not as glamorous as subsequent books and films have made it appear.'

In 1960, Jean Fforde's mother, the Dowager Duchess of Montrose, died. Saddled with enormous death duties, Lady Jean was forced to move out of Brodick Castle which was given in lieu to the National Trust for Scotland. She moved into a cottage on the estate, the former estate office.

And then in 1994, Lady Jean did something that no one had ever done before – she sold the family title. The Hamiltons' 'earldom' came with 1,000 acres and the ruined thirteenth-century castle of Lochranza. The fact that the land and the title had been in the family for hundreds of years mattered little. Lady Jean was cold.

She put the earldom on the market to pay for central heating in the cottage. I guess after 30 years in a cold, damp house, the logs and coal the only source of heat, she'd had enough.

The amount the earldom was sold for was never released, but I assume Lady Jean was happy with her choice. When she was asked how she felt about selling the title, she said she was sad, 'but losing it is nothing like when I lost the family castle to the National Trust.

The castle and all its contents were taken from me and it was like losing my whole life.' I imagine that building must have had a better heating system.

As we walked around the estate, John had talked about the family: the men who gambled, the women who, he said, were more switched on and generous historically. Lady Jean's mother had built schools and churches in some of the villages around the island. They also employed a doctor for the people on their estate. But, in the last few years, the family had angered the community when they attempted to evict tenant farmers from the estate to make way, reportedly, for deer stalking. These kinds of stories are repeated across the country. Landless people have struggled for centuries with changing lairds, landowners and landlords – one might be kind and generous to the plight of their tenants; their successor could disregard their woes and eventually their rights as quick as taking off a pair of boots. It was simply your luck which laird or landowner you were tied to.

Back on Arran that January afternoon, not only is the 4 p.m. ferry cancelled but so is the earlier one. I text John, the gardener, as I sit in the car queue alongside timber wagons, rubbish trucks and pick-up trucks while the wind, which has been whipped up seemingly out of nowhere, shakes the quay. It is out of season so he says Rory and I can sleep in the empty bunkhouse on the edge of the estate. He arranges a room to be made up for us. By the time we get there, it is getting dark, the gusts rattling the wooden boards of the building. It is enough to almost make me glad the ferry didn't sail in this weather, especially when I find that the inside of the bedroom and the living room are warm – John must have put on the storage heaters as soon as I messaged him.

I settle in for the night, rocking Rory asleep again and again, standing up in the small dorm room. Whether it is my anxiousness or the storm rolling around the windows, I don't know, but neither of us gets much sleep. I think about John in his cold cottage, wearing three layers of clothes in bed. He doesn't have a handy earldom to pay for central heating. And he isn't a paying tourist, staying in a centrally heated, purpose-built building. He sleeps in woollen jumpers. But he loves his job. That much is clear.

On the face of it, getting a job in a rural area should be as doable as getting a job anywhere. There is employment in tourism, such as working in (or running, if you have the money) pubs, B&Bs, hotels, restaurants. Farming, forestry, building and other vocations such as plumbing are all obvious employment sectors. Technically, you can do anything you want: set up a brewery, an accountancy firm, a garage, a café, a zoo. There were nearly 550,000 businesses registered in rural areas in England in 2020/21, which accounts for 23 per cent of all business in England. The rural economy is worth £260 billion, which is 15 per cent of England's output.

Farming, forestry and fishing still account for a decent slice of the pie in employment (14 per cent in England), and in Wales, around 85 per cent of Welsh land is used for agriculture or forestry. It is a similar story in Ireland where rural businesses are predominantly agriculture, forestry, fishing and construction. It is not surprising, really. When the majority of the country's land mass (an incredible 98 per cent of Scotland's) is classed as 'rural', jobs in those areas should be a given. But with just 17 per cent of the population resident in that 98 per cent of land mass, this isn't always the case. It can be difficult finding the right people for the job; they may need certain qualifications, particular skills, always a driver's licence and, unless they already live in that area, a place to live.

In Shetland in 1975, the local area changed forever, from a mainly crofting and fishing area to the biggest building site in Europe. It took 7,000 workers six years to create the Sullom Voe oil terminal, which was designed to act as a buffer between the oil-producing fields offshore and the tankers waiting to ship the oil worldwide. Local people left their jobs to build the terminal as the pay was so good, and the huge influx of workers from around the country to build the terminal transformed the area. The population of the closest villages soared to house the staff and accommodation camps were built with pubs for the workers to have a drink in at the end of their shifts. When there was no room in the houses, they lodged the men on ferries, which stayed berthed in the bay.

Marabelle Jack, who worked there at the time of construction, and was the first woman employed there, remembers the early days fondly. 'There were three bars in the camp initially, and they always had stuff laid on – bingo, cabarets, films.'

She dealt with admin and arranged transport for the men. 'You were shifting about six thousand men to go home for Christmas, and if the weather was bad it was an absolute nightmare.'

It was a huge change from the traditional industries of crofting and fishing in the area, but Marabelle said on the whole the terminal was welcome. 'It brought jobs. There was very little bother with the guys if they were at the pub. I think the younger ones took it better.'

Another employee, Linda Riddell, whose job was liaising with the council and the local people, said, 'People like me who had been away at university could come back and get a job, so people weren't leaving perhaps in the way that they did before or the way that they are doing now. There certainly were opportunities that we had never envisaged before.'

At its peak production in the 1980s the terminal was producing 1.5 million barrels of oil a week. There were secure jobs, housing and a community. There was also a landmark deal struck. To help mitigate the impact on the local community, the oil industry promised to invest in the area, constructing and maintaining roads, spending on public services and even building a swimming pool. It sounds like a good deal. But they didn't provide energy. The oil that was shipped in here was sent straight down south and then further away to all corners of the earth. Now, Shetland is left with eye-wateringly high energy prices, relying on bottles of gas, coal and peat – there are very few trees to provide logs locally – to heat their homes. Journalist Jen Stout, who is from the area, remembers the mould on the walls and the endless chest infections and coughs. She describes the 'deep irony' that it is 'possible, from certain locations, to see the high flare of burning gas at the Sullom Voe oil terminal – you can watch this spectacle as you shiver in your damp, cold house while the almost constant wind rattles the windows. Round the back of my house, just like most others, a red gas canister is propped up against the wall. Rates of fuel poverty have long been some of the worst in the country.'

This is another issue rural homes and businesses are currently facing. Shetland has it particularly bad, but many rural areas struggle with fuel poverty. Houses are older, poorly built and less energy efficient. It is more difficult to get mains gas to them and many have to rely on heating oil, electricity or solid fuel such as logs and coal. Like so many in rural areas, I remember ice on the inside of my bedroom window and how my parents got up before dawn to light the fire so the water was hot enough for us and the radiators warmed the rooms. In some ways, it is easy to romanticise this way of life. But there is nothing romantic about a hacking cough, asthma and freezing in your bed in the middle of the night. The rising energy prices mean people in poor housing have to choose between heating their home or eating. This should be a problem of the past. It is not.

National newspapers like to romanticise the rural life perpetually. Often, they will write an article about an advertised job and pair it with photos of white sandy beaches for click bait. Headlines such as '*Dream job for island ranger with accommodation included free*' make for plenty of views but I imagine the reality is quite different. This particular ranger job is on Handa Island, on the west coast of Sutherland, a nature reserve where Scottish Natural Heritage are looking for someone to help take care of the bird population. It states, quite far down in the article, that 'weekly trips to Scourie – the nearest, but remote village – are necessary to carry out laundry, banking, shopping and exchange gas bottles. Therefore, a current driving licence and access to a vehicle are both essential for the role.' It doesn't say the nearest village is a ferry ride and, as always, will be dependent on the weather. It takes a special kind of person to work in these isolated environments. For astronauts going to Mars and scientists and engineers heading to Antarctica, they go through training to work with a small team in an isolated place. Yes, it is a beautiful place, and yes, accommodation is provided (where else would you live?), but the job is tough. These articles are really just dream fodder, fairy-tales for people who are bored in their own jobs. But it isn't much of a fairy-tale if the wage doesn't even cover your food or energy bill. As John said, people don't do these jobs for the money. It seems not. The wage for the ranger's job promises a salary of just over £17,000 a year. Jobs in nature, even within an industry such as farming or forestry, are never about the money. It's always a lifestyle.

Farming, forestry, tourism and construction are all obvious industries in rural areas, but there is one development in Sutherland in Scotland that could give people a completely new way to make a living. The Space Hub Sutherland want to launch satellites for observing patterns and changes in the weather, which will help scientists to understand climate change better. They want to do it on a small patch of land owned by the Melness Crofters' Estate. You would think that the locals would be up in arms against the planning of a space port, that they would say it would destroy the peace and quiet of the area, damage the plant and wildlife. This, however, is definitely not the case here. The chair of Melness Crofters' Estate, Dorothy Pritchard, who was born and raised in the area, is the space port's biggest champion. 'There is no one more invested in the area than us,' Dorothy says. 'Why would we do anything that might risk destroying it?'

Dorothy, a retired teacher who has the energy of one of her former pupils, tells me over Zoom that they are hoping to start building in the summer. The space port will only take up 12 acres, in 10,000 acres of the estate. That isn't very much. 'It will be a lot smaller than people imagine,' she says. And it has been designed to be 'carbon-neutral and to blend in with the natural environment'.

As well as the space hub, Dorothy says, eventually they would like to build a science centre. 'We don't want it to just be a tourist trap here; we want to educate people, tell them the story of peat.' She tells me about the old road in the area that was built on peat; it literally floats on top of the boggy land and has been there for generations. The natural world and wildlife are of vital importance. They have taken great care to make sure the space port will not ruin the landscape or harm the creatures that call the area home. She says there will be no fences so deer can still roam freely, and on the day of a launch (which will probably happen 12 times a year) the crofter will collect all animals away from the area.

'Rural areas need industry,' she says decisively.

Dounreay, a nuclear plant and a big employer in the area, is just 40 miles down the coast. 'Two boys from here drive to Dounreay every day to work, but the plant will be decommissioned in the next ten years. And those jobs will dry up.' Nuclear, like oil, can be big employers in rural areas.

Dounreay was built in the 1950s. For the 3,000-strong workforce that built it, they had temporary accommodation camps, but they also built three new estates for the employees who were going to be staying on there. The families that stayed in Dounreay and lived in the prefabricated homes (they were quicker to put up) came to be known in the local area as the 'Atomics'. The population of Thurso, the nearest town, rapidly rose by almost 6,000 in 10 years, and at its peak the number of workers at Dounreay was around 2,400. Now it is less than half of that.

Nuclear plants were often placed, understandably, far away from centres of population. But people do still live and work near them. Sellafield is one of Europe's largest industrial nuclear plants and is only an hour's drive from the tourism hot spots of the Lake District. It currently employs 11,000 people, the majority of those based in the surrounding area of Seascale. From the 1950s to the 2000s,

Sellafield provided nuclear energy – it was also the site of Britain's worst nuclear disaster, when in 1957 a fire inside the plant released radioactive material to the surrounding area. The site now handles almost all the UK's nuclear waste, generated from the other power plants across the country. Sellafield itself is gradually being decommissioned, and by gradually, I mean it will take another 120 years to shut it down, although some of the waste there will remain radioactive for 100,000 years. It's a scary thought. But it provides huge investment to the area. It employs scientists, engineers, nuclear operators; it even has its own police force, the Civil Nuclear Constabulary (CNC), which employs around 1,500 armed police to protect Sellafield and more places like it around the country.

'Tourism is not enough,' Dorothy says. 'It doesn't keep young people in the area. We are losing all our bright, young people.' Here at Melness, they hope the space port will help change that. They are letting the land the space port will be built on, so the money coming in from that will enable them to build 12 new affordable – and, importantly, eco-friendly – houses. These houses will have laws and rules enabling them to stay in the hands of the locals, for a price that people can afford. They won't ever be sold as second homes. The land isn't an issue, and they have already identified a few plots with a view of the harbour, which sounds lovely. Dorothy is keen to stress that it's not about making money, it's about keeping the community alive. We need new industry in places like this, but 'not at any cost'. Dorothy and the other crofters understand; landscape and community are one and the same.

Inevitably, not everyone sees the space port as a good thing. The biggest objector to it is Anders Povlsen, who owns land nearby and is, incidentally, the UK's largest individual landowner. Povlsen, a Danish billionaire who has huge shares in fashion retail, currently owns 230,000 acres of land in Scotland, having bought estate after estate over the last few years. His objections to the space port were on the grounds of 'environmental issues'. He felt so strongly about it that he paid for the lawyers' bills for the (only) three crofters who were also against the proposals. So far, Povlsen and the crofters have lost each appeal and the space port is set to go ahead, creating around 40 jobs in the Melness area and another 200 jobs further afield.

Povlsen runs a company called Wildland, which is based in Glen Feshie in the Cairngorms; it owns three estates in Scotland with the goal of 'rewilding' large areas of the country. The word 'rewilding' can mean different things to people, but the company Wildland says that to them it is 'a 200-year vision of landscape-scale conservation in the Scottish Highlands. Through our custodianship of three significant Scottish estates, we work to let nature heal, grow and thrive.'

Wildland's vision sounds wonderful, important and totally in line with today's climate issues. They say they have a 'commitment to people and place', which is what I like to hear. People and place are, for me, one and the same. There are other companies and rich landowner individuals with similar visions, undertaking similar projects. They aim to 'give nature a chance to fight back' (Wildland). They aim to complete 'extensive native tree planting, peatland restoration, outdoor learning for teenagers, and multiple wildlife projects' (Alladale Wilderness Reserve). Some aim to 'rewild and re-people the Scottish Highlands by increasing carbon sequestration, growing biodiversity, creating green new jobs' (Highlands Rewilding – Bunloit).

I especially like the idea of rewilding and re-peopling going hand in hand. So-called 'green jobs' – roles in ecology, land management and nature tourism – provide much-needed employment alongside improving biodiversity.

So, is there a problem?

In a word, ownership. It matters who owns what, because everyone else has to play by their rules.

Povlsen, and many others like him, have been labelled 'green lairds'. Both individuals and big businesses have bought up huge areas of land in Scotland to rewild. Beer company BrewDog,

Standard Life and Aviva are just three of the huge corporations and pension funds aiming to decarbonise their business emissions by planting trees and capturing carbon. This, on paper, seems to be a good thing. But there is more to it than that. There are further questions about how these companies make their money – if you have made your fortune through fast fashion or some other industry, exploiting people for cheap labour and damaging the environment, should you be allowed to offset that damage by hoovering up land in the north and planting trees? Trees are only beneficial in the right areas. There is no point in planting thousands of saplings if none of them survives due to placement, lack of knowledge when planting and unfavourable habitat. You can't destroy the landscape in one part of the world and then say you're going to make this pocket nice and green instead. It makes me think of Richard Pennant, of Penrhyn Castle, also known as 'Richard the Improver'. Yes, he invested in his village, building schools and businesses, but on the other side of the world, he used slave labour to make his fortune.

Magnus Davidson, a research associate in environment, economy and society, writes that it is not the word 'green' people primarily have an issue with but the word 'laird'. It harks back to the Highland Clearances, from the mid-eighteenth to mid-nineteenth century, when swathes of people were pushed off the land, kicked out of their homes, to make way for mass sheep farming by a few wealthy landowners.

About Povlsen's estates Davidson says, 'Ownership of his estates, found in the Cairngorms, Loch Ness and north Sutherland, have all the hallmarks of the traditional gentry Highland pastime: absenteeism, exclusive high-end stays, usual traditional sporting pastimes, in addition to less traditional ecotourism. Not quite progressive new ownership, rather more of the same but with less deer.'

Protecting our landscape and wildlife is important and I don't think people have a problem with rewilding land at all. It becomes a problem when these things can only be achieved by very rich people and corporations with the finances to buy land, and local people and rural communities are left on the sidelines, or even worse, pushed out of the area entirely due to lack of housing or opportunities.

Màiri McAllan, Scotland's Minister for Environment, Biodiversity and Land Reform, has said, 'We're investing heavily in nature restoration on our land and seas. But we have to do it in a way which is not, frankly, tantamount to a second Clearances.' It is not just here in the Highlands that this is happening. The National Trust in England has also been accused of kicking off tenants who have farmed the land for years for rewilding and tree planting. One land agent said, 'It feels like a re-enactment of the Highland Clearances – a land grab.'

Journalist Dani Garavelli wrote that the space port on Melness 'is a microcosm of Scotland's wider land debate. It pitches locals against incomers; the environment against the economy; preservation against progress. It raises questions about the commodification of "wilderness" and the balancing of economic, social and environmental sustainability.'

Garavelli has summed this up better than I ever could. Growing up rurally did often feel like it was 'locals against incomers', when villages filled up in the summer with people who didn't seem to understand our way of life.

It did sometimes feel like it was the 'environment against the economy' when people angrily asked foresters, 'Why are you chopping down trees?' and then in the same breath asked for logs for their log burner.

It did feel like 'preservation against progress' when planning permissions were denied for new a local business or a house because it would destroy the 'aesthetic' of the place.

And it shouldn't. We need preservation *and* progress, environment *and* economy, locals *and* incomers. It feels as though there has been a financial imbalance over the last couple of hundred years, where nature is valued but not the people who maintain it. Where owning property, or land, makes it so much easier to own more property and land. A job in a rural area is romanticised, as a way to 'get away from it all', but it's never been that. Not only is it hard work, it's erudite work, it's varied and it's often vital to the rest of the population's survival. Rural industries still provide the most basic of human needs – food, shelter, warmth. If we keep kicking our rural workers, who understand the land, off it, I'm not sure what kind of future we will have left at all.

Dorothy and I chat for a long time. We also speak about how Melness Crofters' Estate is run by volunteers, their income relying on the rents 'from their tenants' to fund other things. She tells me how the estate was given to them by the landowner, Michael Foljambe, in 1995. She describes Michael as a friendly presence in the community when he was visiting, a landowner who genuinely knew everyone and used to pop in to see people for a cup of tea or a dram. When he owned Melness, Dorothy's father was the grazings clerk (he dealt with admin for the crofters as a whole) and Mr Foljambe went to see him one day. He talked about getting older and was interested in the community takeover that had happened in Assynt just a few years before. He had no children, just cousins to leave the estate to. Dorothy says, 'They had a big meeting, it was a big community back then, and we all agreed. We'd take it on.' The trust on Assynt helped them and gave them advice on how to run it. 'No one makes a profit, you see,' Dorothy says.

Without Mr Foljambe's kindness and a desire to see the land held by local people, Melness Crofters' Estate would be something else entirely. There was no way they could have afforded to buy it if it came on the open market. Are we always to rely on rich men doing the right thing?

'He was very –' she pauses '– forward-thinking, shall we say.'

After our conversation, I read Mr Foljambe's obituary on the Melness website. He only died in 2021, and I was amazed to read that the other estate he owned was Osberton, Worksop, Nottinghamshire.

The estate my dad grew up on. Grandad was the head forester at Osberton, and Dad remembers Mr Foljambe popping in now and then for that cup of tea (or maybe a dram). And when Dad was at university studying geology, Mr Foljambe gave him a fossil he had lying around in his cellar. It was the mouth of an ichthyosaur, or the first seven inches of it – the whole aquatic dinosaur would have been two or three metres long. The teeth are as sharp and pointed as they were 60 million years ago and the fossil now sits proudly on my bookcase. Whether he was giving away land or dinosaurs,

it seems Mr Foljambe was a generous man indeed. I think he understood the importance of rural workers living on rural land. I may not have drunk a dram with him, but I reckon he'd be quite excited about the idea of firing rockets into space.

11

Our Land

We are on the way to the island of Eigg for a few days away. It's quite a complicated feat. Phil and I are in our car with Rory, and my parents are driving Jessie and Ellis in theirs. We are leaving the cars at Mallaig, the harbour on the mainland where the ferry goes from. Visitors are not allowed to take vehicles over so we have brought three bikes on the roof rack and will hire two more for my parents. Mum and Dad have not cycled for years and Dad's new knee is a worry. He is often still sore and limps. I cross my fingers for dry weather at least. I worry I have expected too much of everyone and hope we can actually get around and see some of the island that made history 25 years ago when the locals became their own landlords.

We reach the ferry port laden with bags carrying everything we need, and pushing the bikes and the buggy. It is sleeting. The island's shop emailed, instructing us to bring our own bread. They haven't had a delivery for a few days, so I nip into the Co-op for some loaves. Dad asks if there is a pub on the island (there is not), I worry we might run out of nappies and Phil thinks about buying more beer. But we can't carry anything else. We traipse into the belly of the ferry and dump our bags.

The Isle of Eigg has been cemented into Scottish history as the first island community buyout. Assynt community buyout had already taken place (through donations) in 1993, and Melness two years later (as a gift from the landowner) in 1995, but Eigg wasn't bought until 1997. So why is it so celebrated? Well, the Trust that was set up on Eigg was conceived in 1991 – the people involved in this, their ideas and their passions, all went into the success of Assynt and Melness too. Allan MacRae of the Assynt Crofters' Trust later said that the 'seed of inspiration' was from Eigg.

Essentially, the people who lived on Eigg had had enough of not knowing who would own their land and their homes next. After a series of landlords who neglected housing, used the island as a holiday home and ultimately made life for the residents very precarious, they decided enough was enough. The trust was set up along with the Scottish Wildlife Trust and the Highland Council to buy the island themselves. Donations came in from far and wide; one person, still anonymous to this day, donated £750,000. It captured the attention of the world's media, and it's not hard to see why. The island, at just 12 square miles, is the stuff of Scottish postcards with white sandy beaches and dramatic cliffs. The estate agent described the islands on the West Coast of Scotland, Eigg being one of them, as 'Van Goghs' – collectable jewels in a wealthy client's crown. It seems it didn't matter that people actually lived there.

The deal was finally sealed in June 1997 when the islanders purchased it for £1.5 million from the owner, a self-proclaimed German professor and artist 'Maruma', who had bought it only a year previously. History was made and since then, the story of Eigg has inspired other community buyouts. In the words of Linsay Chalmers, development manager at Community Land Scotland, 'They quickly demonstrated what can be achieved when a community owns its land and has control over its own destiny.'

We are staying in the small settlement of Cleadale, which is nearly four miles from the harbour. We clamber off the ferry, pulling and pushing all our baggage. Mum, Dad and the kids get picked up by Charlie, the one minibus driver on the island, and Phil, Ellis and I set off on our bikes. Straight off out of the harbour, it turns out to be one long, bendy hill and I struggle immediately. We cycle past camping pods, old white cottages and wooden bothies with huge glass windows dotted about the hillside. Sheep lie half on the grass, half on the tarmac, their stomachs rounded, almost ready to lamb. The lambs come so much later this far north. The hill is never-ending, and I have to get off and push the bike up some of the way. The views over the top to the mainland are stunning and I nearly drop my phone down a cattlegrid trying to film while cycling. My knees burn but the freedom is wonderful. Ellis is just ahead of me, but we can't see Phil anymore; he has shot ahead, used to cycling these kinds of hills.

We cycle past the primary school, which currently has seven kids enrolled. Its playground and garden have a vegetable patch and a play area. We pass the old post office and shop, which is now a museum, its door unlocked. Later on in the week, I spend a while

reading all the information inside the museum: stories from old residents about the way of life, information on the geology. There are exhibits made by the school kids on climate change and the plastic waste that washes up on the shores. The other half of the old wooden shop is a swap shop – a jumble sale of books, games, toys and clothes that the islanders don't need anymore. Anyone is welcome to pick something up if they need to.

We pass a simple green shed, which we learn later is the only cooperative brewery in Scotland. The beer is very good.

And then we start to go downhill to the collection of houses in Cleadale. We cycle past a small Sitka spruce woodland. 'It should never have been planted here,' Dad complains later. It's the wrong place for it, planted as a tax break when, in the 1970s, the rich could buy land to plant trees to offset their high tax rates. Later on, in the museum, we read that when the current woodland is harvested, a more natural one will be planted, with species of trees that do belong here, such as hazel.

Suddenly, on the horizon, the mountains of Rum, the second Small Hebridean Island in this cluster, announces itself like a key change in a song. Rum looks like it could've been the film location for *Jurassic Park*; its huge, craggy mountains rise from the sea and tower above it, pure rock – jagged, crumbling, sharp. As we start to freewheel down the hill, we can just see the white strip of sand from Laig Beach. The road hairpins once and then we are at the bottom of Cleadale. This is the most fertile land on the island and where most of the crofters currently live. We reach the gate of the house we are staying in, out of breath and red in the cheeks but exhilarated. Jessie is running around the garden. 'There are chickens and rabbits! Come, look!' Mum has put the kettle on already.

Eigg has a rich and complicated history. People have been living on it for thousands of years. After clan rule ended in 1828, there followed a long line of lairds and landowners. The island was bought and sold so many times by so many different personalities, it reads like a novel or a play. Its owners include a surgeon in the Indian

Medical Service, an international arms dealer, a shipping magnate and an Olympic bobsleigher. Like all land, sometimes it was in the hands of people who cared for and looked after it. Sometimes it was abandoned and left to ruin.

Eigg's population has swelled and contracted many times, but the highest reported population in 1841 was 546 people. By the mid-eighteenth century, it had started to fall. Families either left of their own accord (due to famine, or in search of better prospects) or were forced to leave during the Highland Clearances. On Rum, the island we can see so clearly from our windows here, 400 people were sent to America and Canada, literally rounded up off their own land and onto the waiting ships to cross the Atlantic. They had no homes left, no way to make a living, and America was the only option. On the island of Benbecula, the Clearances were so barbaric that crofters were 'hunted down with dogs' if they were unwilling to go onto the ships. The landowners cleared the land so effectively, there was hardly anyone left. Families reached the other side of the Atlantic malnourished and dressed only in rags. It's a wonder anyone survived the passage across, but some clearly did. The Highlands and Islands often have Americans and Canadians with Scottish roots travelling back to see where 'home' might have been.

On Eigg, in 1852, 14 families from the Grulin townships were shipped off to America. Three crofting families were able to stay but moved from the rich land of Grulin to the Cleadale area to stay with family. One girl never recovered from these evictions and threw herself in the sea from the cliffs. I think of her as we walk to the beach one day, the waves crashing against the caves beneath. In Camille Dressler's book *Eigg, The Story of an Island*, she writes of the Clearances that, 'In the Grulin area, houses were plundered for their stones to build a wall for the sheep farm until all but one remained intact, kept for the shepherd, one solitary house in a ghost village.' The Highland Clearances not only destroyed populations in these areas; they decimated centuries of culture.

Eigg's record lowest population was just 39 people in the 1960s under naval commander Bernard Farnham-Smith, who by the end of his time as laird had stopped the free milk and coal that came with estate jobs and kept the community hall locked. After him, the island was then bought in 1975 by Keith Schellenberg, a successful car dealer and power-boat racer. One resident likened him to Mr Toad. 'Keith actually wears those round goggles and he's always arriving in places with a lot of noise and clouds of dust.'

Initially, Schellenberg had grand ideas for the island and he invited people to move to Eigg to contribute to its community. The late Seventies saw the population rise to 60. There was a tearoom and a craft centre, and the school roll rose to 12. But it was a short-lived golden age. Schellenberg was temperamental. He evicted people from houses when he felt like it, or simply 'froze' them out, banning the residents from felling firewood. Some houses were left with only polythene on their windows, Schellenberg unwilling to maintain and repair them.

Dressler notes, 'One person would be in a tied cottage, the other would have to make do with a caravan to house his family, even though both worked for the estate.' One resident stated, 'People relied on him for so much. He owned the houses, he owned the shop, he owned the hall. I remember thinking, "Well, he doesn't own me."'

The conditions of the houses were terrible. The charity Shelter surveyed the accommodation in the Eighties and found it downright hazardous to people's health – some had no running water. Eigg was declared a housing action area and grants were made available for improvements. Unfortunately, the grants were only available to people with secure leases, rendering them useless here as so few people were granted them. In the early 1990s, a friend of Schellenberg's wife, Liz Lyon, saw how bad the conditions were when she witnessed an 80-year-old widow in a house that was literally falling in around her. She persuaded Schellenberg to offer the widow an empty house in Cleadale. But this wasn't enough to satisfy Liz Lyon. She was so appalled at the state of the housing that she spoke to Tom Forsyth, a crofter who had been working at the regeneration of crofting in his local area of Scoraig on the mainland. Tom and Liz (along with a Borders farmer, Robert Harris, who had experience in community affairs, and Alastair McIntosh, who was an academic) launched the Isle of Eigg Trust in 1991. Their aim was to 'remove Eigg in perpetuity from private ownership and provide a novel approach in landownership'. It would be some years before they would have the chance to buy the island, but this trust was important; it was the beginning of land reform in Scotland and would change the way land is bought and sold forever.

In the mid-Nineties, the trust had a chance like never before. Schellenberg was forced to sell due to an acrimonious split from his third wife. Without the islanders' knowledge Eigg was sold to

'Maruma', the German artist and self-styled 'professor', but, as he was gradually uncovered as a fake with little money behind him, the island went up for sale again in 1996 for the total sum of £2 million. The trust began raising attention for their cause. Donations began flowing in; fundraising concerts took place in Scotland and further afield. At one point, it was rumoured that Italian opera singer Luciano Pavarotti was interested in buying it.

Then, finally, after years of insecurity, absent landlords, unfeeling landlords, difficult landlords, the Isle of Eigg Trust bought the island for £1.5 million on 4 April 1997. There are now around 110 people living on it. You can still buy a house here – a small bothy was sold by the trust recently, but they take great pains to state that they will not necessarily take the highest price, and will only sell it to someone who will be an 'active member of the community'. The house was also 'subject to a Rural Housing Burden, which means it cannot be used as a holiday or second home, must be used in perpetuity as a primary full-time residence'.

The island has its own renewable energy, which is community owned, managed and maintained. Eigg Electric comes from all three sources – water, sun and wind – and provides power 24 hours a day. They have built more houses, improved older, less efficient homes and are still hoping to build more. Businesses are flourishing. There is a record label on the island. The brewery is going from strength to strength. With widespread and speedy internet, I guess many kinds of companies could be run here. Certainly, there are more opportunities than a hundred years ago. The population is stable and, unsurprisingly, people come from all around the world to visit it.

Alastair McIntosh, who helped the island to form the trust, said, 'It's not about just wanting to be landowners, it's about the community having life and individuals having life within that community. In Scotland, we spit the word out – "property". You can't own the land; the land owns you.'

Every day we come back from the beach with wet clothes. Ellis and Jessie cannot resist the water, no matter how cold the wind is. They start by paddling in their wellies and boots but then kick them off in the sand and get wet from the knees down. A dead seal, eyes hollowed out by flies and whatever else, rests at the top of the beach. Jessie is fascinated by it and brings us back to it again and again. It looks like a fishing rope is wrapped around its tail but the carcass is so covered in sand we can't quite tell if the rope is just part of the flotsam and jetsam of the beach or not. The sand is soft and white at the dry edges. Rory's socks fall off repeatedly and I place his tiny toes on the sand. He frowns, an expression so comical on a baby we all coo and laugh.

Mum and Dad cycle once or twice on the road but going uphill is hard work and going down is, admittedly, terrifying. But thankfully the two best beaches, Laig and the Singing Sands, are only a short walk from the house. Mainly, we sit on the rocks and watch the kids in the water, shaking our heads at the pure joy and madness the sea water instils in them. They run with the waves, in and out

towards the mountains of Rum in the distance and then back to us. The tide pushes us back further and further up the beach and, finally, the children admit defeat and come back to us shivering. Mum gives Jessie her jumper because she is wet from head to toe. She wears it like a dress.

One evening we walk down to the beach at sunset and Ellis takes photo after photo of the changing colours of the sky and the clouds. The orange of the sun deepens to the red-hot embers of a fire. He has never seen a sunset like it. I tell him about one of my favourite poems, by Carol Ann Duffy, 'Away and See', which describes the sun sinking into the sea.

I'm thankful he's not quite at the stage yet where he'll roll his eyes when I talk about poetry. I know it won't be long. The rabbits run like ribbons flapping in the wind in the field above the sands.

Tourism is one of the main incomes on the island now, just like in most rural places. We are part of the first wave of visitors of the year to come, and in some ways, we can feel it. Everyone always smiles when they pass us on the road, but there is a slight feeling of, oh, here we go again. In the shop or in the queue for the ferry, we feel a little … in the way, shall we say. And I understand that. The shop, the hills, the roads, the beaches: they aren't really 'their own' anymore when the tourists start coming. People who live in beautiful places such as the Lakes, Wales, the Highlands have all said, sheepishly but truthfully, how wonderful lockdown was. Their land was their own for the first time in years.

Rural people often share the warmer months with people who don't understand their way of life – who use it as a playground and are not always respectful of that environment. Everyone should be given the chance to experience these places – and we know we need tourists; livelihoods depend on people coming over to experience a slice of this life. But sometimes, it's nice to have the place you call home to yourself.

After our five days on Eigg, we drop the bikes we have rented back off at the harbour and we chat to Owain who runs the bike and kayak hire. He says we should stick around for the first ceilidh of the season on Saturday, but we need to get home. There has been an excellent music scene on the island for many years now. The parties and ceilidhs are legendary. The ceilidh after the community buyout lasted days.

Owain tells us about the building work going on behind him – they have nearly completed a new community hub at the harbour. There will be new premises for the shop, a café, a play area for the kids. And Owain and his bikes and kayaks will have new premises too. He says we should come back when it's done. Have a pint.

Then Charlie, the minibus driver, meets us at the harbour and Mum and Dad climb out with Rory. Dad realises he's left his walking stick with the forked antler by the front door of the house. 'You'll have to come back for it,' Charlie says. I guess we will now.

There are now 562,000 acres of land, which is 2.9 per cent of the total land area of Scotland, in community ownership. The Scottish government passed the Land Reform Act in 2003, which enshrined in law the 'right to roam' and also introduced the community 'right to buy'. Communities can now apply for up to £1 million in grants to help take ownership of land and buildings. This is a good start, but with the price of land rising every month, it's getting harder and harder to raise the funds needed to purchase anything.

Whereas the community buyout in Scotland is now firmly established, in England things work slightly differently. There are 'community buyouts' but they tend to be for smaller businesses such as shops, pubs or football clubs. In England, there are also community land trusts (CLTs), through which people can develop land for the benefit of a community. They generally provide permanently and genuinely affordable homes and community gardens. There are currently over 500 community land trusts in place with over a thousand homes built. Having the community front and centre in making decisions is becoming more widespread. And whichever document or website you read about community and land, whether it is in England or Scotland or UK wide, one word pops up again and again: stewardship. The act of taking care of or managing something. So much hangs off this term. The word 'steward' first appeared in the Middle Ages, meaning the manager of a household. 'A steward is someone who has the responsibility for looking after property.' You don't own the house, but you look after it. Maybe if more of us had a chance to be stewards of the land, we'd look after it a bit better than we do now.

It's my birthday tomorrow and we are all in Tom's woods again. The sun has warmed the air enough to take our big coats off, but only while you are moving about. It is cold when you sit down for a few minutes. Tom lit the bonfire a few hours ago. He has been waiting to burn some of the brash off one of the wind-blown trees from the storm last November. Storm Arwen floored woods all across the country. It was the direction of the wind, everyone kept saying. So unusual. By Esthwaite Water, on the way to Hawkshead, the wind simply pushed a bank of larch down like old bottles. They lay among the orange needles on the floor, the aftermath of a good party. This image is replicated in forests everywhere.

A number of trees fell in Tom's wood. He had to leave the woods in the dark of the night, for fear a tree would fall on the cabin and crush it. It was the first time in years he'd slept at our parents' house. He was lucky – a veteran oak fell a few metres away from his front door, onto his apple trees and over the well he'd dug, but it missed the cabin by a few feet. Foresters say they have years' worth of work just clearing up after Arwen. Today, the thin, spiny branches of the oak that won't do for firewood or carving spit and sizzle in the fire. The massive trunk of the oak lies like a fallen giant behind us. It looks like an art installation, its branches, which once reached up to the sky, claw into the earth like a hand. Ellis climbs up and walks along the thick arm of the horizontal trunk.

The ashes of the fire are already burnt so low it's too hot to stand near. Lesley arrives a little later than us. She was unhooked from chemo only a few days ago and is a little woozy. She has chemo every two weeks, and some rounds are good enough to let her come to the woods for a few days. When she is here, they carve, paint, garden and plant saplings. It seems to give her more energy, being here.

There are huge patches of frogspawn in the watercourse Tom has dug. He is victorious and pleased as punch. By creating this environment for them, it is like they have accepted an invitation to a well-planned party. We put burgers and sausages on the low embers and watch them burn. Lesley paints Jessie's nails and Mum throws the ball for Tom's dog, Oscar. Dad's sister Lin and I drink Prosecco. And I marvel at the fact that we own this land now. How crazy is that?

Firstly, my parents bought a house.

When I was 20 and away at university, Dad turned 50 and Mum figured, well, if they wanted to stop renting, time was running out.

Banks didn't hand out mortgages to people set to retire soon. They used all their savings and found a three-bedroom terraced house in the nearest market town of Ulverston. It wasn't surrounded by fields, by deer rutting in autumn, by trees in the garden you could hang a rope swing on. It didn't even have a garden, just a backyard, a thin strip of paving stones with a washing line slung above them. But, through the other houses, it had a view of the local hill. It had the original tiles in the hallway, Victorian coffee brown and lapis blue. The house had a nice feel to it, the gas fire was easy to light and it was theirs.

My parents are baby boomers, but only in age. I could never work out why most people of that generation had expensive holidays and were living mortgage free by their late fifties. Then I realised. It was because we had lived in tied accommodation for so long. Mum and Dad have not benefited from the things that normally go alongside the baby-boomer definition. Dad had a free education but the hike in house prices from the Eighties was only advantageous if you had the option of selling and buying. The baby boomers are said to have had more secure jobs and better pensions. But for my parents, there were no decent pensions. In some ways, my parents have had the same issues that my generation has. Low wages, difficulty buying houses and a lack of security. But they've nearly caught up with their peer group. For the first time ever, they have a house that can't be taken from them. Finally, just last year in fact, at Dad's age of 65, they paid off their mortgage.

Then came the land.

We have been visiting Tom's woods since we were young. They are part of a bigger woodland that Dad has managed since he became self-employed. Dad has thinned these woods and introduced more species, which has benefited the wildlife over 20 years, all the while making the landowner a bit of money. When Tom finished university, he took over the role of managing this woodland, and asked the landowner if, instead of money, could he get paid in timber? She agreed. First, he brought in a small caravan and kept it there, sleeping in it occasionally. Then he built a small cabin, had chickens and started to carve wood with the chainsaw. When the landowner died (she was a lovely old lady) the woods went to her son. He wanted to sell them, all 300 acres of them. Tom was scuppered. He couldn't afford that; it would amount to hundreds of thousands of pounds. He would need to leave.

But one night, Mum called me.

'The son's offered us a small bit of the woods. Eight acres.'

'How much?'

'Market value. Which will probably be about twenty grand.'

'But Tom can't afford that. Can he?'

No, he couldn't. But Mum could.

Dad said later, 'You could have knocked me over with a feather when your mum told me we could afford that wood.'

They could only afford it as Mum took out the money she had in her small private pension. It made more sense to use the money for this than to live off it later in life. My parents will never retire, not properly anyway. Dad believes he'll die in the woods, like an old forester he knew from childhood. The man just sat down against a tree one day to have his lunch and never got up again. He was found a few weeks later by a walker.

The eight acres they bought were a mile or so down from where Tom was originally based. The site bordered the edge of the wood, the next-door farmer's field and the single-track road in. We paid the market value for it, but it still felt like a kindness. The landowner didn't have to cordon off those eight acres for Tom. It would have been easier to sell the land as one big block. We are grateful he didn't. Tom carried all his carvings to his new plot, took down the cabin, one plank at a time, and rebuilt a better one in his new space. It gave him the chance to really plan it all. He built store houses for the logs to dry at the top of the wood, where his carving workshop is situated. There are wooden tiki men, totem poles, four-foot chess pieces and elegant hares looking up to the moon dotted around the forest. There are also a Gruffalo and a panda peeking through the leaves. When we visit, we park and walk up the rough road, which is too rough for our suburban cars, and Oscar the dog bounds down the path to greet us.

Is it odd, owning land? I ask Tom. He thinks a while and says it doesn't matter too much that he owns it. 'I look after this patch of land like a nature reserve. Personally, it doesn't matter too much in terms of stewardship. But I am now much more secure. Before, I just had a verbal contract. But now I can plan for the long term. The ownership of it means it gives me the security. And the control.'

Tom's woods have always been used for forestry operations. He tells me they were intensively managed until the First World War, for hazel, charcoal and coppicing. Bill Hogarth, who was integral in protecting the practice and heritage of coppicing throughout the UK, also lived in the woods here. At one point, Bill was the only coppice merchant left in the Lakes. He made hundreds of different coppice products, including hedging stakes, barrel hoops, walking sticks and hurdles, and was an important source of knowledge on the vanishing practice. The Bill Hogarth Memorial Apprentice Trust was set up to pass on his skills and expertise, and it still teaches people today about coppicing.

Tom talks about a plan for the future and, like the patronising big sister I am, I'm surprised. I didn't realise he might have a plan. 'I'd love to teach people to live like this. I live on eight acres and can make a living. Although,' he acknowledges, 'you can't really support a family.'

So many woodlands like the one Tom owns are not managed. If they were, we could support a much more diverse range of plant species and wildlife and a better connection to the land ourselves. 'With the right training, you can live off a plot like this.' Tom has solar panels, which provide power to the lights and his laptop. He brings in water and food from the village, stocking up when he goes shopping every few days. There is no toilet, but he has rigged up a shower system using rainwater and sometimes just takes a dip in the well he dug in front of the cabin. The water there is as fresh as it gets. He makes money by providing firewood and creating carvings for people. He has his own tree nursery, caring for the saplings until they are big enough to sell. It is a lifestyle that is difficult to imagine and it is not for everyone. But it is for him.

Do you need to buy the land, I ask him, to make it work?

'No, being a tenant is a perfect way to get into it. That's what I did.' Owning it means he can apply for liability insurance, which makes bringing people in – whether it is to teach carving or to teach sustainable forest management – possible. They had students in from a nearby university to study the pine martens that they think live there too.

He laughs when I ask him if growing up in the environment we did, on Graythwaite Estate, made him want to live like this. 'Of course … I literally play in the woods like we did when we were kids.' Tom has been to university to study ecology and has been around the world taking study groups in Costa Rica, Romania and Cambodia. I know there is more to this than just 'playing in the woods', but sometimes, when I see him with a spade, knee deep in a pool of clay and mud, he looks just like the 10-year-old kid from the estate.

The wonderful writer Anna Pavord writes in the introduction to her book *Landskipping*:

Roots, if you are lucky enough to have them, still have an influence on the way you respond. That landscape, which I knew so closely, predisposed me to feel a connection with certain landscapes later on. This isn't an unusual trait, this almost animal response to a new place. Do you feel comfortable here? Could you be sustained by this view?

Tom has never really lost his roots. He knows the landscape he has a connection to. He doesn't want a big car, a fancy house or a big TV. He doesn't go on holiday. He really is 'sustained' by the woods. And I find it interesting that it also sustains Lesley, who grew up in a mining town on the edge of a big city. But it makes no difference, really. She has found her home in the woods, alongside Tom.

Back in the woods that day on my birthday, I go for a pee on the other side of the hill. It is so quiet away from the kids, from the chatter of the adults and the fire. The birds are louder and feel incredibly close. The air feels kind of electric. I wander back slowly to the fire as we start to pack up. Lesley is staying for a few days. Tom is helping Dad this week, away all day on the other side of the Lakes planting trees and Lin asks if Lesley will be OK in the woods on her own.

'I'll be fine,' she smiles. 'The other day, it was the first day of the year when you could really feel the sun on your face. I sat outside the cabin and watched the blue tits and two hours passed. I didn't even notice. I looked at my watch and couldn't believe it.' She looks at Tom, who is standing next to me. 'Time is funny here, isn't it?'

*

At home in Scotland, I wash the clothes that smell strongly of woodsmoke and hang them on the washing line, hoping they'll dry before the rain comes. I think of Tom and Lesley in the woods. I hope Lesley is warm enough in the cabin. They have booked their wedding, after postponements due to Covid, for the end of the summer. It will be in the Town Hall in Hawkshead, the big building that sits across from the square and the Kings Arms pub. We are hoping we can all stay at the pub but we don't know who will run it at that point. Ed is long gone and the building and the business are currently up for sale. Maybe we can commandeer it ourselves. A temporary community buyout for the duration of the wedding.

Rory woke me up last night at around 2.45 a.m. He pulled me from a dream. I can't remember what happened in it, but I know I was back on the old estate in the second house we lived in. In my sleep, I am often there in the back garden, by the beck. I remember nothing else about the dream, but I know, if I think about it, I can feel the grass, feel the shade of the big trees where the death slide set off from. I have been back to the estate in real waking life a few times, but it always feels odd. It doesn't feel like mine. I couldn't sit for long or explore the dens I wanted to. I stuck to the paths. It felt like I was trespassing. I didn't feel comfortable there because it wasn't mine anymore. But it doesn't matter. I think I am rooted in some places whether we own them or not, whether I am still there or not. Maybe it's like being a dandelion. I can settle almost anywhere, as long as there is a bit of soil. I worry my kids won't have that tether to the land, but then there's still time. I hope.

Epilogue

Not long after Rory was born, they decided to blow up Longannet chimney, the last bit of the old coal-powered power station that dominated the skyline in this area.

They scheduled it for 9 a.m., so Phil took Jessie and Ellis to school while Rory and I walked up the hill behind the house. I wanted to see it happen. There were a few other people watching too, their phones out ready to record. It was cold but there was no wind. Rory was wrapped up in the sling on my front.

At nine on the dot, the tower crumpled like a tablecloth trick. The stack of bricks bent and fell to the ground, crashing and colliding in slow motion. It happened in silence, with just a few intakes of breath from the onlookers. A few seconds later, maybe as many as 10, we heard the boom of the explosion. A cloud of brick dust, laced with all sorts of dangerous particles, lingered close to the ground like mist. That was it. The last coal-fuelled power station in Scotland fully demolished. Here's to a better way of making energy. Maybe in rural areas we'll have more space ports, more renewable-energy companies, more record labels, more breweries. We need more than tourism in the countryside, that's for sure. And maybe there'll be more communities buying their own land so they can make their own decisions on how to run it. Maybe there'll be more homes built, more opportunities for families to move back to where they call home.

We nod goodbye to each other, the odd collection of people on the hill and their dogs, and I walk back home and put the kettle on.

Phil gets back from school and looks out of Ellis's window and says, 'It's like we've lost a tooth.'

Tom and Lesley had their wedding in the Town Hall in Hawkshead where we used to have the village pantomime and the jumble sales. The Kings Arms, which you could see from the Town Hall, was empty, its windows dark and its doors locked. Adam, who painted the playhouse with Tom with white gloss paint, who ran around the estate with us as kids, was there. We stood outside the Town Hall with our cans of beer and wine and looked at the mountains behind the village. 'I went to the Himalayas,' Adam said, 'and was like, "Nice." No wonder. Look what we grew up with.'

Lesley looked beautiful, luminous and free. Tom wore a suit and

trimmed his beard. They danced all night with their friends. You could not tell that the chemo had stopped working over the summer.

It is nearly December now and she has not made it back to the woods.

They asked me to read something at the wedding so I wrote this for them.

Instructions on how to build a log cabin

Step 1: Set a Good Foundation
You will know as soon as you see it that this is the place for you. You feel at home when you are present. Everything you have been looking for slots into place. All the places before fade into insignificance. The view is nice, and you are excited to get to work.

Step 2: Prepare the Logs
A chainsaw is handy at this point. This is where you start the journey of understanding how things fit alongside each other. You might find you need to adapt to the different grooves and character of the wood. Be patient, as the wood will change shape as you mill or dry it. Have snacks handy.

Step 3: Installing the Subflooring and Joist
These will be your second foundations – you will need to rely on these joists to hold you up more often than you realise. You will be spending a lot of time in here, laughing, cooking, carving and sword fighting. It is OK to leave gaps in the floorboards, but remember the mice might find it a nice place to live too.

Step 4: Log Joinery
This is the stage where you start to really understand the nitty-gritty of your log cabin. What fits where and how. What doesn't work so well. Whatever you decide to use – nails, screws or

joints – to secure the cabin, bear in mind things don't always go to plan. There will be arguments, awkward bits of wood that do not fit. There may be some injuries to extremities at this time. Remember to wear safety equipment.

Step 5: Frame the Roof

The roof is another vital element to the cabin. This will shelter you from the storm and the sun. Remember to leave some beams exposed to wrap fairy lights around them. You will require assistance to install the roof. Always ask for help when you need it. Log cabins are never built by just one person.

Step 6: Assemble the Windows and Door

When installing the windows, give yourself time to think about how far you have come. Look out of the new glass and see the birds on the feeder. When the door is installed, open it and sit on the step and listen. The sun will shine through the windows and the foxgloves will appear in the disturbed ground again. A log cabin that has been built with love and care and set on the best of foundations will stand the test of time. It will survive through the storms of winter and the weeks when there is no rain forecast.

Step 7: Have a Party

Enjoy your home. Invite the people you love most to dance and drink under the boughs of the oak tree that the last storm toppled. Look around at what you have achieved. Despite the bumps in the road, despite nature's crippling curve balls she threw at you, despite the sheer bad luck you had to wade through, you have built something beautiful. You have built a life together. Nothing anyone throws at you now can take that away.

References

Chapter 1: Land

The National Trust now looks after 300 historic houses in England alone: Information available on website: https://www.nationaltrust.org.uk/houses-and-buildings

2,000 stately homes have been demolished or ruined: Matthew Beckett, Lost Heritage: England's Lost Country houses: http://www.lostheritage.org.uk

340 sporting estates in the Highlands and Islands: Andy Wightman, *The Poor Had No Lawyers: Who Owns Scotland (And How They Got It)*, Birlinn (2015), p. 219. Also available at: http://www.andywightman.com/docs/culture_sport_society_2002.pdf

twisted and turned as a serpent and **lovelier than I had ever dreamed:** Daphne du Maurier, *Rebecca,* Virago Modern Classics (2021), pp. 71–73.

a major messenger between the Scottish Jacobites: and all following information and quotes regarding Muiravonside: Geoff Bailey, taken from the website: https://falkirklocalhistory.club/around-the-area/houses-and-estates/muiravonside-house/

report naming 93 properties: National Trust. Full report available: https://nt.global.ssl.fastly.net/documents/colonialism-and-historic-slavery-report.pdf

Everyone's thinking, you've got a house there that you live in: quoted in Jenna Watt, *Hindsight*, Birlinn (2022), p. 183.

estimated that 35 million pheasants: Information available at Game & Wildlife Conservation Trust: https://www.gwct.org.uk/research/species/birds/common-pheasant

The past was tangible: Nicola Chester, *On Gallows Down*, Chelsea Green Publishing (2022), p. 95.

The work was straightforward but the cultural practices were out of the Edwardian period: Andy Wightman, *The Poor Had No Lawyers*, Birlinn (2015), p. 219.

Chapter 2: Wood

We want ours to burn good and slow: Arthur Ransome, *Swallows and Amazons*, Puffin Books (1962), p. 147.

to cover only 15 per cent of England: *British Forests: The Forestry Commission 1919–2019*, Profile Editions (2019), p. 12.

The survival of almost any large tract of woodland: Oliver Rackham, *The History of the Countryside*, Dent Paperbacks (1987 edition), p. 91.

Between one fifth and a quarter of all settlements: Cal Flyn, *Islands of Abandonment*, William Collins (2021), p. 82.

forest cover in England was at 4 per cent: *British Forests: The Forestry Commission 1919–2019*, Profile Editions (2019), p. 12.

importing 90 per cent of its timber: *British Forests: The Forestry Commission 1919–2019*, Profile Editions (2019), p. 12.

nearly lost the war for want of timber than of anything else: David Lloyd George, widely quoted in 1919, taken from 'Forestry', Rogart Heritage: https://rogartheritage.co.uk/working-lives/forestry/

acquired over 100,000 acres: Mairi Stewart, *Voices of the Forest: A Social History of Scottish Forestry in the Twentieth Century*, Birlinn (2016), p. 39.

enclosed agricultural or cultivable land: *British Forests: The Forestry Commission 1919–2019*, Profile Editions (2019), p. 47.

more expensive business than the planting of trees: *British Forests: The Forestry Commission 1919–2019*, Profile Editions (2019), p. 48.

the disadvantages of urban life: Mairi Stewart, *Voices of the Forest*, Birlinn (2016), p. 205.

one shop and that sort of thing: Mairi Stewart, *Voices of the Forest*, Birlinn (2016), p. 214.

dump them in the middle of nowhere: Mairi Stewart, *Voices of the Forest*, Birlinn (2016), p. 216.

I would cycle two miles: Mairi Stewart, *Voices of the Forest*, Birlinn (2016), p. 183.

such societies in the UK: Mairi Stewart, *Voices of the Forest*, Birlinn (2016), pp. 48–49.

supporting children's parties: *British Forests: The Forestry Commission 1919–2019*, Profile Editions (2019), p. 49.

consumed by midges from the forests and the trees: Sir Rupert Speir, parliamentary speech (28 July 1960). Whole speech available at: https://api.parliament.uk/historic-hansard/ commons/1960/jul/28/forestry-commission-villages#column_2007

there are no trained nurses: Sir Rupert Speir, parliamentary speech (28 July 1960). Whole speech available at: https://api.parliament. uk/historic-hansard/commons/1960/jul/28/forestry-commission-villages#column_2007

It was marvellous: Mairi Stewart, *Voices of the Forest*, Birlinn (2016), p. 209.

those who would soon be retiring: Mairi Stewart, *Voices of the Forest*, Birlinn (2016), p. 210.

maintenance work getting into arrears: Mairi Stewart, *Voices of the Forest*, Birlinn (2016), p. 204.

At this point, it was the UK's biggest landowner, managing around 2.2 million acres: 'Who owns the UK?', ABC Finance Limited: https://abcfinance.co.uk/blog/who-owns-the-uk/; Scottish stats from Andy Wightman, *The Poor Had No Lawyers*, Birlinn (2015), p.256; English stats from Guy Shrubsole, 'Who owns England's Woods?', Who Owns England (2 November 2020): https://whoownsengland.org/2020/11/02/who-owns-englands-woods/

Many people think our work is timber production: 'What We Do', Forestry and Land Scotland: https://forestryandland.gov.scot/what-we-do

Chapter 3: Coal

4 million tonnes of coal per year: 'Scottish Power Accelerates Towards Net Zero with Demolition of Chimney at Longannet, Scotland's Last Coal-Fired Power Station', Scottish Power media centre (9 December 2021): https://www.scottishpower.com/news/pages/scottishpower_accelerates_towards_net_zero_with_demolition_of_chimney_at_longannet_scotlands_last_coal_fired_power_station.aspx

Scotland's biggest polluter: survey completed by SEPA: 'Watchdog names worst polluting factories', *Herald* (2 June 2003): https://www.heraldscotland.com/news/11985046.watchdog-names-worst-polluting-factories/

piped to nearby Preston Island in the Firth of Forth: some places say 4,500 tonnes of ash a year but there is nothing to confirm this apart from this information from Scottish Power, which states: 'Valleyfield Lagoons are used for the storage and disposal of pulverised fuel ash created during the combustion of coal at Longannet Power Station.' Longannet Power Station: Biodiversity Information: https://www.scottishpower.com/userfiles/file/Longannet-Bioversity-2014.pdf

an Egyptian water wheel: 'George Bruce: Engineering Achievements', Scottish Engineering Hall of Fame: https://engineeringhalloffame.org/profile/george-bruce

He became a piece of mining equipment: T. C. Smout, *A History of the Scottish People*, 1560–1830, Collins (1969), p. 180.

They had privileges which slaves have not: T. C. Smout, *A History of the Scottish People*, 1560–1830, Collins (1969), p. 432.

state of slavery and bondage: more information available from the Scottish Mining Website, which has published a speech entitled 'Slavery in the coal mines of Scotland' by James Barrowman, a mining engineer (1897), which was presented at the Annual General Meeting of the Federated Institution of Mining Engineers, 14 September 1897: http://www.scottishmining.co.uk/429.html

steam rising from the floor: 'Notes on Miners' Houses Part IV', Scottish Mining Website: http://www.scottishmining.co.uk/403.html

during the night the people, while in bed, hear the miners blasting underneath: 'Notes on Miners' Houses Part XIII', Scottish Mining Website: http://www.scottishmining.co.uk/414.html

If the dreams of some social reformers are true: from the letter published in 'The Worst Village in England', *Christian Budget* (8 November 1899), Conisbrough & Denaby Main Local History: https://conisbroughanddenabyhistory.org.uk/article/the-worst-village-in-england-2/

good and well-managed football club: J. F.'s response in the *Mexborough & Denaby Times* (24 November 1899), Conisbrough & Denaby Main Local History: https://conisbroughanddenabyhistory.org.uk/article/the-worst-village-in-england-certainly-not/

In the absence of a benevolent coal owner: Catherine Bailey, *Black Diamonds*, Penguin (2007), p. 80.

For the sake of the wives and children: Catherine Bailey, *Black Diamonds*, Penguin (2007), p. 79.

'e carn't hurt ya, 'e's dead: Catherine Bailey, *Black Diamonds*, Penguin (2007), p. 6.

In 1878, the *Evening Telegraph* in Scotland: from various newspaper articles all found on the Scottish Mining Website: http://scottishmining.co.uk/488.html

large parts of the village had to be evacuated: Melvyn Jones, *South Yorkshire Mining Villages: A History of the Region's Former Coalmining Communities*, Pen & Sword History (2017), p. 114.

soaked to the skin: taken from newspaper articles at the time, available on Conisbrough & Denaby Main Heritage Group: https://www.conisbroughheritage.com/bag-muck-strike

one of the most determined contests between capital and labour: Melvyn Jones, *South Yorkshire Mining Villages: A History of the Region's Former Coalmining Communities*, Pen & Sword History (2017), p. 24.

Armed with pistols, some with bludgeons: Melvyn Jones, *South Yorkshire Mining Villages: A History of the Region's Former Coalmining Communities*, Pen & Sword History (2017), p. 26.

85,000 men were killed: statistic widely available. Taken from 'Mining accidents and safety', Mining Institute website (January 2016): https://mininginstitute.org.uk/wp-content/uploads/2016/02/Mining-accidents-and-safety-Jan16.pdf

Senghenydd in Glamorgan in 1913: 'Senghenydd, Glamorgan', National Archives: https://www.nationalarchives.gov.uk/pathways/census/pandp/places/seng.htm

Cresswell pit disaster: 'Prologue: The Cresswell Colliery Disaster', Mining Heritage: https://miningheritage.co.uk/the-1950-creswell-colliery-disaster-seventy-years-on/

Grandad Edward worked as a 'ripper': information on jobs available at: http://www.healeyhero.co.uk/rescue/glossary/glossary.htm#R

Bevin Boys were picked out of a hat: information taken from 'Remembering the Bevin Boys in the Second World War', Museum of Wales, but widely available: https://museum.wales/articles/1020/Remembering-the-Bevin-Boys-in-the-Second-World-War/

Women as well as children worked in British pits until 1842: information taken from 'Women in Mining – Then & Now', MRS Training & Rescue (formally Mines Rescue service) (25 February 2021), but widely available: https://www.mrsl.co.uk/news/women-mining-then-now

I draw with the ropes and chain: Elizabeth Dickson, from the report by R. F. Franks to the Children's Employment Commission on the East of Scotland District published in 1842, available (along with many more shocking ones) on the Scottish Mining Website: http://www.scottishmining.co.uk/257.html

Redding pit disaster: all information available on the Scottish Mining Website: http://scottishmining.co.uk/240.html

Chapter 4: Water

It took over 3,000 men: Norman Hoyle and Kenneth Sankey, *Thirlmere Water: A Hundred Miles, A Hundred Years*, Centwrite (1994), p. 38.

effective and economical dams anywhere: Norman Hoyle and Kenneth Sankey, *Thirlmere Water: A Hundred Miles, A Hundred Years*, Centwrite (1994), p. 23.

at a speed of 2 miles an hour: Norman Hoyle and Kenneth Sankey, *Thirlmere Water: A Hundred Miles, A Hundred Years*, Centwrite (1994), p. 29.

enhance its natural beauty: Harriet Ritvo, *The Dawn of Green: Manchester, Thirlmere, and Modern Environmentalism*, University of Chicago Press (2009), p. 5.

The deeper opposition to the Thirlmere Scheme: Harriet Ritvo, *The Dawn of Green: Manchester, Thirlmere, and Modern Environmentalism*, University of Chicago Press (2009), p. 104.

should be put at the bottom of the Lake of Thirlmere: John Ruskin, quoted in Harriet Ritvo's *The Dawn of Green: Manchester, Thirlmere, and Modern Environmentalism*, University of Chicago Press (2009), p. 88.

Apart from living apart in their own communities: Dick Sullivan, *Navvyman*, Coracle Books (1983), p. 55–6.

They could shift up to 20 tonnes of muck: Dick Sullivan, *Navvyman*, Coracle Books (1983), p. 57.

The huts themselves were bleak and bare: Alen McFadzean, *Wythburn Mine and the Lead Miners of Helvellyn*, Red Earth (1987), p. 50.

They lived the best they could in their cramped and squalid conditions: Ian Taylor, *Thirlmere Mines and the Drowning of a Valley*, Blue Rock Publications (2005), p. 166.

stood the same chance of being killed as an infantryman in the Boer War: Dick Sullivan, *Navvyman*, Coracle Books (1983), p. 34.

the deaths of six men and one woman: Alen McFadzean, *Wythburn Mine and the Lead Miners of Helvellyn*, Red Earth (1987), p. 51.

'clean green power' to provide electricity: 'SIMEC Highland hydro station produces enough energy to power a city the size of Inverness', SIMEC (20 April 2020): http://www.simec.com/news/ simec-highland-hydro-station-produces-enough-energy-to-power-a- city-the-size-of-inverness/

held around 1,000 men, including German and Belgian: C. Herbert, Highland Historic Environment Record, Highland Council (2004). ID 18243: https://her.highland.gov.uk/ monument/MHG27947

While looking after sheep a shepherd: Patrick MacGill, *Children of the Dead End,* Lightning Source UK Ltd (1913), p. 158.

escape the Glasgow police: Guthrie Hutton, *Old Kinlochleven and the Highland Aluminon Industry* (2012), p. 12, booklet available at Kinlochleven Post Office.

Navvies were well known for 'hard work all week': Francis John Taylor, 'Scottish Navy Mission' (1908), published in *Life and Work: The Magazine of the Church of Scotland*: https://www.lifeandwork.org/features/looking-back-scottish-navvy-mission

The English mounted a full-scale attack: Dick Sullivan, *Navvyman*, Coracle Books (1983), p. 129.

impact on a tranquil rural population: Dick Sullivan, *Navvyman*, Coracle Books (1983), p. 91.

in the northern section on one year alone was 681: Ian Taylor, *Thirlmere Mines and the Drowning of a Valley*, Blue Rock Publications (2005), p. 165.

Chapter 5: Food

I want the assurance that I will not be evicted: Andy Wightman, *The Poor Had No Lawyers*, Birlinn (2015), p. 234.

the National Trust that is one of the nation's largest farm owners: facts and figures taken from the National Trust website: https://www.nationaltrust.org.uk/features/information-to-journalists

A croft is a small agricultural unit: 'About Crofting', Scottish Crofting Federation: https://www.crofting.org/about-scf/about-crofting/

The crofting system of the Highlands is borne forward: John McPhee, *The Crofter and the Laird*, Daunt Books (1969), p. 124.

no concern being shown for the impact: John MacKenzie, 'The Realisation of the Dream', Assynt Crofters' Trust (1998). All information and a thorough history on the Assynt Crofters' Trust website: http://www.theassyntcrofters.co.uk/history/

By the year 2000, 144,000 acres of land were in community ownership: Andy Wightman, *The Poor Had No Lawyers*, Birlinn (2015), p. 199.

The big thing that we have done is survived: quoted in 'The Assynt Crofters who shook up history 25 years ago', *Scotsman* (9 July 2018): https://www.scotsman.com/arts-and-culture/assynt-crofters-who-shook-history-25-years-ago-277552

I think that it can be fairly said that the pattern of land ownership: John MacKenzie's opening address at the 25th Anniversary Celebrations of Assynt Crofters (July 2018), available on the Assynt Crofters' Trust website: http://www.theassyntcrofters.co.uk/25th-anniversary-speeches/key-speeches-from-the-events/

Chapter 6: Slate

insert wooden wedges into natural cracks in the slate: Mary Withall, *Easdale, Belnahua, Luing and Seil: The Islands that Roofed the World*, Luath Press (2001), p. 14.

19 million slates were being exported annually: Mary Withall, *Easdale, Belnahua, Luing and Seil: The Islands that Roofed the World*, Luath Press (2001), p. viii.

Women and children carried the slate on their backs: Mary Withall, *Easdale, Belnahua, Luing and Seil: The Islands that Roofed the World*, Luath Press (2001), p. 8.

The roof space, although hardly high enough for a man to stand upright at the centre: Mary Withall, *Easdale, Belnahua, Luing and Seil: The Islands that Roofed the World*, Luath Press (2001), p. 22.

Children at the school had to bring a piece of coal: Mary Withall, *Easdale, Belnahua, Luing and Seil: The Islands that Roofed the World*, Luath Press (2001), p. 54.

In this crude shelter: Mary Withall, *Easdale, Belnahua, Luing and Seil: The Islands that Roofed the World*, Luath Press (2001), p. 16.

tidal wave that swamped most of the quarries: Mary Withall, *Easdale, Belnahua, Luing and Seil: The Islands that Roofed the World*, Luath Press (2001), p. 10.

step lightly on the growing plants: Mary Withall, *Easdale, Belnahua, Luing and Seil: The Islands that Roofed the World*, Luath Press (2001), p. 52.

153 kinds of lichen: facts from 'Conserving and Investigating Coniston', Lake District National Park, Archaeology Information: https://www.lakedistrict.gov.uk/learning/archaeologyhistory/coniston-copper/conserving-coniston

He gave out winter clothing to his workers: for facts and figures and more information go to 'Miners and the mining community', Lake District National Park: https://www.lakedistrict.gov.uk/learning/archaeologyhistory/coniston-copper/history-of-coniston-copper/miners-and-the-mining-community2

chance to explore the fascination of the fells: from the Coppermines Lakes Cottages website: https://www.coppermines.co.uk/accommodation/the-coppermines-mountain-cottages-sawyers-carpenters-pelton-wheel-sleeps-18

It started with a dozen of us: interview with Steely D, Simon Doherty, 'The Legendary "Cave Raves" of the Acid House Era', *VICE* (16 October 2018): https://www.vice.com/en/article/vbkn4y/the-legendary-cave-raves-of-the-acid-house-era

We needed some light so we could see the sheep: comments on theconiston blog pages remembering the rave caves of Coniston: https://theconiston.typepad.com/theconiston/2005/09/the_rave_scene_.html

men climbed rock faces with nothing but a chain: Anthony Coulls, *The Slate Industry*, Amberley (2019), p. 13.

natural but invisible grain: Anthony Coulls, *The Slate Industry*, Amberley (2019), p. 14.

experience could not be taught in a college: Anthony Coulls, *The Slate Industry*, Amberley (2019), pp. 9–13.

Slate was its dominant industry: facts and figures from the press release 'Welsh Slate landscape becomes newest UNESCO World Heritage Site', Cyngor Gwynedd (28 July 2021): https://www.gwynedd.llyw.cymru/en/Council/News/Press-releases/Gorffennaf-2021/Welsh-Slate-landscape-becomes-newest-UNESCO-World-Heritage-Site.aspx

90 per cent of the rock extracted: taken from an information board onsite but also available online at Wales Slate website: https://www.llechi.cymru/slateareas/ffestiniog

move them into the disused quarry on Manod: Steffan Rhys, 'How Britain's art treasures were hidden in Welsh caves to protect them from German bombs – a remarkable true story', Wales Online (8 August 2017): https://www.walesonline.co.uk/lifestyle/ nostalgia/remarkable-true-story-how-britains-13447121; 'Dark Secrets', Guardian (3 March 2001): https://www.theguardian.com/ travel/2001/mar/03/unitedkingdom.guardiansaturdaytravelsection2

Chapter 7: Textiles

New Lanark was classed as a UNESCO World Heritage Site: for facts and figures about New Lanark, go to the website: https:// www.newlanark.org/about-new-lanark/timeline

by 1850, Britain was producing half of the world's cotton: Gregory Clark, 'The British Industrial Revolution 1760–1860', World Economic History (ECN 110B, Spring 2005). Available online: http://faculty.econ.ucdavis.edu/faculty/gclark/ecn110b/ readings/ecn110b-chapter2-2005.pdf

Factory work demanded submission: T. C. Smout, *A History of the Scottish People, 1560–1830*, Collins (1969), p. 406.

Employers found they proved restless: T. C. Smout, *A History of the Scottish People, 1560–1830*, Collins (1969), p. 407.

If caught young they could be bent like saplings: T. C. Smout, *A History of the Scottish People, 1560–1830*, Collins (1969), p. 407.

in well aired rooms: T. C. Smout, *A History of the Scottish People, 1560–1830*, Collins (1969), p. 409.

every householder in the village: T. C. Smout, *A History of the Scottish People, 1560–1830*, Collins (1969), p. 421.

By 1850, this area produced 40 per cent of the world's cotton output: Gregory Clark, 'The British Industrial Revolution 1760– 1860', World Economic History (ECN 110B, Spring 2005). Available online: http://faculty.econ.ucdavis.edu/faculty/gclark/ ecn110b/readings/ecn110b-chapter2-2005.pdf

Have you much business among the factory classes?: report from the Commissioners, 1833. Available online: https://play.google. com/books/reader?id=cW9bAAAAQAAJ&pg=GBS.RA3-PA10 &hl=en

During the American Civil War there was a shortage of cotton: information on the decline of the cotton industry in brief in 'The

cotton famine', National Museums Liverpool: https://www.
liverpoolmuseums.org.uk/cotton-decline

The numbers attached to the fashion industry are shocking: these
specific facts and figures are taken from the Clean Clothes
Campaign website but are available widely online: https://
cleanclothes.org/issues/working-hours

Chapter 8: Tourism

**17 per cent of existing housing stock in the Lake District
National Park is made up of second homes:** figures taken from
the LDNP Authority website, who quote them as coming from
the Census 2001 (LDF Technical Report Nos. 2): https://www.
lakedistrict.gov.uk/planning/planningpolicies/affordablehousing

one in four properties is now an Airbnb: Niko Kommedna, Helen
Pidd and Libby Brooks, 'Revealed: the areas in the UK with one
Airbnb for every four homes', *Guardian* (20 February 2020):
https://www.theguardian.com/technology/2020/feb/20/revealed-
the-areas-in-the-uk-with-one-airbnb-for-every-four-homes

landlady admitting they get four times the money doing Airbnb:
Sirin Kale with data by David Blood, '"I wanted my children to
grow up here": how Airbnb is ruining local communities in north
Wales', *Guardian* (10 August 2022): https://www.theguardian.
com/technology/2022/
aug/10/i-wanted-my-children-to-grow-up-here-how-airbnb-is-
ruining-local-communities-in-north-wales

The Lakes. The Highlands, Snowdonia: Anna Pavord,
Landskipping, Bloomsbury (2016), p. 13.

a sort of national property: William Wordsworth, *Guide to the
Lakes*, Oxford University Press (Fifth Edition 1835), p. 92.

Go to a pantomime, a farce, or a puppet-show: William
Wordsworth, *Guide to the Lakes,* Oxford University Press (Fifth
Edition 1835), p. 154.

15.8 million people visit the Lake District every year: figures
from Lake District National Park Authority: https://www.
lakedistrict.gov.uk/learning/forteachers/ks2tourists

sort of nonsense scribbled by the passer-by: Allan McNee, 'The
New Tourists', *History Today*, Vol. 71, Issue 8 (August 2021).

reported that a party of 17 gentlemen ascended the mountain: 'The hotel that once stood on the summit of Ben Nevis', *Scotsman* (1 February 2017): https://www.scotsman.com/sport/hotel-once-stood-summit-ben-nevis-1457027

The Ben Nevis Observatory: information taken from 'Scotland's History: The Ben Nevis Observatory, Scotland's People (18 December 2017): https://www.scotlandspeople.gov.uk/article/our-records-ben-nevis-observatory

the calm confidence, yet submissiveness, of our wise Man of the Mountains: Dorothy Wordsworth, *Guide to the Lakes,* Oxford University Press (Fifth Edition 1835), p. 115.

On the summit of the Pike: Dorothy Wordsworth, *Guide to the Lakes,* Oxford University Press (Fifth Edition 1835), p. 113.

Taking the latest government advice: 'Coronavirus in Scotland: Tourism boss left "speechless" by Highland hotel's decision to sack and evict workers', *Herald* (20 March 2020), widely reported and available here: https://www.heraldscotland.com/news/18321030.coronavirus-scotland-tourism-boss-left-speechless-highland-hotels-decision-sack-evict-workers/

Chapter 9: Development

half of Scotland's rural land is owned by only 432 landowners: James Hunter, Peter Peacock, Andy Wightman and Michael Foxley, '432:50 – Towards a comprehensive land reform agenda for Scotland', Briefing paper for the House of Commons Scottish Affairs Committee (2013): https://www.parliament.uk/globalassets/documents/commons-committees/scottish-affairs/432-Land-Reform-Paper.pdf

the aristocracy and gentry still own roughly 30 per cent of England today: facts and figures available from: Guy Shrubsole, *Who Owns England? How We Lost Our Land and How We Take it Back*, William Collins (2020); Rob Evans, 'Half of England is owned by less than 1% of the population', *Guardian* (April 2019): https://www.theguardian.com/money/2019/apr/17/who-owns-england-thousand-secret-landowners-author

have led me to conclude that an elite of less than 1 per cent: Guy Shrubsole, quoted in 'Who owns England? History of England's

land ownership and how much is privately owned today',
Countryfile (April 2019): https://www.countryfile.com/news/
who-owns-england-history-of-englands-landownership-and-how-
much-is-privately-owned-today/

if you built a house in London without a licence: information
taken from 'The Long History of British Land Use Regulation',
Create Streets (26 April 2019): https://www.createstreets.com/
the-long-history-of-british-land-use-regulation/

'lack of society' but 'beauty of nature': Ebenezer Howard, *Garden
Cities of Tomorrow*, Dodo Press (Second Edition, 1902),
Introduction, p. 6.

The fortunate community living on this estate: Earl Grey's words
on the opening of Letchworth Garden City, quoted in 'The
History of Letchworth Garden City', Discover Letchworth:
https://www.discover-letchworth.com/
visiting/a-brief-history-of-letchworth

The first rural council houses were in Ixworth in Suffolk: John
Boughton, information and much more like it from the
Municipal Dreams website. Specifically, on the first rural
council houses see 'Stow Road, Ixworth: "Thingoe's Follies"',
Municipal Dreams (22 January 2019): https://municipaldreams.
wordpress.com/2019/01/22/stow-road-ixworth-thingoes-follies-
update/

**in the 1920s and 30s an average of 300,000 houses were built
every year:** figures taken from 'The Long History of British Land
Use Regulation', Create Streets (26 April 2019): https://www.
createstreets.com/the-long-history-of-british-land-use-regulation/

Only three years later, there were 159,000 council houses: Trevor
Wild, *Village England: A Social History of the Countryside* (2004),
quoted on the Municipal Dreams website: https://
municipaldreams.wordpress.com/2019/01/22/stow-road-ixworth-
thingoes-follies-update/

**the Conservative Party's manifesto in 2019 was to build 300,000
houses a year:** available from the Conservative Party manifesto
online: https://www.conservatives.com/our-plan/conservative-
party-manifesto-2019

at only 216,000 new homes: 'Housing Supply; net additional
dwellings, England 2020–21', Department for Levelling up,

Housing and Communities (November 2021): https://assets.pub
lishing.service.gov.uk/government/uploads/system/uploads/attach
ment_data/file/1035653/Housing_Supply_England_2020-21.pdf

building 340,000 new homes in England alone: 'Tackling the
under-supply of housing in England', House of Commons
Library, Research Briefings (4 February 2022): https://
commonslibrary.parliament.uk/research-briefings/cbp-7671/

peak of house building in 1968 when 350,000 homes were built:
Jamie Doward, 'Housing crisis hits 1960s levels as tenants battle
to cope, says Shelter', *Guardian* (9 January 2016): https://www.
theguardian.com/society/2016/jan/09/housing-crisis-tenants-
shelter-private-rent

a new, established village, where a vibrant community thrives:
from Calderwood's website: http://www.calderwood.co.uk

in 2020, 52,000 affordable homes were built in England:
'Affordable Housing Supply: April 2020 to March 2021,
England', Department for Levelling Up, Housing &
Communities, UK Government: https://assets.publishing.service.
gov.uk/government/uploads/system/uploads/attachment_data/
file/1034043/AHS_2020-21.pdf

**in England alone more than 1.6 million people are on the list
for social housing:** Lynsey Hanley, 'From Thatcher to Johnson:
how right to buy has fuelled a 40-year housing crisis', *Guardian*
(29 June 2022): https://www.theguardian.com/society/2022/
jun/29/how-right-to-buy-ruined-british-housing

to check the unrestricted sprawl of large built-up areas: 'National
Policy Planning Framework': 13. Protecting Green Belt Land,
Paragraphs 137 to 151 (27 March 2012): https://www.gov.uk/
guidance/national-planning-policy-framework/13-protecting-green-
belt-land

preserved for the people of Scotland and **We should not be
building in the countryside:** quotes taken from Jupiter Artland's
Protect Jupiter Artland website: https://www.jupiterartland.org/
whats-on/protect-jupiter-artland/

Semi-rural is defined as living on the outskirts: definitions
available at Rural Scotland Key Facts 2021: https://www.gov.scot/
publications/rural-scotland-key-facts-2021/

Chapter 10: Business

one of the fashionable Negro footmen: Dr Jennifer Melville, 'Facing Our Past: Interim report on the connections between the properties now in the care of the National Trust for Scotland and historical enslavement', National Trust for Scotland (December 2021; updated April 2022): https://s3-eu-west-1.amazonaws.com/ws-nts/Production/assets/downloads/Facing-our-Past-interim-report-June-22.pdf?mtime=20220615094637

The Beckfords were one of the first families to obtain sugar plantations in Jamaica: 'Beckford and the Slave Trade: The Legacy of the Beckford Family and Slavery', Beckford's Tower and Museum: https://beckfordstower.org.uk/wp-content/uploads/2012/08/Beckfords-and-Slavery-leaflet-2007.pdf

The British government borrowed £20 million: eds Dr Sally-Anne Huxtable, Professor Corinne Fowler, Dr Christo Kefalas and Emma Slocombe, 'Interim Report on the Connections between Colonialism and Properties now in the Care of the National Trust, Including Links with Historic Slavery', National Trust (September 2020): https://nt.global.ssl.fastly.net/binaries/content/assets/website/national/pdf/colonialism-and-historic-slavery-report.pdf

the Pennants, received £14,683 17s. 2d.: 'Penrhyn Castle and slave trade history', National Trust: https://www.nationaltrust.org.uk/penrhyn-castle/features/penrhyn-castle-and-the-transatlantic-slave-trade

He describes the slaves as 'chattels': quote taken from Marian Gwyn's 'Interpreting the Slave Trade: The Penrhyn Castle Exhibition', National Trust: https://www.brunel.ac.uk/creative-writing/research/entertext/documents/entertext071/ET71GwynEDfinal.pdf

was excessively boring: 'Obituary – Lady Jean Fforde, aristocrat, Arran landowner and codebreaker at Bletchley Park', *Herald* (18 October 2017): https://www.heraldscotland.com/opinion/15603075.obituary---lady-jean-fforde-aristocrat-arran-landowner-codebreaker-bletchley-park/

The Hamiltons' 'earldom' came with 1,000 acres: 'Earldom for

Sale', *Herald* (29 December 1994): https://www.heraldscotland.com/news/12538733.earldom-for-sale/

but losing it is nothing like when I lost the family castle to the National Trust: 'Obituary: Lady Jean Fforde, aristocrat said to have auctioned off an earldom to pay for central heating', *Scotsman* (18 October 2017): https://www.scotsman.com/news/obituaries/obituary-lady-jean-fforde-aristocrat-said-have-auctioned-earldom-pay-central-heating-2469417

There were nearly 550,000 businesses registered in rural areas in England: 'Rural business statistics', Department for Environment, Food & Rural Affairs, Official Statistics, UK Government (updated 22 July 2022): https://www.gov.uk/government/statistics/rural-enterprise/rural-business-statistics

around 85 per cent of Welsh land is used for agriculture or forestry: 'A Statistical focus on Rural Wales', 2008 Edition, Welsh Assembly Government: https://gov.wales/sites/default/files/statistics-and-research/2018-12/080515-statistical-focus-rural-wales-08-en.pdf

a similar story in Ireland where rural businesses: 'Key Rural Issues, Northern Ireland, 2021', Department for Agriculture, Environment, and Rural Affairs: https://www.daera-ni.gov.uk/sites/default/files/publications/daera/Key%20Rural%20Issues%202021.pdf

The rural economy is worth £260 billion, which is 15 per cent of England's output: The Rt Hon. Greg Clark MP and the Rt Hon. Lord Benyon, '£110m fund to level up rural communities unveiled', Department of Environment, Food & Rural Affairs, Department for Levelling up, Housing and Communities, UK Government (September 2022): https://www.gov.uk/government/news/110m-fund-to-level-up-rural-communities-unveiled

In Shetland in 1975, the local area changed forever, from a mainly crofting and fishing area to the biggest building site in Europe: EnQuest Fact Sheet (March 2019): https://www.enquest.com/fileadmin/content/operations/ICOP_PDFs/EnQ_ICOP_Sullom_Voe_Terminal_2019_03_28.pdf

an incredible 98 per cent of Scotland's: 'Rural Scotland Key Facts 2021', Scottish Government: https://www.gov.scot/publications/rural-scotland-key-facts-2021/pages/4/

There were three bars in the camp initially: Chris Cope, 'The early days of Sullom Voe: in their own words', *Shetland News* (23 November 2018): https://www.shetnews.co.uk/2018/11/23/the-early-days-of-sullom-voe-in-their-own-words/

Jen Stout, who is from the area, remembers the mould: Jen Stout, 'Oil tankers line Shetland's horizon, but islanders face bitter fuel poverty', *Open Democracy* (6 September 2022): https://www.opendemocracy.net/en/shetland-energy-crisis-fuel-poverty-oil-gas/

Dream job for island ranger with accommodation included free: Jenness Mitchell, 'Dream job for island ranger with accommodation included free – The Scottish Wildlife Trust is looking for a new ranger to join its team on Handa Island', STV News (4 January 2022): https://news.stv.tv/highlands-islands/dream-job-for-island-ranger-with-accommodation-included-free

For the 3,000-strong workforce that built it: 'Dounreay Heritage Strategy: Delivering a Cultural Legacy through Decommissioning', Dounreay Site Restoration LTD (23 August 2010): https://assets.publishing.service.gov.uk/government/uploads/system/uploads/attachment_data/file/718623/Heritage_Strategy_Issue_2_Aug_2010.pdf

Now it is less than half of that: 'Working for Dounreay', UK Government website: https://www.gov.uk/government/organisations/dounreay/about/recruitment#:~:text=We%20employ%20over%201000%20people,allowance%20and%20subsidised%20bus%20travel.

It currently employs 11,000 people: 'The Economic Impact of Sellafield', Oxford Economics (June 2017): https://assets.publishing.service.gov.uk/government/uploads/system/uploads/attachment_data/file/730958/The_economic_impact_of_Sellafield_June_2017_Oxford_economics.pdf

The site now handles almost all the UK's nuclear waste: 'About us, Sellafield Ltd', UK Government website: https://www.gov.uk/government/organisations/sellafield-ltd/about#:~:text=Our%2011%2C000%20strong%20workforce%20is,businesses%20to%20global%20market%20leaders.

Sellafield itself is gradually being decommissioned: Hayley Cox, 'What does the future hold for Sellafield?' University of

Manchester, Science and Engineering (12 March 2020): https://www.mub.eps.manchester.ac.uk/science-engineering/2020/03/12/what-does-the-future-hold-for-sellafield/

Civil Nuclear Constabulary (CNC), which employs around 1,500 armed police: information available on CNC website: https://cnc.jobs

he paid for the lawyers' bills for the (only) three crofters: Dani Garvelli, 'Insight: The battle to Build UK's first Spaceport', *Scotsman* (20 June 2021): https://www.scotsman.com/news/environment/insight-the-battle-to-build-scotlands-spaceport-3279541

a 200-year vision of landscape-scale conservation: Wildland website: https://wildland.scot

extensive native tree planting: Alladale's website: https://alladale.com

rewild and re-people the Scottish Highlands: Highlands Rewilding website. https://www.highlandsrewilding.co.uk

Ownership of his estates, found in the Cairngorms: Magnus Davidson, 'Land, Green Lairds and Rewilding', Bella Caladonia (20 February 2022): https://bellacaledonia.org.uk/2022/02/20/land-green-lairds-and-rewilding/

We're investing heavily in nature restoration: Andrew R. C. Marshall, 'Who Owns Scotland? The Rise of the Green Lairds', Reuters (27 January 2022): https://www.reuters.com/investigates/special-report/scotland-environment-green-lairds/

It feels like a re-enactment of the Highland Clearances – a land grab: Kevin Batemen, quoted in Marianne Curtis's 'National Trust rewilding projects leaves tenants feeling pushed out', *Farmers Weekly* (27 July 2022): https://www.fwi.co.uk/business/business-management/tenancies-rents/national-trust-rewilding-projects-leaves-tenants-feel-pushed-out

is a microcosm of Scotland's wider land debate: Dani Garvelli, 'Insight: The battle to Build UK's first Spaceport', *Scotsman* (20 June 2021): https://www.scotsman.com/news/environment/insight-the-battle-to-build-scotlands-spaceport-3279541

Chapter 11: Our Land

seed of inspiration was from Eigg: Allan Macrae quoted in Alastair
McIntosh, 'How the "People's Republic of Eigg" lit a fire under
land reform in Scotland', *National* (10 April 2022): https://www.
thenational.scot/news/environment/20057564.peoples-republic-
eigg-lit-fire-land-reform-scotland/

Donations came in from far and wide: John Ross, 'Woman who
led Eigg community buyout on keeping the secret of mystery
£750,000 benefactor', *Press and Journal* (30 November 2020):
https://www.pressandjournal.co.uk/fp/news/highlands-
islands/2481070/woman-who-led-eigg-community-buyout-on-
keeping-the-secret-of-mystery-750000-benefactor/

The estate agent described the islands … as 'Van Goghs': Camille
Dressler, *Eigg: The Story of an Island,* Polygon (1998), p. 189.

They quickly demonstrated what can be achieved: Linsay
Chalmers, quoted in John Ross, 'Eigg marks 25 years of
community buyout and inspires others to take control', *Press and
Journal* (10 June 2022): https://www.pressandjournal.co.uk/fp/
news/highlands-islands/4401513/eigg-marking-25-years-of-
community-buyout-and-inspiring-others/

the highest reported population in 1841 was 546 people: Camille
Dressler, *Eigg: The Story of an Island,* Polygon (1998), p. 71.

**On the island of Benbecula, the Clearances were so barbaric that
crofters were 'hunted down with dogs':** Camille Dressler, *Eigg:
The Story of an Island,* Polygon (1998), p. 83.

**One girl never recovered from these evictions and threw herself
in the sea from the cliffs:** Camille Dressler, *Eigg: The Story of an
Island,* Polygon (1998), p. 84.

'In the Grulin area, houses were plundered for their stones:
Camille Dressler, *Eigg: The Story of an Island,* Polygon
(1998), p. 84.

**as laird had stopped the free milk and coal that came with estate
jobs:** Camille Dressler, *Eigg: The Story of an Island,* Polygon
(1998), p. 154.

Keith actually wears those round goggles: Widely quoted but
taken from Patrick Barkham, 'This island is not for sale',
Guardian (26 September 2017):

https://www.theguardian.com/uk-news/2017/sep/26/this-island-is-not-for-sale-how-eigg-fought-back

or simply 'froze' them out: Camille Dressler, *Eigg: The Story of an Island,* Polygon (1998), pp. 157–162.

One person would be in a tied cottage: Camille Dressler, *Eigg: The Story of an Island,* Polygon (1998), p. 168.

remove Eigg in perpetuity from private ownership: Camille Dressler, *Eigg: The Story of an Island,* Polygon (1998), p. 171.

they will not necessarily take the highest price: Information on the Isle of Eigg's website (September 2021): http://isleofeigg.org/2021/09/sandamhor-bothy-for-sale/

It's not about just wanting to be landowners: Alastair McIntosh quoted in Patrick Barkham, 'This island is not for sale', *Guardian* (26 September 2017): https://www.theguardian.com/uk-news/2017/sep/26/this-island-is-not-for-sale-how-eigg-fought-back

There are now 562,000 acres of land: 'Community Ownership', Scottish Land Commission: https://www.landcommission.gov.scot/our-work/ownership/community-ownership

There are currently over 500 community land trusts: 'What is a community land trust (CLT)?' Community Land Trust Network: https://www.communitylandtrusts.org.uk/about-clts/what-is-a-community-land-trust-clt/

A steward is someone who has the responsibility for looking after property: Collins Dictionary Definition of the word 'Steward': https://www.collinsdictionary.com/dictionary/english/steward

Roots, if you are lucky enough to have them: Anna Pavord, *Landskipping,* Bloomsbury (2016), p. 4.

Acknowledgements

So many people have helped me with the research for this book.

Firstly, thanks to James Squires (my Uncle Jim) who, luckily, has been exploring our family history for years. Thank you for all your hard work and answering so many of my questions patiently.

To Geoff Bailey and his inexhaustible research at the Falkirk Historical Society, to my father-in-law, Fergus, for help with old books, for taxiing Jessie around the area and her never-ending supply of chocolate coins.

To Paul from United Utilities who was very helpful with the Thirlmere research and introduced me to John Butcher – and to John whose passion for the history of the area is unparalleled. To Tony Evans, whose knowledge and love for Catcleugh reservoir shines through. The book he wrote and produced himself is fascinating. And to Alan McNee who very kindly shared his excellent research on Victorian visitor books.

For being part of the book, I will be eternally grateful to Dick and Doreen for speaking to me over their kitchen table about the past (and for the parties we had there), to Rose, Christine and Matt who work so hard and still found the time to tell me their stories. I have so much respect for what you do. To Margaret for some of the best childhood memories of being on her farm, thank you for talking to me about it all. And to Auntie Lin, thank you for sharing your memories of Grandad and for your unwavering hospitality –

you have always shown me that life has more possibilities than what's in front of you and for that, I will be forever grateful.

To Ed, a brilliant boss (and Van and Lee) and to Claudia for their stories of working in hospitality. To Ruth and Dougal who were so generous when we stayed with them on Easdale with their time and knowledge of such a beautiful place. To John at Brodick, thank you for the captivating walk around the gardens but more than anything, thank you for the lifesaving bed during the storm. To Dorothy from Melness Crofters' Estate, for her love of community and her incredible fight for it. Thank you for our conversation. And to Helen from Mull and Iona Community Trust for sharing their hopes for the future. There is so much hope out there.

To my friends Fiona, Joanne, Evonne, Lyndsay and Helen who had no idea they would play a part in the book when I went to their houses for a cup of tea or to stay the night. I am so grateful for your never-ending generosity. To Jen for coming on adventures with me. You are an excellent co-adventurer. To Grant, not only for his help with research, but for being part of it in more ways than one. Thanks always to my friends who have always supported me, believed in me, provided childcare, phone calls when I needed them most, night outs, tea and cake – Rachel, Sarah, Lyndsay, (Auntie) Louise, Fiona, Jen, Jess, Ruth, Lizzie, Gill, Claire, Kirsty, Rachael and Anna. To Graeme (you always said I'd do it) and to Harry and Yvonne for everything they do for Ellis. To Jacqueline Baird for the indispensable use of her farm office when the edits were due and to Mark and Jaqueline for their interest in the book over cups of tea.

It takes a long time to get to a stage where writing an actual book is possible and support and love from the very beginning are essential. So firstly, my thanks go to Anna Miles with whom I used to sit in the back corridor of work and share small pieces of writing together. To Claire Askew and the wonderful Write Like a Grrrl crew whose encouragement and support kick-started something in so many writers, thank you. To Kirsty Logan, my first mentor, whose feedback on my writing was so useful and has led to wonderful things. To the staff at the Glasgow University Creative Writing Masters, namely Colin Herd, Elizabeth K. Reeder and Sophie Collins, and the students, Carolyn, Lizzie, Angus, Martha, James, my first readers for the beginnings of this book. It's been an honour to share this journey with you. To Jen, fellow writer and mum (and all the other writers who are parents) – we're in the thick of it but we'll get there. To Rachelle Atalla who is my go-to for advice on that magical thing of becoming an author, thank you for keeping me sane.

I want to give a huge thank you to Cal Flyn (and to Malachy Tallack for introducing us) who took me on as a mentee before I knew this was a book. Every email, every conversation with you settled my worries and inspired me to keep going. The book would not exist without you.

Huge thanks to my agent, Jenny Brown – they all said she was the best agent – they were right. To my editor, Jo Thomson, who has kept me on the right path in more ways than one and made the book what it is today with her excellent eye and experience.

To Creative Scotland, for the funding to finish the book. It enabled me to concentrate on the final stages of it and for that I will be forever grateful.

To Lesley who makes Tom happy and to Tom who welcomes people into his life with open arms, thank you.

To Mum and Dad (Shirley and Mike to everyone else), for coming with me on research trips, for looking after the grandkids when we needed to get away, for letting me write their story and for the biggest thing of all, supporting me in everything I do. Thank you for giving us this life, this stuff of dreams.

To my children, Ellis, for always being kind and asking intelligent questions. Keep asking them. To Jess, who brightens up everyone's day, thank you for making us smile, and to Rory, I guess you were with me, on every research trip, each time I sat down to write. Thank you for keeping me company.

And to Phil, who said one day as he was passing the dining table as I wrote about the tied house I grew up in, 'Didn't coal miners live in tied housing too?' the seed of which became this book. Thank you for giving me the children, for believing in me, for supporting me, for being patient. It wouldn't be possible without you. Thank you.